Liners

gettyimages

Liners

The Golden Age
Die große Zeit der Ozeanriesen
L'Âge d'Or des Paquebots

Text by Robert Fox

Consultant: Clive Harvey

Picture research by
Alex Linghorn

h.f.ullmann

The *Empress of Britain*, 42,348 tons, introduced to the Canadian Pacific fleet in 1931; sunk by German bomber and submarine attack off Ireland, October 1940. A classic photograph by Sasha.

Die *Empress of Britain*, 42.348 Tonnen, war 1931 bei der Canadian Pacific Line in Dienst gestellt worden und sank im Oktober 1940 nach einem deutschen Bomber- und U-Boot-Angriff vor der irischen Küste. Eine klassische Aufnahme von Sasha.

L'*Empress of Britain* (42 348 tonneaux), intégré à la flotte de la Canadian Pacific en 1931, coula en octobre 1940 après avoir été attaqué par un bombardier et un sous-marin allemands au large de l'Irlande. Une photographie classique de Sasha.

© 2006 h.f.ullmann publishing GmbH

Photographs © 1999 Getty Images

Original title: *Liners*
Original ISBN: 978-3-8331-2619-2

For the publisher:
Managing editor: Sally Bald
Assistant editor: Monika Dauer
German translation: Manfred Allié
French translation: Arnaud Dupin de Beyssat

For Getty Images:
Art director: Michael Rand
Design: B+B
Project manager: Alex Linghorn
Editor: Elisabeth Ingles
Proof-reader: Elisabeth Ihre
Scanning: Antonia Hille
Production: Téa McAleer
Special thanks to: Ian Denning, Leon Meyer Ali Khoja, Jim Nye, Alexia Shaw, Laurence Gillett

© 2011 for this edition: h.f.ullmann publishing GmbH

Special edition

Cover design: Simone Sticker

Overall responsibility for production: h.f.ullmann publishing GmbH, Potsdam, Germany

ISBN 978-3-8480-0518-5

Printed in China, 2013

10 9 8 7 6 5 4 3 2 1
X IX VIII VII V IV III II I

www.ullmann-publishing.com
newsletter@ullmann-publishing.com

Contents

Inhalt

Sommaire

Prologue

Steam navigation, 'the only way to travel', was the slogan for the era of the ocean liner. It was an invitation to adventure, luxury, escape; for millions of impoverished migrants it was an invitation to a new life in new worlds. The steamer was to dominate long-distance travel from the 1860s to the 1960s, when it gave way to diesel-driven ships and the commercial jet airliner.

With their liners, troopers, tramps, freighters and tankers, steam navigation companies encircled the world. But on one route above others their ships caught the imagination: the transatlantic crossing from Britain and Europe to America. The Atlantic run was plied by the great liners, the latest, biggest and best in marine engineering and the last word in contemporary design and decor. The rivalry of the companies, ships and captains of the Atlantic dominates the story of steam shipping; it was a tale of romance, elegance, and spectacular disaster.

For all the extravagance of the liners in their heyday, the saga of steam navigation across the Atlantic had a modest beginning. In May 1819 the small sailing packet *Savannah* set out from her eponymous home port for Liverpool. She was a true hybrid of the age of sail and the age of steam, with three masts and a bowsprit, carrying a full weight of sail and a tall, thin funnel. To assist her sails she had two collapsible paddle-wheels driven by steam. The *Savannah* was the first steamship in history to make the Atlantic crossing, although the paddle-wheels were used for only 80 hours out of the 28-day voyage.

The next crossing by steam came in 1833 by the 370-ton *Royal William*, owned by the Quebec and Halifax Steam Navigation Company, which cleared Pictou, Nova Scotia, on 17 August 1833. She was the first to make the voyage almost entirely by steampower; the sails were called on only when the engines had to be cleared of salt. Her engines developed 200 horsepower, and allowed her to make an average of 4.5 knots, clocking up a total time of a very respectable 25 days.

In 1837 Isambard Kingdom Brunel, an engineer for the Great Western Railway, produced one of the first great custom-made transatlantic liners. The *Great Western* sailed from Bristol on 8 April 1838, taking 15 days to New York. She was the largest and fastest ship in the Atlantic, and for a time the only steamer offering a regular service; she completed 64 round trips in eight years. She had a grand saloon decorated in the style of the 18th-century French painter Antoine Watteau, complete with ornate gothic arches. More dramatic still was the appear-

ance of her sister ship, the *Great Britain*, launched in 1843, the first transatlantic liner with a steel hull and driven by a screw propeller from one huge steam boiler. But in her first year of operation she ran aground off the Irish coast, and by the time she was refloated her owners had gone bankrupt.

An even more spectacular failure was Brunel's third great ship, the *Great Eastern*, originally intended for voyages to Australia via Calcutta. At 18,915 gross tons, 693 feet long, and designed to carry some 3,000 passengers, she was to remain the largest ship in the world until she was broken up in 1899. She was so big that she had to rely on a combination of screw and paddle-wheel for propulsion. When she was launched in the Thames, she stuck fast on the slipway, and had to wait a month till she finally entered the water in January 1858. On sea trials she blew off a funnel, and six people died in the explosion. Brunel himself died of a stroke before her maiden voyage in June 1860. By this time she had been switched to the Atlantic route, but she brought her owners little success. She became a cable-laying vessel, laying the first transatlantic telegraphy cable in 1866.

Among the partners of the Quebec and Halifax Steam Navigation Company were the brothers Samuel, Henry and Joseph Cunard. Samuel was to be the father of perhaps the most famous shipping dynasty in the age of steam. He set up the first regular transatlantic service in 1840 with the 1,135-ton *Britannia*. The contract from the British Admiralty for carrying mail across the Atlantic was to ensure that the Cunard Line stayed in business, though it nearly collapsed several times in its first years.

In the early days Cunard had one major rival, the Collins Line of the buccaneering Sir Edward Collins, who signed a mail contract with the American government for the service to Europe. The Collins Line flourished in the era of the great migrations from Europe, when Italians, Irish, Poles, Germans and Scandinavians poured into the United States and Canada by the thousand between 1840 and 1914. Its ships were faster and bigger than the early Cunard liners, and carried more passengers. Most famous were the quartet of *Atlantic*, *Pacific*, *Arctic* and *Baltic*. The Collins story was a classic cocktail of triumph and disaster, both personal and commercial. In September 1854 the *Arctic*, one week out from Liverpool en route to New York, collided in fog with a small steel-hulled Spanish ship, the *Vesta*, and severely damaged her wooden hull. In the chaotic rescue only 86 people were saved and 366

were lost, among them Collins's own wife and two children. In January 1856 the *Pacific*, on the same route, disappeared altogether, and no trace of the ship or the 186 people aboard was ever found; it is believed she hit ice and sank within minutes. In 1858 the Collins Line went bankrupt, and Collins himself died in poverty in 1878. His ships, however, had set a standard for luxury passenger travel across the Atlantic; they were the first to offer the full panoply of staterooms, ballrooms, dining saloons, stewards, and on-board entertainment.

Although for most of their century of glory the ocean-going steam liners competed vigorously with each other in terms of luxury and general excellence, the most coveted prize was the Blue Riband for the fastest crossing of the Atlantic. In the early days two lines dominated the speed challenge, Cunard and its greatest rival, the White Star Line. The first Cunard ship on the winners' list was the *Columbia*, which completed the westbound run in 10 days 19 hours in June 1841, although the Riband was not formally instituted until the 1860s. Occasional interlopers in the list were from the Inman and Guion lines. The challenge had become a deadly commercial contest by the 1890s when such illustrious champions as Inman Line's *City of Paris* and *City of New York*, White Star's *Majestic* and Cunard's giants *Campania* and *Lucania* claimed the trophy.

The Atlantic, glamorous and profitable as it was, was not the only route being developed with the advent of steam. In 1825, six years after the *Savannah* sailed for Liverpool, the 500-ton *Enterprise* left London for Calcutta, the first steam vessel to attempt the voyage to India. It was to take 103 days, far slower than the fastest sailing ships of the day. Ten years later, Arthur Anderson, a Shetland Islander, teamed up with a young London shipbroker, Brodie McGhie Willcox, to form the Peninsula Steam Navigation Company, offering regular services from England to Spain and Portugal. Later it became the Peninsula and Oriental Steam Navigation Company, one of the few firms of that era still trading under the same name. In 1837 the company won the first ever mail contract from the British Admiralty, to carry mail between Falmouth in Cornwall and Vigo in Spain. By 1857 P & O had established itself as the principal line to Australia. Then, in 1866, an engineer called Alfred Holt launched the *Agamemnon* to ply the route to China and the Pacific. Followed by her sisters *Ajax* and *Achilles*, she provided the first reliable modern steamship service to the East. Their success was based on Holt's revolutionary innovation of the high-pressure boiler and double-expansion engine.

As the century closed, two new names appeared on the Atlantic run, the *Kaiser Wilhelm der Grosse* and the *Deutschland*. For the best part of half a century the route had been dominated by British and American lines. Now it was the turn of the Germans, in particular the Hamburg Amerika Line, the creation of another shipping entrepreneur of genius, Albert Ballin. Under his direction the Hamburg Amerika was to dominate the North Atlantic in the first years of the new century.

D
ie Dampfschiffahrt, »die einzig wahre Art zu reisen«, das war der Slogan für die große Zeit der Ozeandampfer. Eine Schiffsfahrt versprach Abenteuer, Luxus, Exotik; für Millionen Auswanderer war sie auch Hoffnung auf ein neues Leben in einer neuen Welt. Wer eine Fernreise machte, der fuhr zwischen den 1860er und 1960er Jahren mit ein Dampfschiff, bis Dieselmotoren und der kommerzielle Flugverkehr die Dampfer ablösten.

Mit ihren Linienschiffen, Truppentransportern, Trampschiffen, Frachtern und Tankern waren die Dampfschiffahrtsgesellschaften rund um den Erdball unterwegs. Doch eine Route beschäftigte die Phantasie der Menschen mehr als alle anderen: die Atlantikroute von England und Europa nach Amerika. Auf der Atlantikroute fuhren die Ozeanriesen, die neuesten, größten und besten Schiffe der Weltmeere, in Technik und Ausstattung immer auf der Höhe der Zeit. Der Wetteifer der Schiffahrtsgesellschaften, der Schiffe und Kapitäne auf dem Nordatlantik beherrscht die Geschichte der Passagierschiffahrt – eine Geschichte voller Romantik, Eleganz und großer Katastrophen.

Doch so extravagant die Schiffe auf dem Höhepunkt dieser Ära auch waren, so bescheiden waren die Anfänge der Atlantik-Dampfschiffahrt. Im Mai 1819 brach das kleine Segel-Dampfschiff *Savannah* aus seinem gleichnamigen amerikanischen Heimathafen nach Liverpool auf. Zwei Zeitalter der Seefahrt vereinten sich in diesem Dreimaster mit Bugspriet und vollständiger Betakelung und einem hohen, dünnen Schornstein, denn zur Unterstützung ihrer Segel war die *Savannah* mit zwei einziehbaren, von einer Dampfmaschine angetriebenen Schaufelrädern versehen. Ihre Fahrt ging als erste Atlantiküberquerung per Dampfschiff in die Geschichte ein, auch wenn die Schaufelräder nur 80 Stunden der 28tägigen Reise in Betrieb waren.

Die nächste Dampfüberfahrt unternahm im Jahre 1833 der 370-Tonner *Royal William* der Quebec and Halifax Steam Navigation Company, der am 17. August im neuschottischen Pictou ablegte. Es war die erste Überquerung, die fast ganz mit Dampfkraft erfolgte; die Segel wurden nur gesetzt, wenn die Maschinen vom Salz befreit werden mußten. Mit 200 PS erreichte die *Royal William* eine Durchschnittsgeschwindigkeit von 4,5 Knoten und eine sehr respektable Überfahrtszeit von 25 Tagen.

1837 konstruierte Isambard Kingdom Brunel, Ingenieur der englischen Great Western Railway, das erste große Atlantik-

schiff. Die *Great Western* unternahm ihre Jungfernfahrt am 8. April 1838 von Bristol aus und erreichte in 15 Tagen New York. Sie war das größte und schnellste Schiff auf dem Atlantik und zunächst der einzige regelmäßig verkehrende Dampfer; in den nächsten acht Jahren brachte sie es auf insgesamt 64 Hin- und Rückfahrten. Der große Salon war mit Spitzbogenfenstern und Bildern im Stil Antoine Watteaus geschmückt, des französischen Malers aus dem 18. Jahrhundert. Noch eindrucksvoller war das Schwesterschiff *Great Britain*, das 1843 vom Stapel lief, der erste Atlantikliner mit einem Schiffskörper aus Metall und mit Schraubenpropeller; den Antrieb besorgte eine einzige gewaltige Dampfmaschine. Doch schon im ersten Dienstjahr lief sie vor der irischen Küste auf Grund, und bis sie wieder flottgemacht war, war die Gesellschaft bankrott.

Noch spektakulärer war der Mißerfolg von Brunels drittem großen Schiff, der *Great Eastern*, die ursprünglich für Fahrten nach Kalkutta und Australien gedacht war. Mit ihren 18915 Bruttoregistertonnen, einer Länge von 211 Metern und Platz für fast 3000 Passagiere blieb sie bis zu ihrer Abwrackung im Jahr 1899 das größte Schiff der Welt. Der Rumpf war so riesig, daß sie neben der Schiffsschraube noch Schaufelräder als zusätzlichen Antrieb brauchte. Beim Stapellauf in die Themse verkeilte sie sich auf der Helling, und es dauerte einen ganzen Monat, bis sie schließlich im Januar 1858 ins Wasser kam. Bei der Probefahrt forderte eine Schornsteinexplosion sechs Menschenleben. Brunel selbst starb wenige Tage vor der Jungfernfahrt im Juni 1860 an einem Schlaganfall. Inzwischen war das Schiff für den Atlantikdienst bestimmt, doch auch dort hatten seine Besitzer damit keinen Erfolg. Schon bald baute man die *Great Eastern* zum Kabelleger um, und 1866 verlegte sie das erste Transatlantikkabel.

Gesellschafter der Quebec and Halifax Steam Navigation Company waren unter anderem die Brüder Samuel, Henry und Joseph Cunard. Samuel sollte der Vater der wohl berühmtesten Schiffahrtsdynastie des Dampfzeitalters werden. 1840 richtete er mit dem 1135-Tonner *Britannia* den ersten Linienverkehr auf dem Atlantik ein. Der Vertrag mit der britischen Admiralität, in deren Auftrag Cunard die Post über den Atlantik beförderte, sicherte die Existenz des Unternehmens, das in seinen ersten Jahren mehr als einmal an den Rand des Untergangs geriet.

In jenen Anfangstagen hatte Cunard nur einen einzigen ernstzunehmenden Konkurrenten, die Collins Line des

Norwegian emigrants aboard SS *Hero*, bound for America, about 1870. This was the era of mass migration to America, important passenger traffic until laws of 1924 brought strict regulation of new arrivals.

Norwegische Emigranten auf dem Weg nach Amerika, aufgenommen an Deck der SS *Hero* um 1870. Auswanderer kamen in großer Zahl in die Neue Welt und stellten einen Großteil der Schiffspassagiere, bis die Vereinigten Staaten 1924 den Zustrom drastisch begrenzten.

Des émigrants norvégiens à bord du SS *Hero*, en partance pour les États-Unis, vers 1870. Ce fut la grande époque d'émigration vers les États-Unis jusqu'à ce que les lois américaines de 1924 limitent strictement le nombre des nouveaux arrivants.

abenteuerlustigen Sir Edward Collins, der in amerikanischem Auftrag Post nach Europa beförderte. Die Collins Line profitierte von den Auswandererströmen, die zwischen 1840 und 1914 von Italien, Irland, Polen, Deutschland und Skandinavien in die Vereinigten Staaten und nach Kanada gingen. Ihre Dampfer waren größer und schneller als die frühen Cunard-Schiffe und konnten mehr Passagiere befördern. Am berühmtesten war das Quartett *Atlantic, Pacific, Arctic* und *Baltic*. Die Geschichte von Collins bot die klassische Mischung aus Triumph und Katastrophe, sowohl persönlich als auch gesellschaftlich. Im September 1854 kollidierte die *Arctic*, eine Woche zuvor von Liverpool nach New York aufgebrochen, im Nebel mit einem kleineren spanischen Schiff, der *Vesta*, deren stählerner Rumpf den hölzernen der *Arctic* schwer beschädigte. In einem chaotischen Rettungsunternehmen überlebten nur 86 Menschen, 366 ertranken, darunter Collins' Frau und seine beiden Kinder. Im Januar 1856 verschwand die *Pacific* auf derselben Route, und weder vom Schiff noch von den 186 Personen an Bord fand sich je eine Spur; man nimmt an, daß sie nach dem Zusammenstoß mit einem Eisberg binnen Minuten sank. 1858 ging die Collins Line in Konkurs, und Collins starb 1878 als armer Mann. Doch seine Schiffe hatten neue Qualitätsstandards im Passagierverkehr über den Atlantik gesetzt; sie waren die ersten, die die ganze Palette der Salons, der Tanz- und Speisesäle, der Stewards und der Bordorchester boten.

Während des ganzen Jahrhunderts der Ozeanriesen lagen die Linien miteinander im Wettstreit um den größten Luxus und den besten Service; doch woran allen am meisten lag, das war das Blaue Band, die Trophäe für die schnellste Atlantiküberquerung. Zunächst wetteiferten vor allem Cunard und sein Erzrivale White Star miteinander. Den ersten Erfolg konnte Cunard mit der *Columbia* verbuchen, die im Juni 1841 die Westroute in 10 Tagen und 19 Stunden absolvierte. Gelegentlich errangen Außenseiter den Preis, der seit den 1860er Jahren offiziell verliehen wurde, etwa die Inman- und Guion-Linien. Zum Ende des Jahrhunderts, als die Trophäe an prachtvolle Schiffe wie Inmans *City of Paris* und *City of New York*, an die *Majestic* der White Star Line und die *Campania* und *Lucania* von Cunard ging, nahm der Wettbewerb mörderische Ausmaße an.

Doch die Atlantikroute, soviel sie auch an Ansehen und Profit einbrachte, war nicht die einzige, die im Zeitalter der Dampfschiffahrt entstand. 1825, sechs Jahre nachdem die

Savannah nach Liverpool gekommen war, brach der 500-Tonner *Enterprise* aus London nach Kalkutta auf, das erste Dampfschiff, das sich auf die Reise nach Indien machte. Die *Enterprise* brauchte 103 Tage dafür, weit mehr als die schnellen Segler der Zeit. Zehn Jahre später gründete der von den Shetland-Inseln stammende Arthur Anderson zusammen mit dem Londoner Schiffsmakler Brodie McGhie Willcox die Peninsula Steam Navigation Company, die einen Liniendienst von England nach Spanien und Portugal einrichtete. Später wurde daraus die Peninsula and Oriental Steam Navigation Company, eines der wenigen Unternehmen aus jener Zeit, die noch unter ihrem ursprünglichen Namen firmieren. 1837 erhielten sie den ersten überhaupt vergebenen Postkontrakt der britischen Admiralität und richteten den Postschiffdienst zwischen Falmouth in Cornwall und dem spanischen Vigo ein; 1857 hatte P & O sich bereits als wichtigste Linie nach Australien etabliert. 1866 brachte der Ingenieur Alfred Holt die *Agamemnon* auf den Weg nach China und auf die Pazifikroute, und bald folgten die Schwesterschiffe *Ajax* und *Achilles*, und so entstand die erste zuverlässige Dampfschiffverbindung in den Fernen Osten. Ihren Erfolg verdankten sie Holts revolutionärer Erfindung des Hochdruck-Dampfkessels und der Expansionsmaschine.

Als das Jahrhundert seinem Ende zuging, tauchten auf der Atlantikroute zwei neue Namen auf, die *Kaiser Wilhelm der Große* und die *Deutschland*. Gut ein halbes Jahrhundert lang hatten britische und amerikanische Linien diese Route beherrscht; nun traten die Deutschen auf den Plan, allen voran die Hamburg-Amerika-Linie, auch sie das Geschöpf eines einfallsreichen Unternehmers: Albert Ballin. Unter seiner Führung schwang sich die Hamburg-Amerika in den ersten Jahren des neuen Jahrhunderts zur führenden Linie auf dem Nordatlantik auf.

La navigation à vapeur, c'est, d'après son slogan au début de l'ère des paquebots transocéanique, « le seul moyen de voyager ». Si, pour les plus riches, c'est une nouvelle invitation à l'aventure, au luxe, à l'évasion, pour des millions d'émigrants, c'est l'occasion d'aller vers une nouvelle vie dans de nouveaux mondes. Ces navires vont dominer le voyage au long cours pendant près d'un siècle, entre 1860 et 1960 environ, date à laquelle ils seront remplacés par des paquebots à propulsion diesel et, surtout, par l'avion.

Alors que paquebots, navires transport de troupes, caboteurs, cargos et pétroliers sillonnent les mers du monde entier, une route particulière emporte l'imagination de tous : la traversée de l'Atlantique de l'Europe aux États-Unis. La ligne de l'Atlantique a été desservie par les plus grands paquebots, les plus modernes, les plus gros et les meilleurs conçus par les ingénieurs de marine et offrant le nec plus ultra de la décoration et des aménagements contemporains. La rivalité qui oppose compagnies, navires et capitaines sur l'Atlantique marque toute l'histoire de la navigation à vapeur – une histoire pleine de romance, d'élégance et de désastres spectaculaires.

Malgré l'extravagance des paquebots dans leurs années glorieuses, la navigation à vapeur dans l'Atlantique fait des débuts plutôt modestes. En mai 1819, un petit paquebot à voiles, le *Savannah*, appareille de son port éponyme pour Liverpool. Ce navire hybride appartient à la fois à l'époque de la voile et à celle de la vapeur, puisqu'il s'agit d'un véritable trois mâts, entre lesquels s'élève une haute cheminée étroite, qui dispose de deux roues à palettes rétractables mues par une chaudière à vapeur. Le *Savannah* fut le premier navire à vapeur à effectuer la traversée de l'Atlantique, même si ses roues à aubes ne fonctionnèrent que 80 heures sur un voyage de 28 jours.

Le 17 août 1833, c'est au tour du vapeur *Royal William* (370 tonneaux), armé par la Quebec and Halifax Steam Navigation Company, de franchir l'Atlantique au départ de Pictou en Nouvelle-Écosse. C'est en fait le premier navire à réaliser cette traversée entièrement mû par la vapeur, les voiles n'étant envoyées que lors du dessalage des machines. Ses chaudières, développant 200 chevaux, lui permettent d'atteindre une vitesse de croisière de 4 à 5 nœuds et d'effectuer la traversée dans le temps très respectable de 25 jours.

En 1837, Isambard Kingdom Brunel, un ingénieur de la Great Western Railway, construit l'un des premiers grands paquebots transatlantiques. Le *Great Western*, qui part de Bristol le 8 avril 1838 et atteint New York 15 jours plus tard, est alors le navire le plus grand et le plus rapide sur l'Atlantique et, pendant un temps, le seul steamer proposant un service régulier ; il effectua 64 voyages aller-retour en huit ans. Son grand salon, orné d'arcs gothiques, était décoré dans le style XVIIIᵉ siècle du peintre français Antoine Watteau. Plus spectaculaire encore, son frère d'armement, le *Great Britain*, lancé en 1843, est le premier paquebot transatlantique bénéficiant d'une coque en fer et d'une propulsion par hélice, actionnée par une grosse chaudière à vapeur. Il s'échoue malheureusement dès la première année de son exploitation au large des côtes irlandaises et ses armateurs font banqueroute au moment de son renflouement.

Le troisième grand navire de Brunel, le *Great Eastern*, à l'origine conçu pour des voyages vers l'Australie via Calcutta, est un échec commercial plus spectaculaire encore. Jaugeant 18 915 tonneaux, mesurant 211 mètres de longueur et conçu pour transporter près de 3 000 passagers, il allait rester le plus grand navire du monde jusqu'à sa mise à la ferraille en 1899. Il était si gros que, lors de son lancement sur la Tamise, il resta coincé sur son ber et il lui fallut attendre un mois avant d'être finalement mis à l'eau en janvier 1858. Son déplacement était si important qu'il avait besoin d'une propulsion mixte – hélice et roue à aubes. Lors des essais en mer, une de ses cheminées explosa, provoquant la mort de six personnes. Brunel lui-même décéda d'une attaque avant le voyage inaugural du navire en juin 1860, où il fut mis en service sur l'Atlantique. Son faible succès commercial poussa ses armateurs à le transformer en navire câblier et c'est lui qui posa le premier câble télégraphique transatlantique en 1866.

La Quebec and Halifax Steam Navigation Company avait pour associés les frères Samuel, Henry et Joseph Cunard. Samuel, le père fondateur de ce qui est peut-être la plus célèbre dynastie maritime, assure dès 1840 le premier service régulier transatlantique avec le *Britannia*, un navire de 1135 tonneaux. Le contrat qu'il passe avec l'Amirauté britannique pour le transport de la poste à travers l'Atlantique allait garantir les activités de la Cunard, qui aurait sinon failli disparaître plusieurs fois lors de ses premières années d'exploitation.

La Cunard a pour principal concurrent la Collins Line, créée par un intrigant, sir Edward Collins, qui signa un contrat de poste avec le gouvernement américain pour la desserte de l'Europe. La Collins Line prospère particulièrement entre 1840 et 1914, lorsque Italiens, Irlandais, Polonais, Allemands et Scandinaves émigrent en masse vers les États-Unis et le Canada. Ses navires – dont les plus célèbres furent l'*Atlantic*, le *Pacific*, l'*Arctic* et le *Baltic* – sont alors plus rapides et plus grands, et peuvent transporter plus de passagers, que ceux de la Cunard. L'histoire de Collins est un mélange, classique à l'époque, de gloires et d'échecs, tant personnels que commerciaux. En septembre 1854, une semaine après son départ de Liverpool pour New York, l'*Arctic* entre en collision dans le brouillard avec le *Vesta*, un petit navire espagnol en acier, et endommage gravement sa coque en bois. Il n'y aura que 86 rescapés dans ce naufrage qui, à cause d'un sauvetage mal organisé, verra disparaître 366 passagers, parmi lesquels la femme et les deux enfants de Collins. En janvier 1856, sur la même route, le *Pacific* disparaît corps et biens sans que l'on trouve jamais aucune trace du navire ni de ses 186 passagers ; on suppose qu'il a heurté un iceberg et sombré en quelques minutes. La Collins Line fait faillite en 1858, et sir Edward meurt dans la misère en 1878. Ses navires ont donné l'exemple aux autres compagnies en proposant à leurs passagers tout le confort possible, avec salons, salles de bal et salles à manger somptueux, stewards pour les servir et spectacles pour les distraire lors des longs voyages transatlantiques.

Tandis que les différentes compagnies se font une sévère concurrence pour offrir à leurs passagers une atmosphère luxueuse, elles se lancent avec plus d'acharnement encore dans la course au Ruban bleu, un trophée attribué au navire ayant réalisé la traversée de l'Atlantique la plus rapide. Deux compagnies britanniques dominent alors toutes les autres : la Cunard et la White Star Line, sa plus dangereuse rivale. En juin 1841, le *Columbia* est le premier navire de la Cunard à s'inscrire sur la liste des lauréats (bien que le Ruban ne fut pas officiellement institué avant les années 1860) en accomplissant la traversée d'est en ouest en 10 jours et 19 heures. Les compagnies Inman et Guion jouent parfois les trouble-fête. Dans les années 1890, la quête du trophée devient une compétition implacable entre des champions aussi illustres que le *City of Paris* et le *City of New York* de la compagnie Inman, le *Majestic* de la White Star et les géants *Campania* et *Lucania* de la Cunard.

Mais l'Atlantique, aussi valorisant et rentable qu'il puisse être, n'est pas la seule ligne qui se développe grâce à la vapeur. En 1825, six ans après l'appareillage du *Savannah* pour Liverpool, l'*Enterprise* (500 tonneaux) quitte Londres en direction de Calcutta et devient le premier navire à vapeur à tenter le voyage vers les Indes ; il va mettre 103 jours pour y parvenir, bien plus lentement que les voiliers les plus rapides de l'époque. Dix ans plus tard, Arthur Anderson, un habitant des îles Shetland, s'associe avec un jeune armateur de Londres, Brodie McGhie Willcox, pour créer la Peninsula Steam Navigation Company, qui assure un service régulier entre l'Angleterre, l'Espagne et le Portugal. Cette compagnie va devenir la Peninsula and Oriental Steam Navigation Company, l'une des rares entreprises de cette époque à continuer de nos jours sous le même nom : P & O. En 1837, la P & O remporte le contrat de transport de la poste auprès de l'Amirauté britannique entre Falmouth, en Cornouailles (Écosse), et Vigo, en Espagne. En 1857, la P & O devient la principale compagnie à desservir l'Australie. En 1866, un ingénieur du nom de Alfred Holt lance l'*Agamemnon* pour assurer la liaison avec la Chine et les îles du Pacifique. Bientôt secondé par ses frères d'armement l'*Ajax* et l'*Achilles*, la compagnie offre le premier service régulier de paquebot à vapeur vers l'Orient. Leur réussite est due à l'adoption par Holt d'un moteur à chaudière à haute pression et double expansion de conception révolutionnaire.

Si l'Atlantique a été dominé par les compagnies anglaises et américaines pendant plus d'un demi-siècle, c'est désormais la Hamburg Amerika Linie, une compagnie développée grâce au génie commercial d'Albert Ballin, qui va les supplanter dans les premières années du XXᵉ siècle grâce à deux de ses navires : le *Kaiser Wilhelm der Grosse* et le *Deutschland*.

The genius of the new era of steam navigation, Isambard Kingdom Brunel (1806–1859), designer of the *Great Western*, the first steamer to cross the Atlantic, and the *Great Britain*, the first driven by screws.

Der Mann, der das neue Zeitalter der Dampfschiffahrt begründete: Isambard Kingdom Brunel (1806–1859), Konstrukteur der *Great Western*, die als erstes Dampfschiff im Liniendienst den Atlantik befuhr, und der *Great Britain*, des ersten Zweischraubendampfers.

La navigation à vapeur s'est développée grâce notamment à Isambard Kingdom Brunel (1806–1859), concepteur du *Great Western*, le premier navire à vapeur à traverser l'Atlantique, et du *Great Britain*, le premier bateau propulsé par hélice.

——— 1 ———
The Race Begins

The Race Begins

While the main aims of the lines on the Atlantic route were speed and opulence, another form of traffic had brought the young Albert Ballin into the shipping world. His father, of Danish-Jewish extraction, owned a modest shipping agency for emigrants in Hamburg. The 17-year-old Albert took over when his father died suddenly in 1874. Between 1875 and 1881 the number of migrants leaving Hamburg for the New World went up fivefold, to just under 125,000 a year. This was the era of mass migration, and the beginning of the legend of Ellis Island, described as the toughest interrogation centre this side of the Last Judgment.

The flow across the Atlantic became a tidal wave. Between 1892 and 1920 12 million passed through New York alone, almost all through Ellis Island. Only about two per cent were rejected, but even so this was nearly a third of a million; some 3,000 committed suicide while waiting to be processed. In 1913 almost one and a half million people took ship from Europe for the United States, and that year more than one million Italians left their native shores to emigrate to America, north or south, Australasia and Africa.

Albert Ballin became managing director of the Hamburg Amerika Line in 1899. The German lines had already overtaken their British and American rivals when the *Kaiser Wilhelm der Grosse*, a super-liner of Norddeutscher Lloyd, won the Blue Riband in 1897. On 24 July 1900 the 17,000-ton *Deutschland* of Hamburg Amerika seized the prize with a run to New York of 5 days 15 hours and 5 minutes.

Ballin's plan was simply to have the biggest and best, in sheer size as well as number of ships and quality of service offered. It was a matter of national prestige. The contest between Britain and Germany in commercial shipping mirrored the naval arms race to build the most effective battleships, the dreadnoughts. At times the contest verged on the megalomaniac. It was even said that a monstrously ornate German imperial eagle was added to the bow of the *Imperator*, just to ensure that she would be the longest ship in existence.

By 1914 the Hamburg Amerika Line was by far the largest shipping company in the world, both in terms of gross tonnage and number of hulls in the water and under construction. It had 194 ships on its books, a total tonnage of 1,307,411, against the 135 ships and 907,996 tons of its nearest rival, the Norddeutscher Lloyd of Bremen. Well below it was the White Star Line with 33 ships and 472,877 tons, and the Cunard Steamship Company with 29 ships and 344,251 tons. By this time the Hamburg Amerika had also taken a dominant role in the new route to the Pacific through the Panama Canal, with its *Tirpitz* and *William O'Swald*, the first two ships above 20,000 tons to appear in that region.

The struggle for supremacy on the Atlantic route was a battle between four companies. Hamburg Amerika, once having grasped the Blue Riband, was determined to hang on to it. But in 1904 the *Kaiser Wilhelm II* of Norddeutscher Lloyd took it with a crossing of 5 days 11 hours and 58 minutes eastbound on 20 June. Three years later Cunard took the prize with the *Lusitania*, and later in the same year with the *Mauretania*, which was to hold it until 1929. Though not always the most luxurious liner, the *Mauretania* was to remain a favourite with Cunard passengers in her 30 years of service. She last did the Atlantic run on 30 June 1934, the day Cunard merged with the White Star Line, the fourth and most ill-fated of the companies striving for the North Atlantic prize.

White Star had taken the Blue Riband in 1891 with the *Majestic* and *Teutonic*, both great pioneers in their day. On 23 January 1909 the *Republic* was involved in a fatal collision with the *Florida*, of Lloyd Italiano, outward-bound from Naples. By using the newfangled invention of wireless telegraphy, the *Republic* managed to call up her fleet-mate the *Baltic*, which successfully took 1,650 passengers and crew aboard. But, as later tragedies were to show, the dangers of sea travel were by no means eliminated by the fact that potential salvation was only a distress-call away.

The value of wireless at sea, however, was shown in the dramatic arrest of Dr Hawley Harvey Crippen, a London dentist who murdered his wife and escaped with his mistress to Canada. Having gone aboard the SS *Montrose* at Antwerp, he believed he was safe. But the captain grew suspicious and telegraphed Scotland Yard. The *Montrose* was overtaken by the faster SS *Laurentic*, carrying Chief Inspector Walter Dew. He boarded the *Montrose* in the St Lawrence River and effected the arrest. Crippen was later hanged in Pentonville Prison, London.

With Cunard's *Mauretania* and her sister *Lusitania* established as the fastest ships on the Atlantic run, the White Star Line planned to beat them with three new giants, *Olympic*, *Titanic* and *Gigantic*. Albert Ballin was determined not to be outdone, and conceived a project for building three German super-liners, *Imperator*, *Vaterland* and *Bismarck*. The

Imperator and her sisters were the first class of liner to exceed 50,000 tons. Novel forms of steam propulsion had to be developed, and the *Bismarck*, the last to be launched, had the revolutionary Parsons direct-acting steam turbines to drive her 56,000 tons.

The story of both trios of ships is touched with deep tragedy. The most successful of the six, perhaps, was the first to be commissioned, the *Olympic*. She was to survive the war first as an armed cruiser, then as a troopship. She successfully evaded three direct attacks by submarine torpedo, and rammed and sank one of her would-be assailants, U-boat U-103, in May 1918 off the Lizard in Cornwall. She left service in 1935.

Her fame could never match that of her sister, the *Titanic*, whose dreadful end on her maiden voyage has made her name universally known. *Titanic* was intended to be the largest, most luxurious and above all safest liner in the world. Her story is one of ill luck, human error and heroism.

After embarking passengers at Southampton, Cherbourg and Queenstown, the *Titanic* cleared Ireland on 11 April 1912. Four days later the papers were carrying the first reports of her end. She had already turned south to avoid ice when she grazed an iceberg at 11.40 pm on 14 April. Wireless warnings about the ice had either been ignored or muddled. As the ship began to sink, it was soon realized that there were lifeboats for only half the number of people aboard. Her complement of lifeboats was in fact in excess of Board of Trade requirements – but these rules had not been updated since the 1800s, well before the age of steam.

As she sank the engineers stayed at their posts to ensure that power and light kept running, and on deck the band played on. Some time after 2.10 am on 15 April she began to slip beneath the surface. The nearest ship, the *Carpathia*, arrived after another two hours. By 8.30 am she had taken aboard 705 survivors; the passenger list had some 1308 names registered, plus crew. The accounts of survivors make poignant reading to this day.

The loss of the *Titanic* was devastating for White Star, who were hard pressed to maintain regular services across the Atlantic. The great German liners of the Hamburg Amerika Line were poised to triumph by the summer of 1914, but then came the war, and the three mighty ships were lost forever.

During the war the great British liners became the targets of the U-boat offensive. The *Lusitania* was hit without warning

by torpedoes off Ireland as she was passing ten miles off the Old Head of Kinsale on 7 May 1915. Only 761 passengers of the full company of 1,959 were saved. Among those who perished was the American millionaire yachtsman Alfred Vanderbilt, a confidant of President Woodrow Wilson. American shock at the attack ensured that the United States would eventually join the war on the side of Britain.

The *Britannic*, as it was deemed wise to rename the *Gigantic* after the tragedy of 1912, was commissioned as a naval hospital ship. On 12 November 1916 she hit a mine laid by U-boat U-73 off the Greek island of Kea. Some 21 people died as lifeboats were lowered into the still rotating propellers. The rest of the company, 1,125 crew, medical staff and patients, were saved. The *Britannic*, at 48,158 tons, was the biggest merchant ship Britain was to lose in the war.

Ashtrays abound in the smoking room of the P & O liner *Himalaya*, 1892. She was built for the long journey to India, and furnished accordingly.

Kein Mangel an Aschenbechern im Rauchsalon des P & O-Liners *Himalaya*, 1892. Das Schiff war für die langen Überfahrten nach Indien gebaut und entsprechend ausgestattet.

En 1892, cendriers et crachoirs abondent dans le fumoir de l'*Himalaya*, un paquebot de la P & O meublé de manière confortable pour les passagers effectuant à bord le long voyage vers les Indes.

Auf der Atlantikroute drehte sich alles um Luxus und Geschwindigkeit, doch als der junge Albert Ballin ins Schiffahrtsgewerbe eintrat, hatte er es zunächst mit Reisenden ganz anderer Art zu tun. Sein Vater, dänisch-jüdischer Abstammung, betrieb in Hamburg eine bescheidene Schiffahrtsagentur für Auswanderer. Als der Vater 1874 unerwartet starb, übernahm der 17jährige Albert das Geschäft. Zwischen 1875 und 1881 verfünffachte sich der Strom der Auswanderer, die von Hamburg in die Neue Welt aufbrachen, und stieg auf knapp 125 000 pro Jahr. Es war die Zeit der Massenemigration, die Zeit, in der Ellis Island zur meistgefürchteten Richterbank diesseits des Jüngsten Gerichts aufstieg.

Eine wahre Flutwelle von Auswanderern wälzte sich über den Atlantik. Zwischen 1892 und 1920 kamen allein 12 Millionen in New York an, fast alle davon auf Ellis Island. Nur etwa zwei Prozent wurden abgewiesen, doch selbst das war fast eine Drittelmillion; an die 3000 brachten sich in den Lagern um. 1913 schifften sich fast anderthalb Millionen Menschen von Europa in die Vereinigten Staaten ein, und im selben Jahr wanderten allein aus Italien über eine Million nach Nord- und Südamerika, Australasien und Afrika aus.

1899 wurde Albert Ballin geschäftsführender Direktor der Hamburg-Amerika-Linie. Die Deutschen hatten ihre britischen und amerikanischen Rivalen bereits 1897 überflügelt, als der Ozeanriese *Kaiser Wilhelm der Große* der Gesellschaft Norddeutscher Lloyd das Blaue Band gewann. Am 24. Juli 1900 errang der 17 000-Tonner *Deutschland* der Hamburg-Amerika-Linie die Trophäe mit einer Fahrt nach New York binnen 5 Tagen, 15 Stunden und 5 Minuten.

Ballin wollte aus seiner Linie schlicht die größte und beste machen, sowohl nach Anzahl der Passagiere und Schiffe als auch nach gebotenem Standard. Es war eine Frage des Nationalstolzes. Der Wettlauf zwischen Großbritannien und Deutschland in der Passagierschiffahrt war ein Echo des Wettrüstens um die schlagkräftigste Kriegsmarine. Zum Teil nahm diese Konkurrenz megalomanische Ausmaße an. Spötter sagten, der *Imperator* habe man ihren monströsen Reichsadler nur an den Bug montiert, damit sie zum längsten Schiff der Welt wurde.

1914 war die Hamburg-Amerika mit Abstand die weltgrößte Schiffahrtslinie, sowohl nach Bruttoregistertonnen als auch nach der Zahl der Schiffe im Dienst oder im Bau. Sie verfügte über 194 Schiffe mit einer Gesamttonnage von 1 507 411 Tonnen; ihr größter Rivale, der Norddeutsche Lloyd aus Bremen, bot 135 Schiffe mit 907 996 Bruttoregistertonnen auf. Weit abgeschlagen folgten die White Star Line mit 33 Schiffen und 472 877 Tonnen und die Cunard Steamship Company mit 29 Schiffen und 344 251 Tonnen. Zu jener Zeit beherrschte die Hamburg-Amerika-Linie mit der *Tirpitz* und der *William O'Swald*, den ersten beiden Schiffen über 20 000 Tonnen in dieser Region, auch bereits die Pazifikroute durch den neu eröffneten Panamakanal.

Vier Gesellschaften rangen um die Vorherrschaft auf der Atlantikroute. Nachdem die Hamburg-Amerika-Linie das Blaue Band einmal errungen hatte, war sie fest entschlossen, es nicht wieder herzugeben. Doch am 20. Juni 1904 jagte der Norddeutsche Lloyd es ihr mit der *Kaiser Wilhelm II* und einer Ostfahrt von 5 Tagen, 11 Stunden und 58 Minuten ab. Drei Jahre darauf errang Cunard mit der *Lusitania* die Trophäe und im selben Jahr noch einmal mit der *Mauretania*, die den Rekord bis 1929 hielt. Obwohl sie unter den Ozeanriesen längst nicht die luxuriöseste war, blieb die *Mauretania* unter den Cunard-Schiffen in ihren 30 Dienstjahren stets eines der beliebtesten. Zu ihrer letzten Atlantiküberfahrt brach sie am 30. Juni 1934 auf, dem Tag, an dem Cunard mit der White Star Line fusionierte, dem vierten und am meisten vom Unglück verfolgten Mitstreiter auf dem Nordatlantik.

White Star hatte das Blaue Band 1891 mit der *Majestic* und der *Teutonic* errungen, beide seinerzeit äußerst fortschrittliche Schiffe. Am 23. Januar 1909 sank die *Republic* nach einer Kollision mit der *Florida* des Lloyd Italiano in der Bucht von Neapel. Mit dem jüngst erfundenen drahtlosen Telegraphen konnte die *Republic* ihr Schwesterschiff *Baltic* zu Hilfe rufen, die 1650 Passagiere und Besatzungsmitglieder rettete. Doch wie spätere Katastrophen beweisen sollten, waren die Gefahren der Seefahrt keineswegs dadurch gebannt, daß eine mögliche Rettung nun nur noch einen SOS-Ruf weit entfernt war.

Auf spektakuläre Weise bewies die Verhaftung von Dr. Crippen den Nutzen eines Funkgerätes an Bord. Der Londoner Zahnarzt Dr. Hawley Harvey Crippen hatte seine Frau umgebracht und wollte sich mit seiner Geliebten nach Kanada absetzen. Als er in Antwerpen an Bord des Dampfers SS *Montrose* ging, wähnte er sich in Sicherheit, doch der Kapitän schöpfte Verdacht und telegrafierte an Scotland Yard. Die schnellere *Laurentic* mit Chefinspektor Walter Dew an Bord holte die SS *Montrose* im St.-Lorenz-Strom ein, der Inspektor setzte über und verhaftete Crippen, der später im Londoner Gefängnis Pentonville gehängt wurde.

Nachdem sich die *Mauretania* und ihr Schwesterschiff *Lusitania* von Cunard als die schnellsten Schiffe auf der Atlantikroute etabliert hatten, gab die White Star Line drei neue Ozeanriesen in Auftrag, die ihnen Paroli bieten sollten, die *Olympic, Titanic* und *Gigantic.* Albert Ballin wollte nicht zurückstehen und plante den Bau drei neuer deutscher Großdampfer, *Imperator, Vaterland* und *Bismarck.* Die *Imperator* und ihre zwei Schwestern waren die ersten Passagierschiffe von mehr als 50 000 Tonnen. Neue Maschinen mußten für ihren Antrieb entwickelt werden, und die 56 000 Tonnen der *Bismarck,* die als letzte vom Stapel lief, trieben bereits die revolutionären Parsons-Dampfturbinen an.

Beiden Schiffstrios war ein tragisches Schicksal beschieden. Am erfolgreichsten war noch die älteste von ihnen, die *Olympic.* Sie überstand den Ersten Weltkrieg zunächst als bewaffneter Kreuzer, dann als Truppentransporter. Dreimal entging sie Torpedoangriffen und rammte und versenkte im Mai 1918 vor Lizard Point in Cornwall ihren deutschen Angreifer U-103. Sie blieb bis 1935 im Dienst.

Doch berühmter wurde ihre Schwester *Titanic,* deren schreckliches Ende auf der Jungfernfahrt bis heute die Erinnerung an sie wachhält. Die *Titanic* sollte der schnellste, luxuriöseste und auch sicherste Ozeandampfer der Welt werden. Unglück, menschliches Versagen, aber auch heroische Leistungen kommen in der Geschichte dieses Schiffes zusammen.

Nachdem sie in Southampton und Cherbourg Passagiere an Bord genommen hatte, lief die *Titanic* das irische Queenstown an, von wo sie am 11. April 1912 ablegte. Vier Tage darauf erschienen in den Zeitungen die ersten Berichte über ihren Untergang. Das Schiff hatte bereits einen südlicheren Kurs genommen, um Eisfelder zu umgehen, doch um 23 Uhr 40 am Abend des 14. April kam es zum Zusammenstoß mit einem Eisberg, der das Schiff entlang der Flanke aufriß. Vorherige Funkwarnungen hatte man ignoriert oder falsch verstanden. Als das Schiff zu sinken begann, war bald klar, daß die vorhandenen Rettungsboote nur für die Hälfte der Menschen an Bord reichen würden. Zwar hatte die *Titanic* mehr Rettungsboote, als amtlich vorgeschrieben war, doch diese Vorschriften stammten aus dem 19. Jahrhundert, aus einer Zeit, als das Dampfschiffzeitalter noch gar nicht wirklich begonnen hatte.

Selbst auf dem sinkenden Schiff blieben die Mechaniker auf ihren Posten, um Beleuchtung und Stromversorgung sicherzustellen, und an Deck spielte weiter die Kapelle. Gegen 2 Uhr 10 am Morgen des 15. April versank die *Titanic* in den Fluten. Weitere zwei Stunden vergingen, bis das nächstgelegene Schiff, die *Carpathia,* an der Unglücksstelle eintraf. Bis 8 Uhr 30 hatte sie 705 Überlebende an Bord genommen; auf der Passagierliste hatten 1308 Namen gestanden, und dazu kam die Besatzung. Auch heute noch sind die Berichte der Überlebenden eine erschütternde Lektüre.

Der Verlust der *Titanic* war ein vernichtender Schlag für die White Star Line, die nur mit Mühe einen Liniendienst über den Atlantik aufrechterhalten konnte. Im Sommer 1914 schien nichts den Siegeszug der deutschen Ozeanriesen der Hamburg-Amerika-Linie aufhalten zu können, doch dann kam der Krieg, und die Reederei sollte ihre drei Prachtschiffe nie wiedersehen.

Im Krieg waren die britischen Linienschiffe den Angriffen der deutschen U-Boote ausgesetzt. Die *Lusitania* wurde am 7. Mai 1915 ohne Vorwarnung vor der irischen Küste torpediert und sank zehn Meilen vor Old Head of Kinsale. Nur 761 der insgesamt 1959 Menschen an Bord wurden gerettet. Zu den Opfern gehörte auch der amerikanische Millionär und Jachtbesitzer Alfred Vanderbilt, ein Vertrauter von Präsident Woodrow Wilson. Die amerikanische Öffentlichkeit war schockiert über den Angriff, und der Vorfall trug mit dazu bei, daß die Vereinigten Staaten schließlich auf britischer Seite in den Krieg eintraten.

Die *Gigantic,* nach der Tragödie von 1912 in *Britannic* umbenannt, wurde als Hospitalschiff requiriert. Am 12. November 1916 lief sie vor der griechischen Insel Kea auf eine von U-Boot U-73 gelegte Mine. 21 Menschen kamen um, als die Rettungsboote in die noch laufenden Schiffsschrauben hinabgelassen wurden. Die übrigen 1125 Besatzungsmitglieder, medizinisches Personal und Patienten wurden gerettet. Mit 48 158 Bruttoregistertonnen war die *Britannic* das größte Schiff, das die britische Handelsmarine im Ersten Weltkrieg verlor.

The Hamburg Amerika Line's *Imperator* off the Isle of Wight, June 1913.

Die *Imperator* der Hamburg-Amerika-Linie vor der Isle of Wight, Juni 1913.

L'*Imperator,* de la Hamburg Amerika Linie, au large de l'île de Wight, en juin 1913.

1

La course est lancée

Tandis que les compagnies transatlantiques cherchent avant tout à offrir vitesse et luxe à leurs passagers, c'est dans un tout autre registre que le jeune Albert Ballin pénètre dans le monde du transport maritime. En 1874, il succède à son père, un juif originaire du Danemark, à la tête de la modeste agence de voyages pour émigrants installée à Hambourg. Le nombre de candidats quittant Hambourg pour le Nouveau Monde quintuple en effet entre 1875 et 1881 pour atteindre le chiffre de 125 000 voyageurs par an. C'est à cette époque d'émigration de masse que naît la légende d'Ellis Island, une île située à la pointe de Manhattan que certains ont décrite comme le centre d'interrogatoire le plus sévère en dehors du Jugement dernier.

Le flux d'immigrants traversant l'Atlantique devient rapidement une véritable marée. Entre 1892 et 1920, 12 millions de passagers débarquent à New York, pour la plupart après une escale obligatoire à Ellis Island. Deux pour cent d'entre eux seulement sont refusés – ce qui représente toutefois près de 300 000 personnes – et près de 3000 se suicident en attendant leur admission. En 1913, près d'un million et demi de personnes prennent le bateau pour se rendre d'Europe aux États-Unis, et plus d'un million d'Italiens émigrent en Amérique – du Nord ou du Sud –, en Australasie et en Afrique.

Albert Ballin est nommé directeur général de la Hamburg Amerika Linie en 1899. À cette époque, les compagnies allemandes surclassent leurs rivales britanniques et américaines sur la ligne transatlantique : le *Kaiser Wilhelm der Grosse*, un paquebot géant de la Norddeutscher Lloyd Linie, qui obtient le Ruban bleu en 1897, est à son tour détrôné le 24 juillet 1900 par le *Deutschland*, un navire de 17 000 tonneaux appartenant à la Hamburg Amerika, qui remporte le prix en ralliant New York en 5 jours, 15 heures et 5 minutes.

Ballin ambitionne de posséder ce qu'il y a de mieux et de plus grand, tant en taille qu'en nombre de navires et en qualité de service offert. Il s'agit alors d'une question de prestige national. La concurrence que se livrent la Grande-Bretagne et l'Allemagne dans le domaine de la navigation commerciale reflète parallèlement cette course à l'armement naval où chacun vise à construire les cuirassés d'escadre les plus puissants. La compétition tourne d'ailleurs parfois à la mégalomanie paranoïaque. On a même dit qu'un gigantesque aigle impérial allemand fut posé à la proue de l'*Imperator* simplement pour le rallonger et en faire le plus long navire existant.

En 1914, la Hamburg Amerika Linie est de loin la plus importante compagnie maritime du monde, à la fois quant au tonnage brut et au nombre de navires en service et en construction. Elle possède en effet 194 bâtiments totalisant 1 307 411 tonneaux, sa plus proche rivale, la Norddeutscher Lloyd de Brême, ne disposant que de 135 navires pour un total de 907 996 tonneaux ; viennent ensuite, de taille bien inférieure, la White Star Line (33 navires, 472 877 tonneaux) et la Cunard Steamship Company (29 navires, 344 251 tonneaux). La Hamburg Amerika occupe à cette époque une position dominante sur la nouvelle route du Pacifique, créée grâce à l'ouverture du canal de Panama, où sont mis en service le *Tirpitz* et le *William O'Swald*, les deux premiers navires de plus de 20 000 tonnes à naviguer dans cette région.

La bataille pour la suprématie sur la route Atlantique se déroule entre quatre compagnies et ne connaît aucun répit. Si la Hamburg Amerika est bien déterminée à conserver le Ruban bleu, elle se le fait reprendre le 20 juin 1904 par le *Kaiser Wilhelm II*, de la Norddeutscher Lloyd, qui effectue la traversée d'ouest en est en 5 jours 11 heures et 58 minutes. Trois ans plus tard, la Cunard s'arroge deux fois le prix la même année grâce, successivement, au *Lusitania* et au *Mauretania*, ce dernier le conservant jusqu'en 1929. S'il est loin de compter parmi les navires les plus luxueux, le *Mauretania* allait demeurer l'un des favoris des passagers de la Cunard pendant ses 30 années de service, jusqu'au 30 juin 1934, date à laquelle il effectue sa dernière traversée de l'Atlantique et où Cunard fusionne avec la White Star Line, la quatrième compagnie à concourir pour le prix de l'Atlantique Nord et la plus malchanceuse de toutes.

La White Star a remporté le Ruban bleu en 1891 avec le *Majestic* et le *Teutonic*, deux des grands navires pionniers de l'époque. Le 23 janvier 1909, son navire le *Republic* entre en collision avec le *Florida*, de la Lloyd Italiano, alors qu'il appareille de Naples et commence à sombrer. Utilisant la télégraphie sans fil, d'invention toute récente, le *Republic* parvient à appeler à la rescousse son « sister ship » le *Baltic*, qui réussit à sauver 1650 passagers et hommes d'équipage. Comme allaient le démontrer malheureusement d'autres tragédies, les dangers inhérents à la navigation ne sont cependant pas éliminés du simple fait qu'un appel de détresse salutaire à la TSF est désormais possible.

Le télégraphe sans fil démontre cependant tout son intérêt en mer à l'occasion de l'arrestation du Dr Hawley Harvey Crippen, un dentiste londonien qui, après avoir assassiné sa

The launch of the 45,324-ton White Star *Olympic* from the Harland and Wolff yard, Belfast, 1910. She was briefly the world's largest liner.

Belfast, 1910: Stapellauf der *Olympic* der White Star Line bei Harland and Wolff. Mit 45 524 Tonnen war sie für kurze Zeit das größte Schiff der Welt.

L'*Olympic* (45 524 tonneaux), appartenant à la White Star, sur son ber de lancement des chantiers Harland & Wolff de Belfast, en 1910. Ce fut brièvement le plus grand paquebot du monde.

femme, s'enfuit avec sa maîtresse et embarque à Anvers sur le SS *Montrose*, en partance pour le Canada. Malheureusement pour eux, le commandant du navire, nourrissant quelques soupçons, télégraphie alors à Scotland Yard qui dépêche aussitôt l'inspecteur principal Walter Dew à la poursuite des fugitifs à bord du SS *Laurentic*. Le *Montrose*, plus lent, est rattrapé sur le Saint-Laurent, où le policier procède à l'arrestation du meurtrier et le ramène en Angleterre, où il sera pendu à la prison londonienne de Pentonville.

Afin de battre les navires les plus rapides sur l'Atlantique, le *Mauretania* et le *Lusitania* de la Cunard, la White Star Line met en chantier trois nouveaux géants des mers, l'*Olympic*, le *Titanic* et le *Gigantic*. De son côté, Albert Ballin n'est pas prêt à se laisser distancer et décide de construire trois paquebots allemands géants : l'*Imperator*, le *Vaterland* et le *Bismarck*. L'*Imperator* et ses « sister ships » étant les premiers navires à dépasser les 50 000 tonnes, il fallut inventer un nouveau mode de propulsion à vapeur ; c'est ainsi que le *Bismarck*, dernier navire lancé, dispose des révolutionnaires turbines à vapeur Parsons pour déplacer ses 56 000 tonnes.

L'histoire de ces deux trios de navires est marquée du sceau de la tragédie. Le plus chanceux des six est sans doute l'*Olympic*, le premier mis en chantier, qui traverse la Première Guerre mondiale en tant que croiseur puis navire transport de troupes. En mai 1918, après avoir échappé à trois torpillages, il réussit à éperonner et couler un de ses probables assaillants, le sous-marin allemand U-103, au large du cap Lizard, en Cornouailles. Il est désarmé en 1935.

Sa renommée est toutefois moindre que celle de son « sister ship » le *Titanic*, qui doit sa tragique célébrité à son dramatique naufrage. Le *Titanic* devait être le plus grand, le plus luxueux et le plus sûr de tous les paquebots du monde. Son histoire est celle de la malchance, de l'erreur humaine et de l'héroïsme.

Après avoir embarqué ses passagers à Southampton, Cherbourg et Queenstown, le *Titanic* quitte l'Irlande le 11 avril 1912 pour son voyage inaugural ; quatre jours plus tard, les journaux diffusent les premiers comptes-rendus de son naufrage. Le paquebot, qui s'est déjà dérouté vers le sud pour éviter les glaces, heurte un iceberg le 14 avril à 23 h 40. Les messages d'alerte diffusés par le télégraphe concernant la présence de banquises flottantes sur sa nouvelle route ont été soit ignorés, soit brouillés. Ce n'est que lorsque le navire commence à sombrer qu'on s'aperçoit que si le nombre des canots de sauvetage à bord dépasse toutefois les exigences du Board of Trade – une réglementation datant des années 1800, bien avant l'âge de la vapeur, et jamais depuis mise à jour –, ils ne peuvent embarquer que la moitié des passagers à bord.

L'orchestre joue inlassablement sur le pont et les mécaniciens du bord continuent d'assurer la production d'électricité et de lumière tandis que le *Titanic* s'enfonce lentement. Peu après 2 h 10 du matin, le 15 avril, le paquebot est englouti sous les eaux et disparaît. Le plus proche navire, le *Carpathia*, arrive deux heures plus tard. À 8 h 30, il n'a pu recueillir que 705 survivants sur un total de 1308 passagers, membres d'équipage non compris. Leurs récits sont aujourd'hui encore d'une lecture poignante.

La perte du *Titanic* est un vrai désastre pour la White Star, qui a déjà du mal à maintenir un service régulier sur l'Atlantique, et les grands paquebots allemands de la Hamburg Amerika Linie s'apprêtent à triompher. Mais la guerre éclate pendant l'été 1914 et la compagnie va bientôt perdre ses trois puissants navires.

Pendant la guerre, les paquebots britanniques deviennent évidemment la cible privilégiée des U boote. Le 7 mai 1915, le *Lusitania* est ainsi torpillé sans sommation par un sous-marin allemand alors qu'il passe au large de l'Irlande, à dix milles de Old Head, près de Kinsale. Il n'y a que 761 rescapés sur les 1 959 passagers. Au nombre des disparus figure l'Américain Alfred Vanderbilt, le yachtsman millionnaire et ami intime de Woodrow Wilson, le président des États-Unis. Le choc subi par les Américains les détermine alors à entrer en guerre aux côtés des Britanniques.

Sagement rebaptisé *Britannic* après la tragédie qu'a connue son « sister ship » en 1912 et transformé en hôpital naval, le *Gigantic* touche le 12 novembre 1916 une mine posée par le U-boot U-73 au large de l'île grecque de Kéa. Si 1125 patients, hommes d'équipage et membres du personnel médical sont sauvés, 21 d'entre eux périssent broyés dans leurs canots de sauvetage, malheureusement descendus trop près des hélices encore en mouvement. Le *Britannic*, de 48158 tonnes de déplacement, est le plus gros navire marchand que les Britanniques perdront pendant la Première Guerre mondiale.

German giant
The *Kaiser Wilhelm der Grosse* was
one of the great German 'four-stackers',
introduced in 1897 on the North Atlantic
route by Norddeutscher Lloyd.

Der deutsche Riese
Die *Kaiser Wilhelm der Große*, eines der
gewaltigen »Vier-Schornstein-Schiffe«,
mit denen der Norddeutsche Lloyd von
1897 an die Nordatlantikroute befuhr.

Un géant allemand
Le *Kaiser Wilhelm der Grosse* est l'un
des grands paquebots allemands à « quatre
cheminées ». Il fut mis en service en
1897 sur la route transatlantique par la
Norddeutscher Lloyd.

The early 'express' liners

The Cunard liner *Campania*, 12,950 tons, was launched in September 1892, and won the Blue Riband a year later. The SS *Orsova* (bottom left) was launched on the Clyde in 1909. Few surpassed in elegance the Hamburg Amerika *Kaiserin Augusta Viktoria* (centre), here entering New York habour or for speed the *Deutschland*, Blue Riband winner in 1900.

Die frühen Expreßdampfer

Der Cunard-Dampfer *Campania*, 12 950 Tonnen, lief im September 1892 vom Stapel und errang im folgenden Jahr das Blaue Band. Die SS *Orsova* (unten links) verließ 1909 die Werften am Clyde. An Eleganz konnten es nur wenige mit der *Kaiserin Augusta Viktoria* der Hamburg-Amerika-Linie aufnehmen, hier bei der Einfahrt in den New Yorker Hafen (Mitte), oder an Geschwindigkeit mit der *Deutschland*, an die das Blaue Band im Jahre 1900 ging.

Les premiers paquebots « rapides »

Le *Campania* (12 950 tonneaux), mis en service en septembre 1892 par la Cunard, remporte le Ruban bleu un an plus tard. Le SS *Orsova* (en bas, à gauche) est lancé sur la Clyde en 1909. Peu de navires de l'époque dépassent en élégance le *Kaiserin Augusta Viktoria* (au centre, entrant dans le port de New York) de la Hamburg Amerika, ou en vitesse le *Deutschland*, lauréat du Ruban bleu en 1900.

Contrasting lifestyles
Lascar stokers in the boiler rooms of a P & O liner swelter as they shovel coal. The Duke of Marlborough (fourth from left) and his American duchess, Consuela (second from left), relax on the promenade deck of the P & O liner *Arabia* en route from Marseilles to Bombay for the Delhi Durbar, 1902.

Das schöne und das harte Leben
In der Gluthitze des Kesselraums schaufeln Laskaren auf einem P & O-Liner die Kohle in die Kessel. Der Herzog von Marlborough (vierter von links) und die amerikanische Herzogin Consuelo (zweite von links) entspannen sich auf dem Promenadendeck des P & O-Liners *Arabia* auf der Fahrt von Marseille nach Bombay, unterwegs zu einem Empfang beim Vizekönig in Delhi, 1902.

Des styles de vie opposés
Les chauffeurs de ce paquebot de la P & O pelletaient le charbon jour après jour dans une chaleur étouffante. Le duc de Marlborough (quatrième à partir de la gauche) et Consuelo, son épouse américaine (deuxième à partir de la gauche), se reposent sur le pont-promenade du paquebot *Arabia* de la P & O, en service sur la ligne Marseille-Bombay, en se rendant au darbâr de Delhi en 1902.

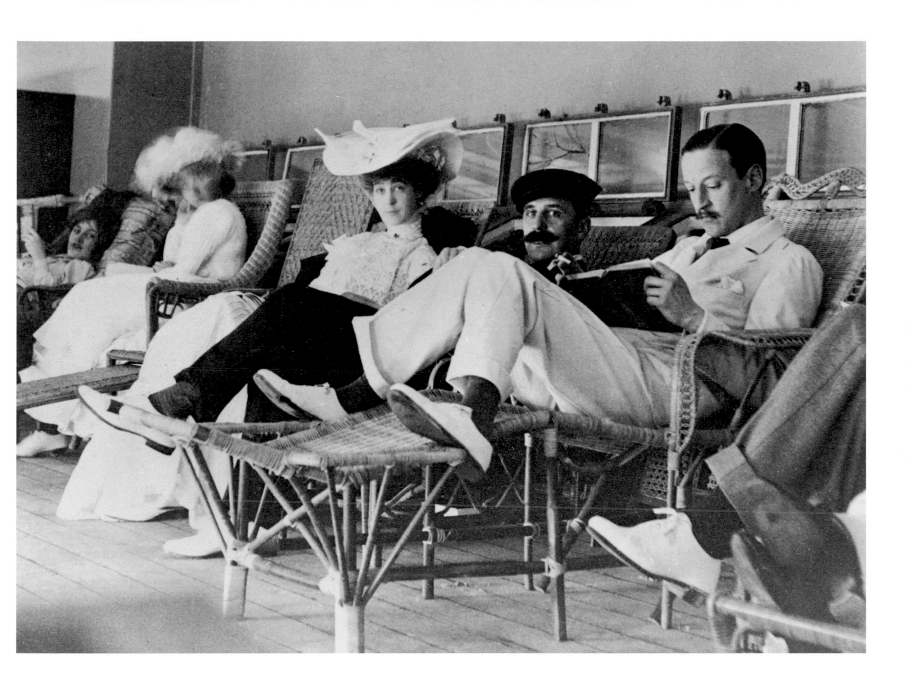

Bound for new lands
Travelling to a new life in steerage class, emigrants crowd aboard the tender *Herald* leaving the quay at Liverpool to board the liner *Zealandic* for Australia, 4 October 1913. (Above) A family of Scottish emigrants sight Canada for the first time from their ship, 1915.

Zu neuen Ufern
Emigranten drängen sich auf dem Leichter *Herald*, der am 4. Oktober 1913 am Kai von Liverpool ablegt, um sie an Bord des Dampfers *Zealandic* und auf dessen Zwischendeck zu einem neuen Leben in Australien zu bringen. (Oben) Eine schottische Emigrantenfamilie sieht 1915 von Bord ihres Schiffes zum ersten Male Kanada.

Le voyage vers de nouveaux mondes
Les émigrants en partance pour une nouvelle vie se pressent à bord du transbordeur *Herald*, quittant ici un quai de Liverpool le 4 octobre 1913, pour embarquer – en troisième classe – sur le paquebot *Zealandic* à destination de l'Australie. (Ci-dessus) Une famille d'émigrants écossais aperçoit enfin les côtes du Canada depuis le pont de leur navire, en 1915.

Despair, hope, trepidation
(Left) Emigrants from central Europe crowd the fo'c'sle of the Red Star *Westernland*, bound from Antwerp to New York, 1901. Millions of migrants headed for the new world on the first liners, and had to pass through the dreaded Ellis Island terminal (above). An immigration inspector sticks labels to the coats of a family from Germany, 1905.

Verzweiflung, Hoffnung, Furcht
(Links) Mitteleuropäische Auswanderer auf dem Vorderdeck des Red Star-Liners *Westernland*, mit dem sie im Jahre 1901 von Antwerpen nach New York aufbrechen. Mit den ersten Ozeandampfern gelangten Millionen von Emigranten in die Neue Welt, wo sie zunächst die gefürchtete Einreisekontrolle in Ellis Island passieren mußten (oben). Ein Beamter der Einwanderungsbehörde steckt 1905 einer deutschen Familie Etiketten an den Mantel.

Désespoir, espoir, inquiétude
(À gauche) Ces émigrants d'Europe centrale s'agglutinent sur le gaillard d'avant du *Westernland*, un navire de la Red Star reliant, en 1901, Anvers à New York. Les millions de migrants partis pour le Nouveau Monde doivent passer par le redoutable terminal d'Ellis Island (ci-dessus). Un inspecteur de l'immigration épingle une étiquette sur les manteaux d'une famille venue d'Allemagne (1905).

Travellers' favourite

The RMS *Mauretania* clearing Liverpool docks on her maiden voyage, 16 November 1907. Despite storms and heavy fog, she made a good time of under six days for the crossing. She captured the Blue Riband from her sister, the *Lusitania*, in 1907 and 1909, and held it until 1929. She was to remain one of the most popular liners on the North Atlantic.

Der Liebling der Passagiere

Die RMS *Mauretania* verläßt auf ihrer Jungfernfahrt am 16. November 1907 den Hafen von Liverpool. Trotz Unwettern und schwerem Nebel gelang ihr die Atlantiküberquerung in der beachtlichen Zeit von weniger als sechs Tagen. 1907 und 1909 jagte sie ihrem Schwesterschiff *Lusitania* das Blaue Band ab und behielt es bis 1929. Bis zuletzt zählte sie zu den populärsten Schiffen auf der Nordatlantikroute.

Le favori des voyageurs

Ce 16 novembre 1907, le RMS *Mauretania* quitte les quais de Liverpool pour son voyage inaugural. Malgré le mauvais temps et un fort brouillard, il réalisa une traversée assez rapide de l'Atlantique en moins de six jours. Il reprit le Ruban bleu à son « sister ship » le *Lusitania* en 1907 et 1909 et le conserva jusqu'en 1929. Ce fut sans doute un des paquebots les plus populaires sur l'Atlantique Nord.

Cunard classic

Stewards, passengers and bystanders aboard the *Mauretania* anchored off the Pembrokeshire coast, Wales, June 1911. She carried 563 first-class, 464 second-class and 1,158 third-class passengers, though she would carry roughly double this number as a troopship from 1915 to 1919. The view of her high rounded stern was to be one of the classic silhouettes of a Cunard liner, imitated but never surpassed.

Der Cunard-Klassiker

Stewards, Passagiere und Besucher an Bord der *Mauretania*, die im Juni 1911 vor der Küste von Pembrokeshire, Wales, vor Anker liegt. Sie konnte 563 Erster-, 464 Zweiter- und 1138 Dritter-Klasse-Passagiere unterbringen, und zwischen 1915 und 1919 beförderte sie als Truppentransporter etwa doppelt so viel Mann. Das hohe, runde Heck zählte zu den großen klassischen Cunard-Silhouetten, oft kopiert, doch nie erreicht.

Un « classique » de la Cunard

Stewards, passagers et spectateurs du *Mauretania*, à l'ancre au large des côtes du Pembrokeshire (Pays de Galles), en juin 1911. Le paquebot pouvait transporter 563 passagers en première classe, 464 en seconde classe et 1138 en troisième classe ; il put toutefois en embarquer près du double de 1915 à 1919 après avoir été transformé en transport de troupes. Sa haute poupe ronde est une des caractéristiques, souvent imitée mais jamais dépassée, des paquebots de la Cunard.

Welsh greeting

In 1909 the *Mauretania* was the first of the great transatlantic liners to call at Fishguard on the Pembrokeshire coast – because it offered a fast rail connection with London. (Left) Well-wishers on a tender greet the ship on her first visit, 30 August 1909. Another group watches from the decks of a local ferry (right).

Begrüßung in Wales

Die *Mauretania* war 1909 der erste Transatlantikliner, der in Fishguard an der Küste von Pembrokeshire Halt machte, von wo es eine schnelle Eisenbahnverbindung nach London gab. (Links) Am 30. August 1909 fährt ein Empfangskomitee mit einem Leichter dem Schiff entgegen und begrüßt es zu seiner ersten Ankunft. Andere sehen von Deck einer Fähre zu (rechts).

L'accueil gallois

En 1909, le *Mauretania* est le premier des grands paquebots transatlantiques à desservir Fishguard, sur la côte du Pembrokeshire, qui avait l'avantage d'offrir une rapide liaison par rail avec Londres. Depuis un transbordeur, ces admirateurs viennent saluer le navire lors de sa première escale, le 30 août 1909 (à gauche), tandis qu'un autre groupe observe le paquebot depuis le pont d'un ferry local (à droite).

One for the road
Passengers aboard the *Mauretania* have a last
drink at the bar before disembarking at Fishguard,
20 September 1909. Note the decor of the bar: it was
made to look like a country house, a common
theme in the interior design of later great Cunarders
such as the *Queen Mary* and *Queen Elizabeth*.

Ein Schlückchen zum Abschied
Reisende der *Mauretania* genehmigen sich am
20. September 1909 noch einen letzten Schluck,
bevor sie in Fishguard von Bord gehen. Die Bar ist
im Stil eines Landhauses aufgemacht, ein Motiv,
das auch bei den späteren großen Cunard-Linern
wie der *Queen Mary* und der *Queen Elizabeth* immer
wieder auftaucht.

Un verre pour la route
Ces passagers du *Mauretania* prennent un dernier
verre avant de débarquer à Fishguard, le 20 septembre
1909. Notez le décor du bar qui évoque la maison de
campagne, thème récurrent dans la décoration
intérieure des futurs grands navires de la Cunard
comme le *Queen Mary* et le *Queen Elizabeth*.

Life-saving drill
Two crewmen man a lifeboat
trailed astern of the *Mauretania*.
After the *Titanic* disaster of April
1912, lifeboat training was increased
on all passenger liners. (Right)
Crowds onshore watch the arrival
of the *Mauretania* at Fishguard,
30 August 1909.

Rettungsübung
Zwei Seeleute an Bord eines
Rettungsbootes im Schlepptau
der *Mauretania*. Nach der *Titanic*-
Katastrophe im April 1912 wurden
auf allen Passagierdampfern ver-
stärkt Rettungsübungen durch-
geführt. (Rechts) Schaulustige
verfolgen an Land die Ankunft
der *Mauretania* in Fishguard am
30. August 1909.

Exercice de sauvetage
Deux hommes d'équipage
manœuvrent sur un canot de
sauvetage à la remorque du
Mauretania. Les exercices de canot
de sauvetage se multiplièrent sur
tous les paquebots après le naufrage
du *Titanic* en avril 1912. La foule
assiste à l'arrivée du *Mauretania* à
Fishguard, le 30 août 1909 (à droite).

44

Happy landings
Passengers from the *Mauretania* coming ashore at
Fishguard after the liner has called there for the first
time, 30 August 1909. (Right) Passengers disembarking
from the tender *Sir Francis Drake*. Liners like the
Mauretania had to stand off at anchor because of their
great draft, particularly if the tide was not right.

Glückliche Ankunft
Passagiere der *Mauretania* gehen in Fishguard an
Land, als sie dort am 30. August 1909 zum ersten Mal
Station macht. (Rechts) Umstieg in den Leichter *Sir
Francis Drake*. Ozeanriesen wie die *Mauretania*
konnten wegen ihres großen Tiefgangs nicht in den
Hafen einlaufen und mußten je nach Tide mehr
oder weniger weit draußen auf Reede gehen.

Des arrivées heureuses
Ces passagers du *Mauretania* débarquent à Fishguard
le 30 août 1909, à l'ouverture de l'escale. D'autres
ont dû prendre le transbordeur *Sir Francis Drake*
(à droite) car les paquebots comme le *Mauretania*
devaient souvent rester en rade à l'ancre en raison de
leur important tirant d'eau, surtout en cas de faible
coefficient de marée.

Royal Mail Ship
Loading and sorting mail on the decks of the *Mauretania*. Bags are sorted into baskets (left) before going ashore in the tender *Smeaton* at Fishguard. Mail was an essential service of the great liners, for which they earned the title of RMS – Royal Mail Ship. The mail would be distributed by special Royal Mail trains.

Königliches Postschiff
Postsäcke werden auf Deck der *Mauretania* sortiert und verladen. Sie kommen in große Körbe (links), in denen der Leichter *Smeaton* sie in Fishguard an Land bringt. Die Postbeförderung war ein wichtiger Dienst der Ozeanschiffe, wofür sie die Bezeichnung RMS tragen durften – Royal Mail Ship (Königliches Post-schiff). Die Post wurde mit eigenen Postzügen im Land verteilt.

Le navire de la Poste royale
Le chargement et le tri du courrier sur les ponts du *Mauretania*. Les sacs sont répartis dans des paniers (à gauche) avant d'être expédiés à terre à bord du transbordeur *Smeaton* de Fishguard. La poste était un service important rendu par les grands paquebots, ce qui leur valait le titre de RMS – Royal Mail Ship. Le courrier était ensuite distribué par des trains spéciaux de la Poste royale.

Onward journey

Passengers from the *Mauretania* wait at Fishguard station for an express to London. The passengers, judging by the amount of their luggage, are from the better class of berth. (Right) Travel by sea was evidently a major adventure. Here a famous aviator of the day, a Mr Drexel, is surrounded by his impedimenta for the journey.

Zu Wasser und zu Lande

Passagiere der *Mauretania* warten im Bahnhof von Fishguard auf den Expreßzug nach London. Der Menge an Gepäck nach zu urteilen, müssen es Reisende der gehobeneren Klassen sein. (Rechts) Eine Seereise war immer ein Abenteuer. Hier ein gewisser Herr Drexel, seinerzeit ein berühmter Flieger, inmitten seines Gepäcks.

Avant et après la traversée

Ces passagers du *Mauretania* attendent l'express de Londres à la gare de Fishguard. À en juger par le nombre de leurs bagages, ils ont voyagé en classe supérieure. Le voyage par mer représentait évidemment une grande aventure. On voit ici un célèbre aviateur de l'époque, M. Drexel, cerné par tous ses bagages (à droite).

Doomed

(Previous pages) The *Lusitania*, the 31,550-ton sister of the *Mauretania*, departing New York in 1912. Introduced in 1907, she won the Blue Riband in October that year. She came to a terrible end, sunk off Ireland in 1915 with huge loss of life. (Above and right) Gentle games of shuffleboard and skipping on the *Lusitania's* decks. Note how well wrapped up passengers and crew are; this was in June.

Dem Untergang geweiht

(Vorherige Seiten) Der 31550-Tonner *Lusitania*, Schwesterschiff der *Mauretania*, verläßt 1912 New York. Die *Lusitania* wurde 1907 in Dienst genommen und errang im Oktober desselben Jahres das Blaue Band. Zahlreiche Menschen verloren ihr Leben, als sie 1915 vor der irischen Küste unterging. (Oben und rechts) Zeitvertreib mit Shuffleboard und Seilspringen auf den Decks der *Lusitania*. Auffällig ist, wie warm Passagiere und Mannschaft angezogen sind – die Aufnahme entstand im Juni.

Le destin

(Pages précédentes) Le *Lusitania* (31550 tonneaux), « sister ship » du *Mauretania*, quitte New York en 1912. Mis en service en 1907, il remporta le Ruban bleu en octobre de la même année mais connut une fin dramatique en 1915, où il fut coulé au large de l'Irlande, entraînant de nombreuses pertes en vies humaines. Les passagers s'y livraient à de paisibles jeux de palet et de saut à la corde. Notez que tout le monde est habillé chaudement, bien que l'on soit en juin (ci-dessus et à droite).

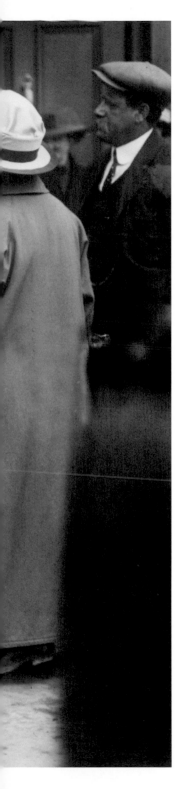

The survivors and the dead
The *Lusitania* was torpedoed by a
German submarine without warning
at about 2.15 pm on 7 May 1915. She
had 1,959 passengers aboard, and
1,198 passengers and crew were lost.
(Left) Survivors in the streets of
Queenstown (Cobh), Ireland. (Above)
A mass burial, with only service
personnel in attendance.

Die Überlebenden und die Toten
Gegen 14 Uhr 15 am Nachmittag des
7. Mai 1915 wurde die *Lusitania* ohne
Vorwarnung von einem deutschen
U-Boot torpediert. Sie hatte 1959
Reisende an Bord, und 1198 Passagiere und Besatzungsmitglieder
kamen um. (Links) Überlebende
in den Straßen des irischen Queenstown (Cobh). (Oben) Bestattung von
Opfern im Massengrab; nur Militär
und Seeleute sind zugegen.

Les survivants et les morts
Le *Lusitania* fut torpillé sans
sommation par un sous-marin
allemand le 7 mai 1915 à 14 h 15
environ. Sur les 1959 passagers
qu'il transportait, 1198 passagers
et membres d'équipage périrent.
(À gauche) On voit ici quelques-
uns des survivants dans les rues de
Queenstown (Cobh) en Irlande.
(Ci-dessus) Les victimes retrouvées
furent enterrées dans une fosse
commune, en présence des seuls
militaires.

Enjoying the sun

Third-class passengers (left) on the Cunard liner
Franconia (above), 18,150 tons. She could carry 2,850
passengers (2,200 in third class), a capacity that
made her suitable as a troopship; she was torpedoed
off Malta on 4 October 1916, with twelve lives lost.
(Right) A galley steward draws a mug of tea, 1911.

Ein Platz an der Sonne

(Links) Dritter-Klasse-Passagiere des Cunard-Liners
Franconia (oben). Der 18150-Tonner konnte 2850
Reisende befördern (davon 2200 in der Dritten Klasse),
eine Kapazität, die ihn als Truppentransporter
interessant machte; am 4. Oktober 1916 wurde er vor
Malta von einem Torpedo getroffen, zwölf Menschen
ließen ihr Leben. (Rechts) Ein Küchenhelfer füllt eine
Teetasse, 1911.

Profiter du soleil

Les passagers de troisième classe (à gauche) sur le
Franconia (18150 tonneaux) (ci-dessus), un paquebot de
la Cunard. Ce navire pouvait transporter 2850 passagers
(dont 2200 en troisième classe), une capacité qui le
rendait particulièrement apte au transport de troupes ;
torpillé au large de Malte le 4 octobre 1916, son naufrage
fit douze victimes. (À droite) Un garçon des cuisines
remplit une tasse de thé, un jour de 1911.

Keeping fit
One of the recreation facilities aboard the *Franconia* was an early multi-gym (left). Note the exercise cycle. The gentleman at the punch-ball still keeps his waistcoat on. (Below left, right) Skipping and a tug of war on the decks in full winter garb on a chilly June day, 1912.

Fit bleiben
Durch ihre Ausstattung mit einem Sportstudio war die *Franconia* ihrer Zeit voraus (links). Auch das Trimmfahrrad ist bemerkenswert, und der Herr am Punchingball behält die Weste an. (Unten links, rechts) Seilhüpfen und Tauziehen auf Deck, im Wintermantel an einem kühlen Junitag des Jahres 1912.

Garder la forme
Le *Franconia* proposait, entre autres distractions, une salle de gymnastique (à gauche) – remarquez le vélo d'exercice et le gentleman au punching-ball qui a conservé son gilet. (En bas, à gauche et à droite) D'autres passagers en vêtements d'hiver, un jour frais de juin 1912, pratiquent le saut et le tir à la corde sur les ponts.

White Star's pride

The huge white hull of the *Olympic*, 45,342 tons, just after her launch at Harland and Wolff's yard, Belfast, on 20 October 1910. *Olympic* was the first of the three 'giants' of the White Star Line. She outlasted her two sisters, *Titanic* and *Britannic*, by a generation. She served in the First World War as a troopship, disguised with dazzle-paint camouflage and equipped with a 6-inch gun.

Der Stolz der White Star Line

Der gewaltige weiße Rumpf der *Olympic*, 45 342 Bruttoregistertonnen, unmittelbar nach dem Stapellauf in der Werft Harland and Wolff in Belfast am 20. Oktober 1910. Die *Olympic* war der erste der drei »Giganten« von White Star und überlebte ihre Schwestern *Titanic* und *Britannic* um eine ganze Generation. Im Ersten Weltkrieg diente sie, mit einer gescheckten Tarnbemalung versehen und einer 15-cm-Kanone bestückt, als Truppentransporter.

La fierté de la White Star

La gigantesque coque blanche de l'*Olympic* (45 342 tonneaux), juste après son lancement aux chantiers Harland & Wolff de Belfast, le 20 octobre 1910. L'*Olympic*, le premier des trois « géants » de la White Star Line, survécut pendant une génération à ses deux « sister ships », le *Titanic* et le *Britannic*. Repeint avec une livrée de camouflage et équipé d'un canon de 152 mm, il servit de transport de troupes pendant la Première Guerre mondiale.

Strike

The *Olympic* alongside in Southampton, 24 April 1912.
The stokers had gone on strike, and 285 crew had
deserted. It was a few days after the loss of her sister,
the *Titanic*. The crew were protesting that the *Olympic*,
too, did not have enough lifeboats. (Right) Preparing one
of the four funnels and scrubbing the decks before her
departure from Belfast, 1911.

Streik

Die *Olympic* am Kai in Southampton, 24. April 1912.
Die Heizer waren in Streik getreten, und von der
Besatzung hatten 285 das Schiff verlassen. Wenige Tage
zuvor war das Schwesterschiff *Titanic* untergegangen,
und die Seeleute protestierten, weil auch die *Olympic*
nicht genügend Rettungsboote an Bord habe. (Rechts)
Vor der Abfahrt wird 1911 in Belfast das Deck geschrubbt, und einer der vier Schornsteine bekommt
noch den letzten Schliff.

La grève

L'*Olympic* à quai à Southampton, le 24 avril 1912. Les
chauffeurs sont en grève et 285 membres de l'équipage
ont déserté quelques jours après la perte du *Titanic*,
son jumeau, pour protester contre le nombre également
insuffisant de canots de sauvetage à bord. (À droite) Des
matelots s'occupent de l'une des quatre cheminées et
nettoient les ponts de l'*Olympic* avant son départ de
Belfast, en 1911.

The unsinkable

One of the huge sea anchors, horse-drawn through the streets of Belfast in 1911, destined for the *Titanic*, order no. 401 at the Harland and Wolff yard. (Right) The huge hulls of the *Olympic* (no. 400) and *Titanic*, seen here, were built side by side. The *Titanic* was believed to be unsinkable because of the revolutionary design of the bulkheads in the new White Star liners.

Die Unsinkbare

Einer der großen Anker für die *Titanic*, Auftragsnummer 401 auf der Werft Harland and Wolff, bei der Anlieferung mit dem Pferdewagen in den Straßen von Belfast. (Rechts) Die gewaltigen Schiffskörper der *Olympic* (Nr. 400) und der *Titanic*, hier im Bild, wurden Seite an Seite gebaut. Die *Titanic* galt aufgrund der neuartigen Schottenkonstruktion der jüngsten Generation von White-Star-Linern als »unsinkbar«.

Insubmersible !

Un attelage de chevaux traîne dans les rues de Belfast l'une des gigantesques ancres destinée au *Titanic*, construit en 1911 aux chantiers Harland & Wolff sous le numéro de commande 401. Les énormes carènes de l'*Olympic* (n° 400) et du *Titanic* (ici à droite) furent assemblées simultanément. On disait le Titanic insubmersible grâce à la conception révolutionnaire – des cloisons étanches – des nouveaux paquebots de la White Star.

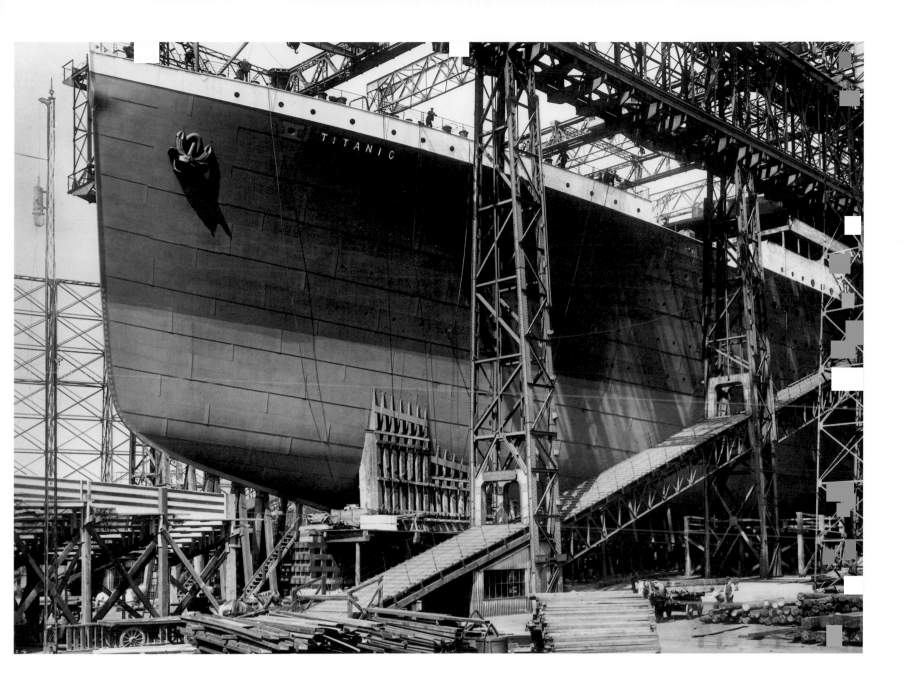

Trials

The graceful lines of the *Titanic* as she is towed from the yard in 1912. Her catastrophic end on the night of 14/15 April, with the loss of 1,503 lives, has made her perhaps the best-known liner of all time. She did not heed the warning of unusual amounts of ice, pack and icebergs, drifting south that year. Outmoded Board of Trade regulations meant she had too few lifeboats.

Probefahrt

Von zwei Schleppern wird die *Titanic* in all ihrer Schönheit 1912 zur ersten Ausfahrt aus der Werft manövriert. Der entsetzliche Untergang dieses Schiffes in der Nacht vom 14. auf den 15. April, bei dem 1503 Menschen ihr Leben ließen, hat sie zum bekanntesten Ozeandampfer aller Zeiten gemacht. Ihr Kapitän schlug die Warnungen vor ungewöhnlich großen Mengen Eis, Packeis und Eisbergen, die in jenem Jahr weit nach Süden drifteten, in den Wind; längst veraltete gesetzliche Regelungen waren dafür verantwortlich, daß sie mit viel zu wenigen Rettungsbooten ausgerüstet war.

Épreuves

On découvre les lignes élégantes du *Titanic* lors de son remorquage au sortir du chantier, en 1912. Il doit à sa fin tragique dans la nuit du 14 au 15 avril, qui fit 1503 victimes, d'être sans doute le paquebot le plus célèbre du monde. L'équipage n'aurait pas tenu compte d'avertissements concernant la quantité inhabituelle cette année là de packs et d'icebergs à une latitude aussi sud. Une réglementation dépassée du Board of Trade prévoyait également un nombre insuffisant de canots de sauvetage.

Disaster

The news of the loss of the *Titanic* hits the streets the next day, 16 April 1912. (Left) The newsboy of the *Evening News* in the City of London. (Right) A woman buys a souvenir picture of the ship just after the disaster. (Below right) Survivors greeted by relatives upon their return to Southampton. Crew members were detained for questioning when they arrived in New York.

Die Katastrophe

Am nächsten Tag, dem 16. April 1912, verbreitete sich die Nachricht vom Untergang der *Titanic* wie ein Lauffeuer. (Links) Ein Zeitungsjunge der *Evening News* in London. (Rechts) Gleich nach dem Unglück kauft eine Frau ein Bild des Schiffes als Souvenir. (Rechts unten) Überlebende werden in Southampton von Verwandten empfangen. Die geretteten Besatzungs-mitglieder wurden zunächst in New York festgehalten und verhört.

Désastre

Les nouvelles de la disparition du *Titanic* furent diffusées le lendemain, 16 avril 1912, par les crieurs de journaux comme celui-ci du *Evening News*, à Londres (à gauche). (À droite) Une femme achète une image souvenir du navire juste après la tragédie. (À droite) À Southampton, les survivants sont attendus par les membres de leur famille. À leur arrivée à New York, les marins seront placés en détention et soumis à des interrogatoires.

Ballin's dream

The *Imperator*, 52,117 tons, launched by the Kaiser in 1913, was one of the three great ships of the Hamburg Amerika line, and was the largest ship in the world. With her sisters *Vaterland* and *Bismarck* she was one of the three 'monster ships' built to fulfil the plan of Hamburg Amerika's Albert Ballin to dominate the North Atlantic. She entered service in 1913, but spent most of the Great War idle in Germany. After a period as an American troopship she was bought by Cunard, who renamed her *Berengaria*. The imperial eagle was added to her prow (right) to ensure she would be the longest ship in the world!

Ballins Traum

Die *Imperator* war eines von drei neuen Großschiffen der Hamburg-Amerika-Linie und mit 52 117 Tonnen das größte der Welt. Mit ihr und den beiden Schwesterschiffen *Vaterland* und *Bismarck*, drei veritablen Ozeanriesen, wollte der Direktor der Linie seinen großen Traum wahrmachen – die Vorherrschaft auf dem Nordatlantik. Die *Imperator* wurde 1913 in Anwesenheit des Kaisers in Dienst gestellt, verbrachte jedoch den größten Teil des Ersten Weltkriegs am Kai in Deutschland. Nach ihrem Einsatz als amerikanischer Truppentransporter erwarb Cunard sie und benannte sie in *Berengaria* um. Erst der am Bug angesetzte Reichsadler machte sie zum längsten Schiff der Welt.

Le rêve de Ballin

L'*Imperator* (52 117 tonneaux) était l'un des plus grands navires de la Hamburg Amerika et le plus grand navire du monde. Avec ses « sister ship » *Vaterland* et *Bismarck*, il était l'un des trois « monstres » construits pour accomplir la volonté de Albert Ballin de dominer l'Atlantique Nord avec sa compagnie. Ce paquebot fut mis en service en 1913 mais passa la plus grande partie de la Première Guerre mondiale à quai en Allemagne. Après avoir servi de transport de troupes pour les Américains, il fut acheté par la Cunard qui le rebaptisa *Berengaria*. Lancé par le Kaiser en 1913, l'aigle impérial lui fut ajouté en figure de proue (à droite) pour en faire le plus long navire du monde.

Floral abundance at sea
(Above) Green fingers on the decks
of the *Imperator* in 1916. (Right)
Dame Clara Butt, the renowned
contralto, comes ashore from the
Imperator, 20 May 1914. As the
Berengaria, the ship was very
popular and very reliable. She was
withdrawn in 1938 as the *Queen
Mary* was coming into service.

Blumenpracht auf See
(Oben) Sogar ein Gewächshaus
hatte die *Imperator*, aufgenommen
1916. (Rechts) Die berühmte Altistin
Dame Clara Butt geht am 20. Mai
1914 von Bord der *Imperator*. Unter
dem neuen Namen *Berengaria*
erwies sich das Schiff als äußerst
zuverlässig und höchst populär;
erst 1938 trat die *Queen Mary*
ihre Nachfolge an.

Fleurs en mer
Les « mains vertes » s'affairent
sur les ponts de l'*Imperator*, en
1916 (ci-dessus). (À droite) Dame
Clara Butt, le célèbre contralto,
débarque de l'*Imperator*, le 20 mai
1914. Sous le nom *Berengaria*, ce
navire était très apprécié et très
fiable. Il fut désarmé en 1938 lors de
la mise en service du *Queen Mary*.

Framework

The laying down of the *Aquitania*, 45,647 tons, at the John Brown yard, Clydebank, where she was launched on 21 April 1913 before a crowd of 100,000. She was the longest-serving of all the great Cunarders and the last of the 'four-stackers', of which only 14 were built. Here are clear views of the first ribs and the first hull plates of the ship.

Die Rippen eines Schiffes

Die *Aquitania* wird bei John Brown in Clydebank auf Kiel gelegt, wo sie am 21. April 1913 vor 100 000 Zuschauern vom Stapel laufen sollte. Der 45647-Tonner blieb von allen Cunard-Schiffen am längsten im Dienst und war das letzte der »Vier-Schornstein-Schiffe«, von denen insgesamt nur 14 gebaut wurden. Die Bilder zeigen deutlich die ersten Spanten und Platten der Beplankung des Schiffskörpers.

En chantier

La construction de l'*Aquitania* (45 647 tonneaux) aux chantiers John Brown de Clydebank, d'où il fut lancé le 21 avril 1913 devant une foule de 100 000 personnes. Ce fut le paquebot de la Cunard qui resta le plus longtemps en service et le dernier navire à « quatre cheminées » d'une série de 14 bâtiments. On distingue ici nettement les premiers couples et les plaques rivetées de la coque du navire.

The making of a ship
(Left) Sidelights being drilled by
pneumatic equipment into the hull
of the *Aquitania*, 1912. (Above) One
of the four funnels being hoisted
into place at the John Brown yard
as she nears completion in January
1913. The *Aquitania*, a classic of
her time, was withdrawn at the
end of 1949, and finally scrapped
in Scotland in the summer of 1950.

Ein Schiff entsteht
(Links) Die Löcher für die Bull-
augen werden 1912 mit einer
pneumatischen Vorrichtung in
die Bordwand der *Aquitania* ge-
bohrt. (Oben) Im Januar 1913 geht
der Bau bei John Brown der Vollendung entgegen, und einer der
vier großen Schornsteine wird an
seinen Platz gehievt. Die *Aquitania*,
einer der großen Klassiker ihrer
Zeit, wurde Ende 1949 außer Dienst
gestellt und im Sommer 1950 in
Schottland abgewrackt.

La construction d'un navire
(À gauche) À l'aide d'une machine
pneumatique, les hublots sont percés
dans la carène de l'*Aquitania* en 1912.
(Ci-dessus) En janvier 1913, le
paquebot est presque achevé et les
chantiers John Brown procèdent à la
mise en place d'une de ses quatre
cheminées. L'*Aquitania*, un bâtiment
classique pour son époque, fut
désarmé fin 1949 et mis à la ferraille
en Écosse à l'été 1950.

Huge components

(Left) An enormous condenser being prepared for hoisting aboard the *Aquitania* and a 62-ton piece of the stern casting (below left). (Right) One of the rotors for the huge steam turbines which drove the four screws of the liner, delivering a cruising speed of 23 knots.

Metallbaukasten für Riesen

(Links) Ein gewaltiger Kondensator hängt am Kran, der ihn an Bord der *Aquitania* hieven soll, ebenso wie ein 62 Tonnen schweres Gußteil für das Heck (unten links). (Rechts) Eines der Schaufelräder für die riesigen Dampfturbinen, die den Antrieb der vier Schiffsschrauben lieferten. Die *Aquitania* erreichte eine Reisegeschwindigkeit von 23 Knoten.

Un mécano géant

Cet énorme condensateur (à gauche) et une pièce du gouvernail de 62 tonnes (ci-dessous, à gauche) sont prêts à être montés à bord de l'*Aquitania*. (À droite) On voit ici l'un des rotors d'une des monstrueuses turbines à vapeur qui entraînaient les quatre hélices du paquebot, lui procurant une vitesse de croisière de 23 nœuds.

The start of long service

Crowds aboard a ferry greet the *Aquitania* on her first arrival at Fishguard, Pembrokeshire, 16 June 1914. (Right) Photographers were part of the regular services of the *Aquitania* for her passengers, here disembarking for the first time at Fishguard. The *Aquitania* was outstanding in that she served as a troopship in both world wars, assisting in the Gallipoli campaign in 1915, and helping to take Australian troops from Suez in January 1943 to defend their country and join the Pacific campaigns.

Der Anfang einer langen Dienstzeit

Schaulustige an Bord einer Fähre begrüßen die *Aquitania*, als sie am 16. Juni 1914 zum ersten Mal in Fishguard in Pembrokeshire eintrifft. (Rechts) Ein Bordfotograf stand den Passagieren, hier unterwegs zu ihrem ersten Landgang in Fishguard, stets zur Verfügung. Die *Aquitania* war eines der wenigen Schiffe, die in beiden Weltkriegen als Truppentransporter dienten; 1915 war sie in Gallipoli dabei, und im Januar 1943 gehörte sie zu dem Konvoi, der australische Truppen durch den Suezkanal zurück zur Verteidigung ihrer Heimat und zum Einsatz im Pazifik brachte.

Le début d'une longue carrière

La foule, entassée sur un ferry, salue la première arrivée de l'*Aquitania* à Fishguard (Pembrokeshire), le 16 juin 1914. (À droite) Des photographes étaient régulièrement conviés à bord du paquebot pour le service des passagers, que l'on voit débarquer ici à Fishguard pour la première fois. L'*Aquitania* eut une carrière bien remplie puisqu'il servit de transport de troupes pendant les deux guerres mondiales, participant à la campagne des Dardanelles en 1915 et assurant en janvier 1943 le rapatriement des soldats australiens stationnés à Suez afin de défendre leur patrie et de participer à la guerre du Pacifique.

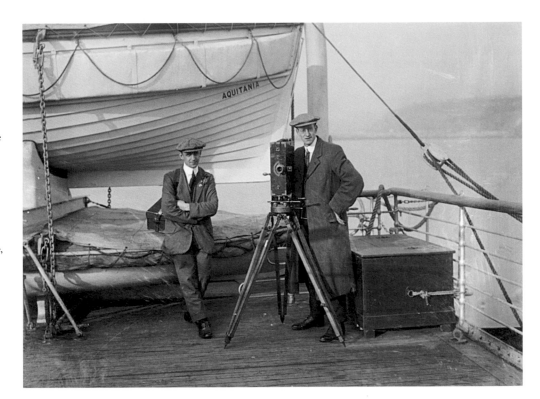

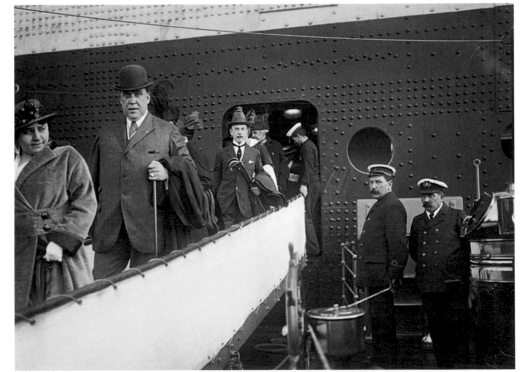

Truly gigantic

The third White Star giant, the *Britannic*, 48,158 tons, leaves for the fitting-out basin after her launch at the Harland and Wolff yard, Belfast, 26 February 1914. The *Britannic* was the sister of *Olympic* and *Titanic*, and was originally to be named the *Gigantic*. She was commissioned as a Royal Navy hospital ship with 3,300 beds. In 1915 she sailed for the Mediterranean, and in November 1916 struck a mine, it is thought, off Kea in the Aegean. At least 21 died, most in a lifeboat accident, but 1,125 were saved.

Ein wahrer Gigant

Der dritte große White-Star-Liner, der 48158-Tonner *Britannic*, wird bei Harland and Wolff in Belfast nach dem Stapellauf am 26. Februar 1914 zum Ausrüstungs-dock geschleppt. Ursprünglich war das Schwesterschiff von *Olympic* und *Titanic* auf den Namen *Gigantic* getauft worden. Die Royal Navy requirierte die *Britannic* mit 3300 Betten als Lazarettschiff. 1915 kam sie im Mittelmeer zum Einsatz, wo sie im November 1916 vor Kea in der Ägäis vermutlich auf eine Mine lief. Mindestens 21 Menschen kamen um, die meisten durch ein verunglücktes Rettungsboot, doch 1125 wurden ge-rettet.

Véritablement gigantesque

Le troisième géant de la White Star, le *Britannic* (48158 tonneaux) est conduit au bassin d'achèvement après son lancement des chantiers Harland & Wolff de Belfast, le 26 février 1914. Le *Britannic*, sister ship de l'*Olympic* et du *Titanic*, s'appelait à l'origine le *Gigantic*. En 1915, il fut transformé en navire hôpital (3 300 lits) affecté à la Royal Navy et fut expédié en Méditerranée. En novembre 1916, il sombra après avoir probablement touché une mine au large de l'île de Kea, en mer Égée. Il y eut au moins 21 victimes – la plupart périrent lors de l'accident d'un canot de sauvetage – et 1125 survivants.

One ship, two names, two flags
The Hamburg Amerika *Vaterland*, 54,282 tons (above), was
one of Albert Ballin's three 'monsters'. Launched in 1913,
commissioned in May 1914, she was caught at her pier in
Hoboken, New Jersey, when war broke out in August that year.
When America entered the war in April 1917 she was seized
and renamed as the troopship USS *Leviathan* (right). She then
became a less than profitable liner, and was scrapped in 1938.

Ein Schiff, zwei Namen, zwei Flaggen
Die *Vaterland* der Hamburg-Amerika-Linie (oben) zählte mit
ihren 54282 Tonnen zu Albert Ballins »großen Drei«. 1913 vom
Stapel gelaufen, im Mai 1914 in Dienst gestellt, mußte sie an
ihrem Pier in Hoboken (New Jersey) bleiben, als im August
jenes Jahres der Krieg ausbrach. Als die Vereinigten Staaten
1917 in den Krieg eintraten, betrachteten sie das Schiff als
Kriegsbeute und rüsteten es unter dem Namen USS *Leviathan*
zum Truppentransporter um. Später fuhr es als Passagierdampfer auf dem Atlantik, war jedoch nie profitabel und wurde
1938 abgewrackt.

Un navire, deux noms, deux pavillons
Le *Vaterland* (en haut), un paquebot de 54 282 tonneaux
appartenant à la Hamburg Amerika, était l'un des trois
« monstres » d'Albert Ballin. Lancé en 1913 et mis en service
en mai 1914, la déclaration de guerre en août entraîna son
immobilisation à Hoboken (New Jersey). Lorsque les États-
Unis entrèrent en guerre en avril 1917, il fut alors réquisitionné
et rebaptisé USS *Leviathan*, sous le nom duquel il servit de
transport de troupes (à droite). Réarmé en paquebot mais
peu rentable, il fut envoyé à la ferraille en 1938.

2

War, Reparations and a New Era: The Twenties

War, Reparations and a
New Era: The Twenties

Previous page: The three monster
ships of Albert Ballin's Hamburg
Amerika Line in new livery and
with new names after the First
World War. The USS *Leviathan*,
formerly the *Vaterland*, is alongside
White Star's *Majestic*, the former
Bismarck, and Cunard's *Berengaria*,
the former *Imperator*. They were
awarded to Britain and America as
part of Germany's war reparations.

Vorherige Seite: Die drei Giganten,
die Albert Ballin für die Hamburg-
Amerika-Linie hatte bauen lassen,
fuhren nach dem Ersten Weltkrieg
unter neuen Namen und in neuen
Farben. Hier die USS *Leviathan*,
vormals *Vaterland*, die *Majestic* der
White Star Line, vormals *Bismarck*,
und die *Berengaria* von Cunard,
die ehemalige *Imperator*. Die
drei deutschen Schiffe gingen
als Reparationsleistungen an
England und Amerika.

Page précédente : Les trois
paquebots géants de la Hamburg
Amerika Linie d'Albert Ballin dans
leur nouvelle livrée et sous leurs
nouveaux noms après la Première
Guerre mondiale. On reconnaît ici
le USS *Leviathan* (l'ancien *Vaterland*), le *Majestic* (l'ancien *Bismarck*) de la White Star et le
Berengaria (l'ancien *Imperator*) de
la Cunard. Ces trois navires furent
attribués à la Grande-Bretagne et
aux États-Unis au titre des
réparations de guerre.

The *Mauretania* returned to normal peacetime duty in 1919. In the early days of the war, in which she had served as troopship and hospital ship, she, like her fellow trooper the *Olympic*, wore a spectacular livery of dazzle-paint camouflage. Craftsmen carefully restored much of the wonderful Edwardian furnishings, the domed ceiling of the two-storey dining saloon and the mahogany panelling with gilt carvings, which had made her decor the last word in chic. But she was much slower than on her pre-war crossings. Following a fire she was extensively modernized, and on her return to service in 1922 she was in many respects a new vessel.

Her former rivals, the 'big three' of the Hamburg Amerika Line, survived the war in rather different fashion. The oldest, the 52,117-ton *Imperator*, was about to sail for New York on 31 July 1914 when the German Imperial Navy forbade her to move. She spent most of the war tied up at a pier in the river Elbe, then became an American troopship before being award-ed to Cunard by the Allied Naval Commission in Paris. Her first voyage as the *Berengaria* was in March 1921. Though she had some early difficulties she worked the Cunard transatlantic service successfully with the *Mauretania* and *Aquitania*. She was finally demolished in Rosyth, Scotland, in 1946.

The story of her sister, the 54,282-ton *Vaterland*, was to be one of the most extraordinary maritime sagas of the entire war. On 31 July she was at her pier at Hoboken waiting to cross the Atlantic. When Britain declared war four days later she was immobilized, after only seven Atlantic crossings. Albert Ballin tried several ruses to free her, including declaring her a neutral 'peace ship'.

When America finally declared war on 6 April 1917, she was seized for war duty. The 300 German crew members were rounded up, taken to Ellis Island, and offered the option of becoming American citizens. The *Vaterland*, re-christened the USS *Leviathan*, was conscripted to carry more than 100,000 GIs to France in some 19 round trips, on one occasion having 14,416 soldiers on board. After the war she was laid up for two years. The second largest ship in the world then became a liner under the flag of the new American Line, a role in which she appeared very uncomfortable. She often traded at a loss, with only 700 or 800 passengers served by a crew of 1,200. In 1938 she too sailed to Rosyth to be scrapped.

The *Bismarck*, the third of Ballin's super-liners, was not even finished when war broke out in 1914. The largest ship of its day was launched at Blohm and Voss yard, Hamburg, on 20 June 1914, eight days before the murder of the Archduke Franz Ferdinand in Sarajevo. For the rest of the war she sat slowly rusting until she was sold to the White Star Line, who renamed her the *Majestic*. The yard workers, reluctant to hand her to a British line, deliberately painted her name as *Bismarck* and her funnels in the Hamburg Amerika colours. She then served alongside one of the giant British liners, the *Olympic*, but after Cunard and White Star merged in 1934 the two were with-drawn. Renamed *Caledonia*, she saw brief service as a training ship, but was damaged by fire and eventually scrapped in 1943.

Albert Ballin's contribution to the development of the great liners had been much more than a race for the biggest and most powerful ship on the Atlantic run. He was responsible for the fabulous interiors, the saloons and staterooms, the fittings, fabrics and furnishings of his ships. On a pre-war visit to London he was so taken with the Ritz-Carlton Grill that he asked its chef and the French designer Charles Mewès to build and run a replica aboard his new ship, the *Amerika*. From the first, he had raged at what he called this 'insane war'. In 1918 he took an overdose and died, one day before the armistice was signed.

The first new liners were of more modest dimension and design compared with the pre-war giants of the *Imperator* and *Olympic* class. Besides the *Mauretania*, another survivor which proved very popular was Cunard's 45,647-ton *Aquitania*. Launched from John Brown's yard on the Clyde in 1913, she was to serve in both world wars as a troopship. She was broken up in 1950, the last of the 'four-stackers' of the North Atlantic route.

The biggest innovation of the Twenties came from France, now a leading competitor on the Atlantic run, with the intro-duction of the Compagnie Générale Transatlantique/French Line's *Île de France*. Launched in 1926, the *Île* was to prove one of the most popular and successful liners: it is thought that none carried more first-class passengers across the Atlantic. The hallmark of the French Line had always been superb com-fort, cuisine and decor, and the *Île de France* was the first great ship furnished in Art Deco style. Her cabins, day-rooms, ball-rooms, staircases and dining rooms were minor masterpieces. Most daring was the flowing grand staircase breaking out into two great wings, faced in grey Lunel stone and yellow marble.

The *Île* was the pace-setter for many of the great liners of the Thirties, including the Art Deco masterpieces *Normandie* and

Queen Mary. Above all she was a lucky ship. On the day of the dock trials of her engines, she broke her moorings and threatened to crash into the dock gates at Saint-Nazaire. By some miracle the gates swung open at the last moment and with masterly handling her captain, Blancart, steered her to safety. She was beloved by American millionaires because, being a foreign ship, she escaped the US federal laws on prohibition. Although the Federal Treasury and excise authorities tried hard to stop the shipping of liquor, the crew and the passengers

continued to enjoy the finest wines, and the gentlemen their post-prandial whisky and cognac.

To cut the mail delivery time the ship was fitted with a catapult for a seaplane. Her charm and panache lasted until the end. Successfully surviving as a trooper throughout the Second World War, she returned to the New York route for nearly ten years from 1949. In 1956 she assisted in the rescue of passengers from the stricken Italian liner *Andrea Doria*. In 1958 she was sold for scrap to Japanese ship-breakers. Her last public appearance was as the *Claridon* in a disaster movie, *The Last Voyage*, for which she was leased at $4,000 a day.

Despite the Great Crash of October 1929 and the subsequent Depression, shipping and to a large extent ship-building survived. Regular and highly successful services were run from Europe to Asia, Australia and India. It was the heyday of the great ships of the Canadian Pacific Line, particularly those out of Vancouver for the Pacific. P & O dominated services to India and Australia, Union Castle to South Africa. The *Viceroy of India* was the last liner built for P & O's London–Bombay scheduled service. She was one of the most graceful and popular ships of the line. The 19,648-ton ship was driven by turbo-electric engines, which ensured a very smooth passage. Typically, she had berths for 415 first-class passengers, and only 258 in second class. In the Second World War she became a troopship and on 11 November 1942 was torpedoed by a U-boat off the Algerian coast, with the loss of four lives. The Nederland Line introduced two smart new liners, *Marnix Van St Aldegonde* and *Johan Van Oldenbarnevelt*, for the Amsterdam–Batavia (now Djakarta) route in 1930.

The most surprising development in the time of economic uncertainty leading up to the Great Crash was the decision by Norddeutscher Lloyd to build two new luxury liners for the North Atlantic. Funds for the *Bremen* were raised on the open market, a sizeable proportion from Americans who wanted to help Germany's postwar recovery. The *Bremen* and the *Europa*, both over 50,000 tons, were launched in 1928. Both had a revolutionary hull design, rounded stems, with a bulbous bow below the waterline. On her maiden voyage the *Bremen* took the Blue Riband from the *Mauretania* with a crossing completed on 22 July 1929 of four days 14½ hours at an average speed of 27.91 knots. The following March and July the *Europa* took the record with a slightly faster average of 27.92. The German ships once more were the fastest in the world but only briefly, as the Thirties were to be the last golden summer of the ocean liner.

Top left: The world's largest screw, weighing 20 tons, built by J. Stone & Co. of Deptford, London, for the Canadian Pacific liner *Empress of Japan*, launched in November 1929.
Below: Clay pigeon shooting aboard the SS *Laconia*, November 1922, a favourite deck pursuit on cruises to this day.

Oben links: Die größte Schiffsschraube der Welt. Der 20-Tonnen-Koloß wurde von J. Stone & Co. in Deptford (London) für die *Empress of Japan* der Canadian Pacific gefertigt, die im November 1929 vom Stapel lief.
Unten: Tontaubenschießen an Deck der SS *Laconia* im November 1922 – auch heute noch eine beliebte Unterhaltung auf Kreuzfahrtschiffen.

En haut à gauche : Cette hélice, la plus grande du monde (20 tonnes), fut construite par J. Stone & Co., de Deptford (Londres) pour équiper l'*Empress of Japan*, un paquebot de la Canadian Pacific lancé en novembre 1929.
En bas : Le tir aux pigeons d'argile est l'un des passe-temps favoris à bord des paquebots, comme ici sur le SS *Laconia*, en novembre 1922.

Die *Mauretania* kehrte 1919 in den Liniendienst zurück. Zu Beginn des Krieges, in dem sie als Truppentransporter und Hospitalschiff diente, hatte sie, genau wie die ebenfalls eingezogene *Olympic*, einen spektakulären Tarnfarbenanstrich bekommen. Nun wurde die edwardianische Pracht ihrer Ausstattung so gut es ging restauriert, einschließlich der Kuppel des zweistöckigen Speisesaals und der Mahagonivertäfelung mit ihren vergoldeten Schnitzereien, die seinerzeit der Gipfel der Eleganz gewesen waren. Doch die Geschwindigkeiten ihrer Vorkriegsüberfahrten erreichte sie nicht mehr. Nach einem Brand wurde sie generalüberholt, und als sie 1922 wieder in Dienst gestellt wurde, war sie in vielerlei Hinsicht ein neues Schiff.

Auch ihre früheren Rivalen, die »großen Drei« der Hamburg-Amerika-Linie, überstanden den Krieg, wenn auch auf andere Art. Der 52 117-Tonner *Imperator*, das älteste der drei Schiffe, sollte am 31. Juli 1914 nach New York ablegen, doch die kaiserliche Marine untersagte die Fahrt. Die *Imperator* verbrachte den größten Teil des Krieges an einem Pier in der Elbe, dann wurde sie in einen amerikanischen Truppentransporter umgewandelt, und schließlich sprach die Alliierte Seefahrtskommission in Paris sie Cunard zu. Ihre erste Fahrt unter dem neuen Namen *Berengaria* unternahm sie im März 1921. Nach anfänglichen Schwierigkeiten befuhr sie später zusammen mit der *Mauretania* und der *Aquitania* erfolgreich für Cunard die Nordatlantikroute. 1946 wurde sie im schottischen Rosyth abgewrackt.

Das Schicksal ihres Schwesterschiffes *Vaterland* (54 282 Tonnen), sollte eines der größten Seefahrtsabenteuer des ganzen Krieges werden. Am 31. Juli lag sie an ihrem Pier in Hoboken (New Jersey) für die nächste Überfahrt bereit. Als Großbritannien vier Tage darauf den Krieg erklärte, erhielt sie Auslaufverbot, nach nur sieben Atlantiküberquerungen. Mit allen erdenklichen Mitteln versuchte Albert Ballin, sie freizubekommen – unter anderem erklärte er sie zum neutralen »Friedensschiff« –, doch vergebens.

Als die Vereinigten Staaten schließlich am 6. April 1917 selbst in den Krieg eintraten, wurde das Schiff requiriert. Die 300 deutschen Besatzungsmitglieder kamen nach Ellis Island, wo man ihnen die amerikanische Staatsbürgerschaft anbot. Unter ihrem neuen Namen USS *Leviathan* schaffte die ehemalige *Vaterland* in etwa 19 Hin- und Rückfahrten über 100 000 GIs nach Frankreich, einmal mit einem Kontingent von 14 416 Soldaten an Bord. Nach dem Krieg lag sie zwei Jahre lang am Kai, bevor sie unter der Flagge der neuen American Line wieder in den Liniendienst kam – und sich als sehr unpopulär erwies. Auf vielen Fahrten machte das zweitgrößte Schiff der Welt Verluste, und eine Besatzung von 1200 Mann versorgte nur sieben- oder achthundert Passagiere. 1938 kam die Verschrottung, ebenfalls in Rosyth.

Die *Bismarck*, der dritte von Ballins Ozeanriesen, lag noch in der Werft, als der Krieg ausbrach. Am 20. Juni 1914, nur acht Tage vor dem Attentat auf Erzherzog Franz Ferdinand in Sarajevo, war das größte Schiff seiner Zeit in Hamburg bei Blohm und Voss vom Stapel gelaufen. Den Rest des Krieges rostete sie vor sich hin und wurde schließlich an die White Star Line verkauft, die sie in *Majestic* umtaufte. Die Werftarbeiter, die nicht wollten, daß sie in britische Hände kam, malten trotzig den Namen *Bismarck* an den Bug und strichen die Schornsteine in den Farben der Hamburg-Amerika-Linie. Das Schiff bediente dann gemeinsam mit einem der großen britischen Ozeanriesen, der *Olympic*, die Atlantikroute, doch nach der Fusion von Cunard und White Star im Jahre 1934 wurden beide außer Dienst gestellt. Unter dem Namen *Caledonia* kam sie noch kurz als Schulschiff zum Einsatz, wurde jedoch durch ein Feuer beschädigt und schließlich 1943 abgewrackt.

Albert Ballin hatte für die Entwicklung der Passagierschifffahrt mehr getan, als nur den Wettlauf um das schnellste und stärkste Schiff auf dem Atlantik anzuheizen. Ihm persönlich waren die märchenhaften Interieurs seiner Dampfer zu verdanken, die Salons und Prunkgemächer, bis hin zur Ausstattung, Möblierung und der Auswahl der Stoffe. Als er vor dem Krieg einmal in London war, war er so beeindruckt vom Ritz-Carlton-Grill, daß er dem Chefkoch und dem französischen Designer Charles Mewès den Auftrag gab, das Lokal für sein neuestes Schiff, die *Amerika*, nachzubauen und es an Bord zu betreiben. Von Anfang an hatte er gegen den »irrsinnigen Krieg« gepredigt. 1918, nur einen Tag vor dem Waffenstillstand, nahm er sich mit einer Überdosis das Leben.

Die ersten Nachkriegsschiffe waren in Ausmaßen und Ausstattung bescheiden im Vergleich zu den Vorkriegsgiganten der Kategorie *Imperator* und *Olympic*. Ein weiterer Überlebender der Kriegszeit, der sich als ähnlich populär wie die *Mauretania* erweisen sollte, war Cunards 45 647-Tonner *Aquitania*. 1913 bei John Brown in Clydebank vom Stapel gelaufen, diente sie in beiden Weltkriegen als Truppentransporter. Als sie 1950 abgebrochen wurde, war sie das letzte der »Vier-Schornstein-Schiffe« auf der Nordatlantikroute.

Die größten Neuerungen der zwanziger Jahre kamen aus Frankreich, das sich inzwischen zu einem ernsthaften Konkurrenten auf dem Nordatlantik entwickelt hatte. 1926 lief die *Île de France* der Compagnie Générale Transatlantique/French Line vom Stapel und zählte binnen kurzem zu den populärsten und erfolgreichsten aller Ozeanriesen – vermutlich beförderte kein anderes Schiff mehr Erster-Klasse-Passagiere über den Atlantik als sie. Markenzeichen der CGT waren seit jeher ihr großer Komfort, die gute Küche und die geschmackvolle Einrichtung, und die *Île de France* war das erste große Schiff, das im Art-déco-Stil ausgestattet war. Ihre Kabinen, Aufenthaltsräume, Ballsäle, Treppenhäuser und Speisesäle waren allesamt kleine Meisterwerke. Aufsehen erregte vor allem die schwungvolle Haupttreppe, die sich in zwei Seitenflügel teilte; das Treppenhaus war mit grauem Lunel-Stein und gelbem Marmor ausgekleidet.

Die *Île* setzte den Standard für die großen Passagierdampfer der dreißiger Jahre, darunter die Art-déco-Meisterwerke *Normandie* und *Queen Mary*. Von Anfang an war die *Île* ein Glücksschiff. Beim ersten Probelauf ihrer Maschinen riß sie sich von der Vertäuung los und drohte in die Hafentore von Saint-Nazaire zu fahren; wie durch ein Wunder öffneten sich die Tore im letzten Moment, und in einem meisterhaften Manöver rettete Kapitän Blancart das Schiff. Amerikanische Millionäre reisten mit Vorliebe auf der *Île de France*, denn da sie unter ausländischer Flagge fuhr, fiel sie nicht unter das Alkoholverbot. Das US-Schatzamt und die Zollbehörden taten zwar alles, um die Mitnahme von Alkohol zu unterbinden, doch an Bord genossen Offiziere und Passagiere auch weiterhin die erlesensten Weine, und die Herren durften sich nach dem Essen einen Whisky oder Cognac genehmigen.

Zur Beschleunigung der Postbeförderung war das Schiff mit einem Wasserflugzeug ausgestattet, das mit Hilfe eines Katapults gestartet wurde. Charme und Stil blieben der *Île de France* bis zuletzt erhalten. Nach erfolgreichem Einsatz als Truppentransporter im Zweiten Weltkrieg kehrte sie 1949 noch einmal für fast ein Jahrzehnt auf die Route nach New York zurück. 1956 half sie bei der Rettung der Schiffbrüchigen der *Andrea Doria*. 1958 wurde sie an eine japanische Firma zum Abwracken verkauft. Ihren letzten Auftritt hatte sie in dem Katastrophenfilm »Die letzte Reise«, wo sie, für $4000 am Tag gechartert, unter dem Namen *Claridon* zu sehen war.

Trotz des Börsenkrachs im Oktober 1929 und der folgenden Weltwirtschaftskrise konnten sich die Schiffahrtslinien und weitgehend auch der Schiffsbau halten. Höchst erfolgreiche Liniendienste von Europa nach Asien, Australien und Indien wurden eingerichtet. Es war die große Zeit der Canadian Pacific Line, die mit ihren Schiffen vor allem von Vancouver aus den Pazifik befuhr. P & O beherrschte die Indien- und Australienrouten, Union Castle die Route nach Südafrika. Die *Viceroy of India* war der letzte Ozeandampfer, der für den P & O-Liniendienst London–Bombay gebaut wurde, und zählte zu den elegantesten und beliebtesten Schiffen der Linie. Der 19648-Tonner war mit einem turboelektrischen Antrieb versehen, der für eine sehr ruhige Überfahrt sorgte. Den 415 Plätzen für Passagiere der Ersten Klasse standen nur 258 Zweiter-Klasse-Plätze gegenüber, eine charakteristische Verteilung für diese Routen. Im Zweiten Weltkrieg wurde das Schiff zum Truppentransporter umfunktioniert und am 11. November 1942 vor der algerischen Küste von einem deutschen U-Boot torpediert, wobei vier Menschen starben. Die niederländische Linie stellte 1930 zwei elegante neue Schiffe in den Dienst von Amsterdam nach Batavia (dem heutigen Jakarta), die *Marnix van St. Aldegonde* und die *Johan van Oldenbarnevelt*.

Es erregte Aufsehen, als der Norddeutsche Lloyd gerade in der wirtschaftlich unsicheren Zeit vor dem Börsenkrach den Bau zweier neuer Luxusdampfer für die Nordatlantikroute ankündigte. Die Geldmittel für die *Bremen* wurden auf dem freien Markt beschafft, und zahlreiche Amerikaner investierten, um Deutschland beim Wiederaufbau nach dem Krieg zu helfen. Die *Bremen* und die *Europa*, beide über 50 000 Bruttoregistertonnen, liefen 1928 vom Stapel. Beide waren nach einer neuartigen Rumpfkonstruktion mit abgerundetem Bug und einem Bugwulst unterhalb der Wasserlinie gebaut. Auf ihrer Jungfernfahrt jagte die *Bremen* der *Mauretania* das Blaue Band ab, als sie am 22. Juli 1929 nach 4 Tagen 14 Stunden und 30 Minuten mit einer Durchschnittsgeschwindigkeit von 27,91 Knoten einlief. Im folgenden März und Juli ging die Trophäe mit einem noch etwas höheren Durchschnitt von 27,92 Knoten an die *Europa*. Nun waren die deutschen Schiffe wieder die schnellsten der Welt – doch nicht für lange, denn mit Beginn der dreißiger Jahre begann auch der letzte goldene Sommer der Ozeanriesen.

A boxing match aboard the Cunard SS *Caronia*, 1921. As well as recreational facilities, some formal sports were scheduled for long voyages.

Ein Boxkampf an Bord des Cunard-Liners SS *Caronia*, 1921. Die Schiffe hatten nicht nur Turnräume unter Deck, sondern auf längeren Überfahrten gehörte Sport auch zum Unterhaltungsprogramm.

Un match de boxe à bord du SS *Caronia*, de la Cunard, en 1921. Des activités et des matches de sport étaient organisés à bord à l'occasion des longues traversées.

Le *Mauretania* reprend un service commercial normal en 1919, après qu'on a fait disparaître la spectaculaire livrée de camouflage qu'il a portée (comme son « sister ship » l'*Olympic*) dès les premiers jours de la guerre lorsqu'il servait de transport des troupes et de navire hôpital. Une théorie d'artisans restaure également son magnifique mobilier édouardien, le dôme du plafond de sa salle à manger à galerie d'étage et ses panneaux d'acajou sculptés et enrichis de dorures qui faisaient de sa décoration le parangon du luxe chic. Le navire se révélant beaucoup plus lent que pendant l'avant-guerre, on profite d'un incendie pour le moderniser si bien que c'est un tout nouveau navire qui sort des chantiers, en 1922.

Ses anciens rivaux, les « trois géants » de la Hamburg Amerika Linie, ont passé les années de guerre de manière différente. Le plus ancien d'entre eux, l'*Imperator* (52 117 tonneaux), se prépare à lever l'ancre pour New York le 31 juillet 1914 lorsqu'il se voit interdire d'appareiller par la marine impériale allemande et doit passer la plus grande partie de la guerre amarré à un quai de l'Elbe. Transformé en transport de troupes par les Américains, il est attribué à la Cunard par la Commission navale alliée et effectue en mars 1921 son premier voyage pour cette compagnie sous le nom de *Berengaria*. Malgré quelques problèmes au début de sa nouvelle carrière, il assure le service transatlantique avec le *Mauretania* et l'*Aquitania* avant d'être détruit à Rosyth (Écosse) en 1946.

L'histoire de son frère d'armement, le *Vaterland* (54 282 tonneaux), compose l'une des sagas maritimes les plus extraordinaires de toute la guerre. Le 31 juillet 1914, il n'a encore effectué que sept traversées de l'Atlantique et attend de repartir d'Hoboken pour un nouveau voyage lorsque la Grande-Bretagne déclare la guerre à l'Allemagne, quatre jours plus tard. Il est aussitôt immobilisé à poste malgré les nombreuses tentatives pour le délivrer d'Albert Ballin, qui le déclare « navire désarmé » neutre.

Il est réquisitionné dès le 6 avril 1917, avec l'entrée dans la guerre des États-Unis, tandis que les 300 membres de son équipage allemand sont rassemblés à Ellis Island, où ils se voient proposer la citoyenneté américaine. Rebaptisé USS *Leviathan*, il va transporter plus de 100 000 GI vers la France en près de 19 voyages, embarquant à son bord jusqu'à 14 416 soldats. Resté désarmé pendant deux ans après la fin de la guerre, le second plus grand paquebot du monde reprend un service commercial aux couleurs de la nouvelle American Line mais navigue souvent à perte, n'embarquant parfois que 700 à 800 passagers que sert un équipage de 1 200 hommes. Il finit également à la casse à Rosyth en 1938.

Le *Bismarck*, troisième des paquebots géants de Ballin, n'est pas encore terminé lorsque la Première Guerre mondiale éclate. Ce navire sort des chantiers Blohm & Voss de Hambourg le 20 juin 1914, huit jours avant l'assassinat de l'archiduc François-Ferdinand à Sarajevo. Pendant la guerre, il reste à quai, rouillant lentement. Lorsqu'il est vendu à la White Star Line, qui le rebaptise *Majestic*, les ouvriers du chantier, rechignant à le céder à une compagnie britannique, repeignent son nom en *Bismarck* et ses cheminées aux couleurs de la Hamburg Amerika. Il est exploité conjointement avec l'*Olympic*, l'un des paquebots géants britanniques, jusqu'à ce qu'ils soient retirés tous deux du service en 1934 à la suite de la fusion de la Cunard et de la White Star. Rebaptisé *Caledonia*, il sert brièvement de navire d'entraînement avant d'être ravagé par un incendie et finalement envoyé à la ferraille en 1943.

La contribution d'Albert Ballin au développement des grands paquebots n'a pas seulement consisté à participer à la course au plus grand et au plus puissant navire sur la route Atlantique. C'est à lui que les paquebots de sa compagnie doivent leurs fabuleux intérieurs, avec leurs salons et cabines luxueux, enrichis de tissus et de meubles extraordinaires. C'est ainsi qu'il demande au décorateur français Charles Mewès de reproduire à bord de son nouveau navire, l'*Amerika*, le décor du Grill du Ritz-Carlton de Londres. Dès le début, il s'élève contre ce qu'il appelle « une guerre imbécile ». En novembre 1918, il meurt d'une overdose, la veille de la signature de l'armistice.

Les premiers paquebots construits après-guerre sont de dimensions plus modestes que les géants de la classe de l'*Imperator* et de l'*Olympic*. Outre le *Mauretania*, l'*Aquitania*, un navire de 45 647 tonneaux appartenant à la Cunard, remporta un grand succès. Lancé en 1913 par les chantiers John Brown, il allait être affecté au transport de troupes pendant les deux guerres mondiales. Avec sa démolition en 1950 disparaissait le dernier des « quatre cheminées » de la route transatlantique nord.

La plus grande innovation des années 1920 est apportée par la France, devenue un des grands concurrents de la course transatlantique, qui met en service l'*Île de France* de la

Compagnie Générale Transatlantique/French Line. Lancé en 1926, ce paquebot allait être l'un des plus populaires et des plus réputés. La CGT s'est toujours fait une règle d'offrir un confort extraordinaire, une cuisine excellente et un décor magnifique à ses passagers. L'*Île de France* est le premier grand navire meublé dans le style Art déco. Le plus surprenant est le gracieux grand escalier à double révolution, élevé sur trois étages et paré de pierre de Lunel grise et de marbre jaune.

L'*Île de France* servira de modèle à nombre de grands paquebots des années 1930, notamment aux chefs-d'œuvre de l'Art déco que sont le *Normandie* et le *Queen Mary*. Ce paquebot est un navire heureux. Le jour de ses essais de moteur au bassin de Saint-Nazaire, il rompt brusquement ses amarres et menace de s'écraser contre les portes de l'écluse … lorsque leurs battants s'ouvrent par miracle au dernier moment. Le commandant Blancart reprend alors le contrôle du navire et réussit, manœuvrant habilement, à le faire accoster en toute sécurité. L'*Île de France* est particulièrement apprécié par les millionnaires américains en raison de son statut de navire étranger qui lui permet d'échapper aux lois fédérales américaines sur la prohibition. Bien que les services du Trésor et l'administration des Impôts américains aient essayé d'empêcher la livraison d'alcool à bord, les passagers et l'équipage peuvent y jouir des vins les plus fins.

L'*Île de France* va conserver tout son charme et son panache jusqu'à son désarmement. Réquisitionné comme transport de troupes pendant la Seconde Guerre mondiale, il reprend son service dès 1949 sur la ligne de New York qu'il va assurer encore près de dix ans. En 1956, il participe au sauvetage des passagers du paquebot italien *Andrea Doria* et, en 1958, est vendu à des Japonais et mis à la casse. C'est en star qu'il fait sa dernière apparition publique, loué 4000 $ par jour sous le nom de *Claridon*, dans le film catastrophe « The Last Voyage ».

Le crack d'octobre 1929 et la Dépression qui s'ensuit touchent relativement peu les transports maritimes et les constructions navales. Des lignes régulières très profitables sont ouvertes entre l'Europe et l'Asie, l'Australie et l'Inde. Cette période est assez faste pour la Canadian Pacific Line, notamment sur les routes du Pacifique au départ de Vancouver, tandis que la Union Castle domine les lignes vers l'Afrique du Sud et la P & O celles vers l'Inde et l'Australie. Le dernier paquebot construit par la P & O pour assurer un service régulier entre Londres et Bombay, le *Viceroy of India* (19648 tonneaux) est l'un des navires les plus élégants et les

plus populaires de la ligne. Il peut accueillir 415 passagers en première classe et 258 en seconde classe. Aménagé en transport de troupes lors de la Seconde Guerre mondiale, il est torpillé le 11 novembre 1942 par un U-boot au large des côtes algériennes (4 tués). De son côté, la Nederland Line met en service deux nouveaux superbes paquebots, le *Marnix Van St Aldegonde* et le *Johan Van Oldenbarnevelt*, sur la ligne Amsterdam-Batavia (l'actuelle Jakarta).

Le plus surprenant dans cette époque d'incertitude économique est la décision que prend la Norddeutscher Lloyd de construire deux nouveaux paquebots de luxe pour desservir l'Atlantique Nord. Pour son *Bremen*, la compagnie obtient les fonds nécessaires auprès du public, dont une notable proportion est composée d'Américains désireux de participer à la reconstruction de l'Allemagne d'après-guerre. Lancés en 1928, le *Bremen* et l'*Europa*, qui dépassent les 50 000 tonneaux de jauge, montrent une carène de conception révolutionnaire, avec une étrave arrondie et un bulbe sous la ligne d'eau. Lors de son voyage inaugural, le 22 juillet 1929, le *Bremen* ravit le Ruban bleu au *Mauretania* en effectuant la traversée de l'Atlantique en 4 jours 14 heures et 30 minutes à une vitesse moyenne de 27,91 nœuds. La même année, en mars et juillet, l'*Europa* s'attribue à son tour de justesse le record, à la moyenne de 27,92 nœuds. Les années 1930 – le dernier bel été des paquebots océaniques – voient ainsi revenir au premier plan la marine marchande allemande.

Leaving port

(Above) *Berengaria* passes the White Star *Olympic*, sister ship of the *Titanic*, leaving Southampton docks, May 1922. The liner had just been converted to oil fuel. (Right) Another view of *Berengaria* leaving Southampton in August 1926, showing her graceful line. She proved highly popular in the Cunard fleet, and perhaps was the most successful of the former Hamburg Amerika liners.

Leinen los!

(Oben) Die *Berengaria* passiert beim Ablegen in Southampton, im Mai 1922, die *Olympic* der White Star Line, das Schwesterschiff der *Titanic*. Kurz zuvor waren ihre Kessel von Kohle- auf Ölfeuerung umgestellt worden. (Rechts) Eine weitere Ansicht der *Berengaria* bei der Ausfahrt aus Southampton im August 1926 zeigt ihre elegante Silhouette. Sie fuhr mit großem Erfolg für Cunard und war wahrscheinlich das beliebteste unter den drei ehemaligen Hamburg-Amerika-Schiffen.

Appareillage

Quittant les docks de Southampton, en mai 1922, après l'adaptation de ses machines au mazout, le *Berengaria* passe bord à bord avec l'*Olympic* (ci-dessus), frères d'armement du *Titanic* et appartenant à la White Star. (À droite) On distingue les lignes gracieuses du *Berengaria* appareillant de Southampton en août 1926. Ce navire fut l'un des plus appréciés de la flotte de la Cunard et peut-être l'un des paquebots les plus réussis de la Hamburg Amerika.

Dry dock maintenance

(Above) *Berengaria* in floating dry dock in Southampton for a seasonal overhaul, February 1927. To the right is the world's largest floating crane. (Left) Two of *Berengaria*'s screws being inspected in dry dock in Southampton. A work platform has been rigged above the rudder for repairs and alignment.

Im Trockendock

(Oben) Die *Berengaria* bei der jährlichen Überholung im Schwimmdock in Southampton, Februar 1927. Rechts der weltgrößte Schwimmkran. (Links) Zwei der vier Schrauben der *Berengaria* bei der Inspektion im Trockendock in Southampton. Über dem Ruder ist zum Reparieren und Justieren eine Arbeitsplattform aufgebaut.

Un entretien périodique

Le *Berengaria* en radoub sur un dock flottant de Southampton, en février 1927 (ci-dessus). On aperçoit sur la droite la plus grande grue flottante du monde. (À gauche) Les œuvres vives du *Berengaria* sont inspectées sur le dock flottant de Southampton. Une plate-forme de travail a été gréée au-dessus du gouvernail pour effectuer les réparations et les ajustages .

Sports day aboard *Berengaria*

(Left) Ladies' sack-race on the main deck. Note the fashionable sports attire – this was July 1923, early in the 'roaring Twenties'. (Right) Ladies' fencing match; the clothing looks more professional, but the shoes give the game away! (Centre) Potato race and (below right) tug of war, other events at the sports day.

Sporttag auf der *Berengaria*

(Links) Sackhüpfen der Damen auf dem Hauptdeck. Auffällig die modische Sportbekleidung – die Aufnahme entstand im Juli 1923, noch zu Anfang der »Goldenen Zwanziger«. (Rechts) Fechtturnier der Damen. Hier wirkt die Kleidung schon professioneller, doch die Schuhe verraten alles! (Mitte) Kartoffelwettlauf und Tauziehen (unten rechts), zwei weitere Höhepunkte des Sporttages.

Du sport à bord du *Berengaria*

Les activités sportives sont nombreuses sur le *Berengaria* : course en sac sur le pont principal (à gauche) – notez la tenue de sport alors à la mode, en juillet 1923, au début des « Années folles » ; (à droite) match d'escrime féminin (si le costume semble adéquat, les chaussures ne sont pas conformes) ; course à la pomme de terre (au centre) et tir à la corde (ci-dessous, à droite).

Professional entertainers

(Above) The impresario Charles B. Cochran and his wife with the playwright Noël Coward and members of their company on the decks of the *Berengaria* returning from a triumphant tour in New York, July 1928. (Right) A chorus line at a charity performance on the liner.

Unterhaltungskünstler

(Oben) Der Impresario Charles B. Cochran und seine Frau mit dem Dramatiker Noël Coward und Mitgliedern der Schauspieltruppe auf der Rückkehr von einer triumphalen Tournee in New York, aufgenommen an Deck der *Berengaria* im Juli 1928. (Rechts) Tänzerinnen bei einem Wohltätigkeits-auftritt an Bord.

Des artistes professionnels du divertissement

L'impresario Charles B. Cochran et son épouse avec l'auteur dramatique Noël Coward et des membres de leur troupe sur le pont du *Berengaria*, au retour d'une tournée triomphale à New York, en juillet 1928 (ci-dessus). (À droite) Les « girls » d'une troupe de music-hall posent à l'occasion d'un spectacle de charité donné sur le paquebot.

Cool opulence

(Above left) A view of *Berengaria*'s elliptical staircase, viewed from the captain's deck. (Above right) Deck-chairs on the saloon deck of the 52,117-ton liner, neatly drilled ten minutes prior to departure from Southampton. (Above) The ship's gardener checks the bay trees that will decorate the main staircase. (Right) Cooling their heels: partygoers at a ship's ball take a break by the indoor swimming-pool.

Kühle Pracht

(Oben links) Blick auf die elliptische Haupttreppe der *Berengaria* vom Kapitänsdeck. (Oben rechts) Liegestühle auf dem Salondeck des 52 117-Tonners in Reih und Glied, zehn Minuten vor dem Auslaufen in Southampton. (Oben) Der Schiffsgärtner prüft die Lorbeerbäume, die das Treppen-haus zieren sollen. (Rechts) Kühlen Fuß bewahren: Gäste eines Bordfestes machen Pause am überdachten Schwimmbecken.

Un luxe raffiné

Vue sur l'escalier elliptique du *Berengaria* (ci-dessus, à gauche) depuis la passerelle de commandement. Dix minutes avant le départ de Southampton, les « transats » du pont salon de ce paquebot de 52 117 tonneaux sont soigneusement alignés (ci-dessus, à droite) tandis que le jardinier du bord vérifie l'empotage des arbustes qui décoreront le grand escalier (ci-dessus). Ces passagers profitent de quelques minutes d'entracte rafraîchissant au bord de la piscine intérieure du navire (à droite).

Serious catering

(Above) Chefs prepare the Christmas menus for *Berengaria*. Food had to be stored and frozen by the ton. One of the signs reads 'Royal Baron of Beef' – an undivided double sirloin. (Right) Father Christmas on parade with guests for the festivities aboard.

Versorgung muß sein

(Oben) Bordköche der *Berengaria* bei der Vorbereitung des Weihnachtsbanketts. Tiefgefrorene Vorräte nahm man gleich tonnenweise an Bord. Das »Royal Baron of Beef«, das die Schilder anpreisen, ist ein ungeteiltes Lendenstück. (Rechts) Auch zum Fest auf See kommt der Weihnachtsmann.

Un avitaillement complet

Les paquebots devaient entreposer au froid des tonnes de nourriture. (Ci-dessus) Les chefs de cuisine du *Berengaria* présentent fièrement l'éventaire des viandes nécessaires aux menus des fêtes de Noël (le « Royal Baron of Beef » est un double aloyau de bœuf). Le Père Noël pose avec ses invités au moment des festivités (à droite).

Party time

(Above) A dance aboard *Berengaria*, April 1929. Balls and dances were held nightly on most of the great liners. The Atlantic liners were an important source of engagements for the big dance bands of the day. (Right) A fancy-dress ball aboard *Berengaria* in July 1923.

Tanzvergnügen

(Oben) Tanz auf der *Berengaria*, April 1929. Die meisten Passagierdampfer boten Abend für Abend Bälle oder Tanz-veranstaltungen. Engagements auf den Atlantiklinern waren eine der Haupteinnahmequellen für die großen Tanzkapellen der Zeit. (Rechts) Ein Kostümfest an Bord der *Berengaria*, Juli 1923.

L'heure du bal

Des bals comme celui-ci, donné à bord du *Berengaria* en avril 1929 (ci-dessus), étaient organisés sur la plupart des grands paquebots transatlantiques. C'était une source d'engagements importante pour les grands orchestres de l'époque. (À droite) Photo de groupe pour les passagers du *Berengaria* lors d'un bal costumé, en juillet 1923.

Edible model and original
The pastry chefs (above) display their prize effort for the Christmas party aboard RMS *Aquitania*, a cake in the shape of the liner, Christmas 1923. (Right) The real thing: the *Aquitania*, the last and longest-serving of the 'four-stackers', alongside at Southampton in the same year.

Abbild und Original
Die Konditormeister (oben) präsentieren ihr Meisterwerk zur Weihnachtsfeier an Bord der RMS *Aquitania*, eine Torte in Gestalt des Schiffes, Weihnachten 1923. (Rechts) Das Original: die *Aquitania*, letztes und dienstältestes der »Vier-Schornstein-Schiffe«, im selben Jahr am Kai in Southampton.

L'original et son modèle
Les chefs pâtissiers du RMS *Aquitania* (ci-dessus) présentent leur chef-d'œuvre – un gâteau représentant leur paquebot (à droite) –, confectionné à l'occasion de Noël 1923. L'*Aquitania*, grandeur nature, en manœuvre d'amarrage à Southampton la même année, fut le dernier des « quatre cheminées » et celui qui resta le plus longtemps en service.

Revels
(Above) Two passengers in fancy dress in an arty
pose for the ship's photographer in one of the air
vents aboard *Aquitania*, January 1927.
(Right) Passengers dancing impromptu as the ship
arrives in port. Note the wonderful Georgian-style
windows giving on to the promenade deck.

Übermut
(Oben) Zwei zum Maskenball verkleidete
Passagiere posieren für den Bordfotografen in
einem Lüftungsrohr der *Aquitania*, Januar 1927.
(Rechts) Ein improvisiertes Tänzchen, als das Schiff
in den Hafen einläuft. Beachtenswert sind die
schönen klassizistischen Schiebefenster zum
Promenadendeck.

Divertissements à bord
Deux passagers costumés, assis dans l'une des prises
d'air de l'*Aquitania*, posent en janvier 1927 pour le
photographe de bord (ci-dessus). D'autres (à droite)
improvisent quelques pas de danse à l'arrivée au port.
Notez les belles fenêtres de style Georgien qui
ouvrent sur le pont promenade.

All part of the service

(Top left) Stevedores loading fresh milk aboard *Aquitania*. (Top right) Food containers being unloaded from a goods train. (Bottom left) Daniel Rudge leading the messenger boys with a £5,000 delivery. They are carrying master gramophone records to New York. (Bottom right) Registering proxy votes for an election, 1923. (Right) The famous four funnels of the *Aquitania*.

Der Service an Bord

(Oben links) Stauer bringen Kannen mit frischer Milch auf die *Aquitania*. (Oben rechts) Die Lebensmittel für die Kombüse kommen mit dem Güterzug. (Unten links) Daniel Rudge führt eine Gruppe von Botenjungen an. Die Pakete, die £5000 wert sind, enthalten Schallplattenmatrizen für New York. (Unten rechts) Zu einer Wahl 1923 werden die Stimmen im voraus abgegeben. (Rechts) Die berühmten vier Schornsteine der *Aquitania*.

Tous les acteurs du service de bord

Des caisses de vivres sont déchargées d'un train de marchandise (en haut, à droite) pendant que les dockers embarquent du lait frais à bord de l'*Aquitania* (en haut, à gauche). Daniel Rudge dirige la colonne des garçons de courses qui convoient les matrices de disques gramophone – d'une valeur de 5 000 £ – jusqu'à New York (en bas, à gauche). Le personnel de bord s'inscrit pour voter par procuration, en 1923 (en bas, à droite). (À droite) Vue du pont supérieur sur les quatre célèbres cheminées de l'*Aquitania*.

Relaxation and refreshment
Visitors to the captain's bridge (above) during a fancy-dress ball aboard *Aquitania*, 25 January 1927. (Right) A drink at the soda fountain for passengers who have just been for a stroll on deck. Note the hats and the design of the glasses, some for early milkshakes.

Entspannung und Erfrischung
Besuch auf der Brücke (oben) während eines Kostümfestes an Bord der *Aquitania* am 25. Januar 1927. (Rechts) Nach einem Spaziergang auf Deck nehmen Reisende eine Erfrischung an der Eisbar. Auffällig sind die Hüte sowie die Gläser, in denen unter anderem eine frühe Form von Milchshake serviert wurde.

Relaxation et rafraîchissement
Des passagers visitent la passerelle de commandement (ci-dessus) lors d'un bal costumé donné à bord de l'*Aquitania*, le 25 janvier 1927. (À droite) Un léger rafraîchissement à la buvette du bord après la promenade sur le pont. Remarquez les chapeaux ainsi que la forme des verres, dans lesquels est servie une sorte de milk-shake.

Nose to stern
Two views of the great pre-war liners at Southampton in July 1923. (Above) To the left *Aquitania*, alongside right the White Star *Olympic*, from the decks of the USS *Leviathan*. (Right) The *Leviathan* with the *Olympic*. The *Leviathan* had just arrived in Southampton in her new guise as a United States Lines passenger liner (she had previously served as an American troopship). Thousands turned out to greet her.

Schiff an Schiff
Zwei Ansichten der großen Vorkriegsliner in Southampton, Juli 1923. (Oben) Links die *Aquitania*, längsseits rechts die *Olympic* der White Star Line, von Deck der USS *Leviathan* aus gesehen. (Rechts) Tausende begrüßten die *Leviathan*, als sie nach ihrem Umbau vom amerikanischen Truppentransporter zum Passagierdampfer erstmals unter der Flagge der United States Lines in Southampton einlief.

Alignés poupe à proue
(Ci-dessus) Deux des grands paquebots d'avant-guerre sont réunis ici à Southampton, en juillet 1923 : à gauche, l'*Aquitania* et, à droite, l'*Olympic* de la White Star, vus depuis le pont du USS *Leviathan*. (À droite) Le paquebot *Leviathan*, repeint à ses nouvelles couleurs des United States Lines (après avoir servi de transport de troupes américain), vient d'accoster à Southampton sous les yeux des milliers de curieux venus le saluer.

Survivors

(Above) Cunard's *Berengaria*, 52,117 tons (foreground),
alongside White Star's *Olympic*, 45,324 tons, in harbour. Both
had been the world's largest liners, had survived war and
disaster, and would serve up to the early Thirties. (Right)
Taking the sun on the upper decks of the *Olympic*, 1929.

Alte Kämpen

(Oben links) Die *Berengaria* von Cunard, 52 117 Tonnen
(vorn), im Hafen längsseits der *Olympic* der White Star Line
mit 45 324 Tonnen. Beide waren seinerzeit jeweils das größte
Schiff der Welt, beide hatten Krieg und Katastrophen überstanden und beide sollten noch bis in die frühen dreißiger
Jahre fahren. (Rechts) Ein Sonnenbad auf dem Oberdeck
der *Olympic*, 1929.

Des survivants

(Ci-dessus, à gauche) On reconnaît au premier plan le *Berengaria*, un paquebot de 52 117 tonneaux appartenant à la Cunard,
bord à bord avec l'*Olympic* (45 324 tonneaux) de la White Star.
Ces deux navires, en leur temps les plus grands paquebots du
monde, ont survécu à la guerre et vont rester en service jusqu'au
début des années 1930. Quelques passagers prennent un bain de
soleil sur le pont supérieur de l'*Olympic*, en 1929 (à droite).

Arrival

Mauretania arrives at Havana (left), a favourite stop for cruise liners. Thousands of the Cuban capital's beau monde have turned out to greet her. (Above) American passengers, heavily laden with luggage, leave *Mauretania* by tender to land at Plymouth, southern England, 30 June 1925.

Ankunft

Die *Mauretania* trifft in Havanna ein (links), ein beliebter Anlaufpunkt für Kreuzfahrten. Tausende aus der *beau monde* der kubanischen Hauptstadt haben sich versammelt, um sie willkommen zu heißen. (Oben) Amerikanische Passagiere mit großen Seekisten verlassen per Leichter die *Mauretania* und gehen im südenglischen Plymouth an Land, 30. Juni 1925.

L'arrivée

Le *Mauretania* arrive à la Havane (à gauche), une des escales favorites des paquebots de croisière, accueilli par des milliers de représentants du beau monde de la capitale cubaine. (Ci-dessus) Des passagers américains du *Mauretania*, lourdement chargés de bagages, empruntent le transbordeur pour débarquer à Plymouth, dans le Sud de l'Angleterre, le 30 juin 1925.

Safety drills

Mauretania, September 1922: (above) Staff Captain Brown helps the Scottish comedian and singer Sir Harry Lauder to adjust his life-jacket. (Right) Necessary adjustments to the fully inflated life-jacket of one of the younger passengers.

Für alle Fälle

Rettungsübung auf der *Mauretania* im September 1922. (Oben) Kaptän Brown hilft dem schottischen Sänger und Komiker Sir Harry Lauder beim Anlegen seiner Schwimmweste. (Rechts) Letzte Justierung an der aufgeblasenen Schwimmweste einer jüngeren Reisenden.

Exercices de sauvetage

Mauretania, septembre 1922 : le maître d'équipage Brown ajuste le gilet de sauvetage, déjà gonflé, de l'un des plus jeunes passagers du bord (à droite) et vérifie celui du comédien et chanteur écossais sir Harry Lauder (ci-dessus).

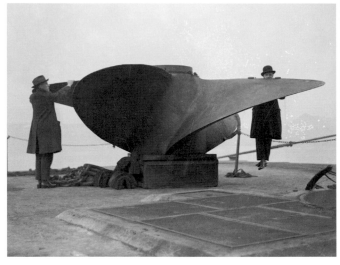

Maintenance

Mauretania undergoing a major refit in the dry dock at Southampton, March 1922. (Left) Maintenance work on the four screws. (Above) One of the four new 18-ton screws for the refit at Liverpool, 1926. (Right) Stripping and painting the rudder at Cherbourg, 1924.

Wartungsarbeiten

Die *Mauretania* bei einer größeren Überholung im Trockendock in Southampton, März 1922. (Links) Arbeiten an einer der vier Schiffsschrauben. (Oben) Eine von vier neuen Schrauben, die 1926 in Liverpool montiert wurden. Jede davon wog 18 Tonnen. (Rechts) Ein neuer Anstrich für das Ruder, Cherbourg, 1924.

Entretien

En mars 1922, le *Mauretania* subit une remise en état approfondie dans la cale sèche de Southampton, où les quatre hélices (à gauche) sont vérifiées. L'une de ses quatre nouvelles hélices (18 tonnes) est prête à être montée à Liverpool, en 1926 (ci-dessus) alors que c'est à Cherbourg, en 1924, qu'il sera procédé au nettoyage et à la peinture du gouvernail (à droite).

Change of name

The White Star Line's newly renamed *Homeric*, 34,351 tons, February 1922. She was formerly the Norddeutscher Lloyd *Columbus*. She had been given to White Star, in a still incomplete state, under the war reparations agreed at the Treaty of Paris, 1919.

Namenswechsel

Der neue 34351-Tonner *Homeric* der White Star Line im Februar 1922. Die ehemalige *Columbus* des Norddeutschen Lloyd war, noch unvollendet, gemäß den Bedingungen des Versailler Vertrages von 1919 als Reparationsleistung an die White Star gegangen.

Rebaptisé

L'*Homeric* (34351 tonneaux), que l'on voit ici en février 1922, est l'ancien *Columbus* de la Norddeutscher Lloyd qui fut attribué – encore inachevé – à la White Star Line au titre des réparations de guerre décidées par le traité de Versailles de 1919.

Newly majestic

(Above) The renamed *Majestic* receives an enthusiastic welcome on arrival at New York. (Near right) Blanche Tucker, chief cashier of the *Majestic*, gives the order to lower the lifeboat. She was the first woman to hold the British Board of Trade's certificate for lifeboat efficiency. (Far right) The *Majestic* in dry dock.

Neue Majestät

(Oben) Die *Majestic*, wie das unter dem Namen *Bismarck* gebaute Schiff nun hieß, wird beim Einlauf in New York enthusiastisch begrüßt. (Rechts) Blanche Tucker, Zahlmeisterin der *Majestic*, gibt Order, ein Rettungsboot zu Wasser zu lassen. Sie war die erste Frau, die das vom British Board of Trade verliehene Diplom eines Rettungsbootführers erhielt. (Ganz rechts) Die *Majestic* im Trockendock.

Le nouveau *Majestic*

Le paquebot *Majestic*, récemment rebaptisé, reçoit un accueil enthousiaste à son arrivée à New York (ci-dessus). Blanche Tucker, la trésorière du navire, donne l'ordre d'affaler le canot de sauvetage (ci-contre, à droite). Elle fut la première femme à obtenir le certificat d'aptitude au sauvetage en mer du Board of Trade britannique. (À l'extrême droite) Le *Majestic* sur un dock flottant.

Inner workings
Preparing new screws for the *Majestic* (above) in dry dock
at Southampton, autumn 1922, at the time of her introduction
to service with White Star. (Right) The engine-room crew
pose by a telegraph.

Ein Blick ins Innere
Neue Schrauben werden für die *Majestic* vorbereitet (oben), die
im Herbst 1922 auf dem Trockendock in Southampton für
den Liniendienst bei White Star hergerichtet wird. (Rechts) Die
Maschinisten vor dem Maschinentelegrafen.

Travail à bord
La préparation de nouvelles hélices pour le *Majestic*
(ci-dessus), en cale sèche à Southampton, à l'automne 1922,
au moment de sa mise en service pour le compte de la White
Star. (À droite) L'équipage de la salle des machines pose près
du transmetteur d'ordres.

From port to port

(Above) Tugs guiding the *Majestic* into the dry dock at Southampton. (One of the Cunard four-stackers is alongside in the mist in the background.) (Right) Cheers as the *Majestic* clears the pier at New York bound for Europe, around 1925.

Von Hafen zu Hafen

(Oben) Schleppkähne bringen die *Majestic* ins Trockendock in Southampton. (Im Hintergrund ist im Nebel ein »Vier-Schornstein-Schiff« der Cunard-Linie auszumachen.) (Rechts) Zuschauer winken zum Abschied, als die *Majestic* in New York zur Fahrt nach Europa ablegt, um 1925.

De port en port

Des remorqueurs guident le *Majestic* vers la cale sèche de Southampton (ci-dessus), tandis qu'on aperçoit dans le brouillard l'un des « quatre cheminées » de la Cunard à l'arrière-plan. (À droite) Les spectateurs acclament le départ du *Majestic*, appareillant de New York pour l'Europe vers 1925.

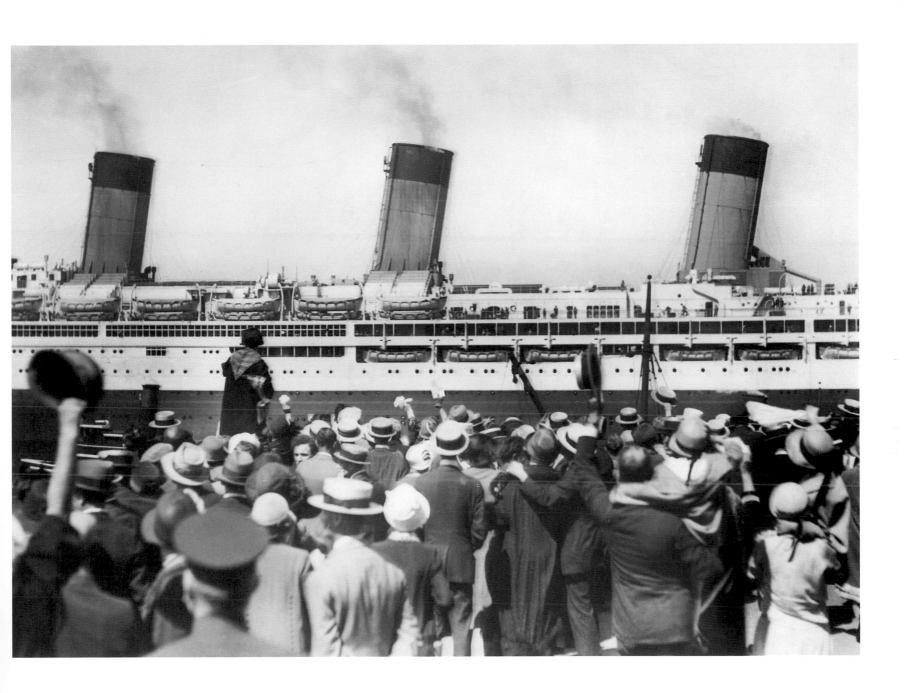

Entertainment, entertainment

(Above) Distinguished guests being welcomed aboard
the SS *Majestic* for an all-night ball after she has tied up
at Southampton, 13 April 1926. (Right) A guided tour of
the captain's bridge by Captain G.R. Metcalf himself, at
the same event, a ball for a hospital charity.

Unterhaltung ist alles

(Oben) Vornehme Gesellschaft kommt zu einem Ball auf die
SS *Majestic*, die im Hafen von Southampton festgemacht hat
am 13. April 1926. (Rechts) Bei derselben Gelegenheit, einer
Wohltätigkeitsgala für Krankenhäuser, zeigt Kapitän
G. R. Metcalf seinen Gästen höchstpersönlich die Brücke.

Plaisirs et spectacles

L'équipage accueille des invités de marque à bord du
SS *Majestic*, à quai à Southampton, à l'occasion du bal de
charité donné le 13 avril 1926 (ci-dessus). Le même soir,
le commandant G. R. Metcalf lui-même guide la visite
de sa passerelle (à droite).

The world's biggest
The USS *Leviathan*, another of the great ships formerly of the Hamburg Amerika Line, entering New York harbour in 1925. She was promoted by her owners, United States Lines, as the world's largest liner.

Das größte der Welt
Die USS *Leviathan*, ebenfalls eines der ehemals »großen Drei« der Hamburg-Amerika-Linie, 1925 beim Einlauf in den New Yorker Hafen. Ihre Eigner, die United States Lines, warben mit ihr als dem größten Schiff der Welt.

Le plus grand du monde
Le USS *Leviathan*, un autre des paquebots ayant appartenu à la Hamburg Amerika Linie, entre dans le port de New York en 1925. Ses propriétaires, les United States Lines, l'annonçaient comme le plus grand paquebot du monde.

Fun and games
(Above left) The New Zealand boxer Tom Heeney training with a medicine ball aboard the *Leviathan*, 1928. (Below left) Heeney playing deck shuffleboard. (Above right) Bellhops playing leapfrog as the *Leviathan* arrives at Southampton. (Below right) Light diversion by passengers, 1925. (Opposite) Passengers playing 'deck ball' on the *Leviathan*, 1926.

Spiel und Spaß
(Oben links) Der neuseeländische Boxer Tom Heeney trainiert 1928 mit einem Medizinball an Bord der *Leviathan*. (Unten links) Heeney spielt Shuffleboard an Deck. (Oben rechts) Pagen vergnügen sich mit Bockspringen, kurz vor dem Einlaufen der *Leviathan* in Southampton. (Unten rechts) Ein Jux an Bord, 1925. (Gegenüber) Passagiere spielen »Deckball« auf der *Leviathan*, 1926.

Jeux et distractions
Le boxeur néo-zélandais Tom Heeney s'entraîne avec un médecine-ball (en haut, à gauche) et joue au palet (en bas, à gauche) à bord du *Leviathan*, en avril 1928. Les chasseurs du navire jouent à saute-mouton lors de l'arrivée du paquebot à Southampton (en haut, à droite). Les passagers de 1925 s'amusent (en bas, à droite), et ceux de 1926 jouent au ballon sur le pont du *Leviathan* (ci-contre).

Laconia luxury

(Above) Three ladies watching the Cunard *Laconia*, the second liner to bear the name, leaving for New York, 1922. (Opposite, top left) B-deck stateroom, *Laconia*, 1922. (Top right, below left) Garden lounge, and second-class saloon with colonnade. (Below right) The first-class smoking room, furnished in the mock-Tudor style of an English pub of the time.

Luxus an Bord der *Laconia*

(Oben) Drei Damen sehen 1922 dem Cunard-Liner *Laconia* zu, der eben nach New York ausläuft. Er war das zweite Schiff dieses Namens. (Oben links) Luxuskabine auf dem B-Deck der *Laconia*, 1922. (Oben rechts, unten links) Der Gartensalon und der Zweiter-Klasse-Salon mit Säulengang. (Unten rechts) Der Rauchersalon der Ersten Klasse war in einem Pseudo-Tudor-Stil gestaltet, wie man ihn damals in englischen Pubs fand.

Le luxe du *Laconia*

Trois femmes observent le départ pour New York du *Laconia*, deuxième paquebot du nom appartenant à la Cunard, en 1922 (ci-dessus). Le salon du pont B du *Laconia*, en 1922 (en haut, à gauche). Le salon de jardin (en haut, à droite) et le salon des deuxième classe, au pourtour rythmé par une colonnade (en bas, à gauche). Le fumoir des première classe, meublé dans le style faux Tudor caractéristique des pubs anglais de l'époque (en bas, à droite).

Egyptian cruise
Cunard's *Caronia* alongside at Alexandria during a
cruise, March 1921. She is surrounded by Nile feluccas.
The 19,324-ton liner was launched in 1905 and served on
the Liverpool–New York route. During the First World
War she was an armed merchantman, and then a
troopship. Built to carry up to 2,650 passengers, she
carried fewer than 600 when cruising.

Auf nach Ägypten
Die *Caronia* von Cunard am Kai in Alexandria,
aufgenommen während einer Kreuzfahrt im März
1921, umgeben von den typischen Nil-Feluken. Der
19324-Tonner war 1905 vom Stapel gelaufen und im
Liniendienst auf der Route Liverpool–New York
im Einsatz. Im Ersten Weltkrieg fuhr er zunächst als
Hilfsschiff, dann als Truppentransporter. Die *Caronia*
konnte bis zu 2650 Passagiere befördern, auf
Kreuzfahrten waren es jedoch nur knapp 600.

Croisière égyptienne
Le *Caronia* (compagnie Cunard) amarré à l'escale
d'Alexandrie lors d'une croisière, en mars 1921,
entouré par des felouques du Nil. Ce paquebot de
19324 tonneaux avait été lancé en 1905 et mis en service
sur la route Liverpool-New York. Pendant la Première
Guerre mondiale, il fut transformé en navire de
commerce armé puis en transport de troupes.
Construit pour emporter 2650 personnes, il
accueillait moins de 600 passagers en croisière.

Fashion in Liverpool
The 20,158-ton Cunard liner *Franconia* at Liverpool, 1923.
She replaced a ship of the same name sunk by torpedo
off Malta, 1916. (Right) A fashion show held on the decks
of *Franconia* during Liverpool's Civic Week, October 1925.

Laufsteg in Liverpool
Die *Franconia* in Liverpool, 1923. Der 20158-Tonnen-Liner
der Cunard trat die Nachfolge eines Schiffes gleichen Namens
an, das 1916 vor Malta von einem Torpedo versenkt worden
war. (Rechts) Eine Modenschau an Deck der *Franconia*,
veranstaltet anläßlich der Liverpooler Festwoche im
Oktober 1925.

Défilé de mode à Liverpool
Amarré sur les quais de Liverpool en 1923, le *Franconia*,
un paquebot de 20158 tonneaux appartenant à la Cunard,
remplaçait un navire homonyme coulé par une torpille au
large de Malte en 1916. À droite, un défilé de mode organisé
sur le pont du *Franconia* à l'occasion de la Civic Week de
Liverpool d'octobre 1925.

Launch day

(Left) The launch of the 19,777-ton *Orama*, May 1924, at the Vickers-Armstrong yard, Barrow-in-Furness. (Above) The moment of launch for the company by Miss Cook. The *Orama* was to work on the London–Australia service; she was sunk by a German warship on 8 June 1940.

Der große Tag

(Links) Stapellauf des 19 777-Tonners *Orama* im Mai 1924 auf der Vickers-Armstrong-Werft im englischen Barrow-in-Furness. (Oben) Miss Cook gibt das Signal zum Start. Die *Orama* befuhr die London-Australien-Route und wurde am 8. Juni 1940 von einem deutschen Kriegsschiff versenkt.

Le jour du lancement

L'*Orama* (19777 tonneaux), construit par les chantiers Vickers-Armstrong de Barrow-in-Furness (à gauche), fut lancé en mai 1924 par Miss Cook (ci-dessus). Il assurait le service Londres–Australie lorsqu'il fut coulé le 8 juin 1940 par un bâtiment de guerre allemand.

Before and after

(Above) The Orient Line's SS *Otranto* as she is launched from the Vickers-Armstrong yard at Barrow-in-Furness, June 1925.
(Right) *Otranto* on her return to Southampton after a collision with a rock, exactly one year later, in June 1926.

Seemannspech

(Oben) Die SS *Otranto* der Orient Line beim Stapellauf auf der Vickers-Armstrong-Werft in Barrow-in-Furness im Juni 1925.
(Rechts) Die *Otranto* genau ein Jahr später, als sie im Juni 1926 nach der Kollision mit einem Felsen in Southampton einläuft.

Avant et après

Le SS *Otranto*, de l'Orient Line, au moment de son lancement en juin 1925 aux chantiers Vickers-Armstrong de Barrow-in-Furness (ci-dessus) et à son retour à Southampton après une collision contre un rocher, exactement un an plus tard, en juin 1926 (à droite).

Dry dock inspection

(Above and right) The new German liner *Bremen*, 51,656 tons, having her screws inspected in the floating dry dock at Southampton in 1929, the year she entered service with Norddeutscher-Lloyd. The *Bremen* was destroyed by fire at Bremerhaven, 16 March 1941, and was scrapped, the lower part of her hull being sunk in the river Weser.

Inspektion im Trockendock

(Oben und rechts) Der neue deutsche Ozeanriese *Bremen* 1929 bei der Inspektion seiner Schiffsschrauben im Schwimmdock von Southampton im selben Jahr, in dem der Norddeutsche Lloyd den 51 656-Tonner in Dienst gestellt hatte. Die *Bremen* brannte am 16. März 1941 in Bremerhaven aus und wurde abgewrackt; den unteren Teil des Rumpfes versenkte man in der Weser.

Inspection en cale sèche

(Ci-dessus et à droite) Inspection des hélices du nouveau paquebot allemand *Bremen* (51 656 tonneaux), en radoub sur un dock flottant de Southampton en 1929, l'année de sa mise en service par la Norddeutscher Lloyd. Le *Bremen* fut détruit par un incendie à Bremerhaven le 16 mars 1941 et la partie inférieure de sa coque coulée dans la Weser.

The Empresses

(Left) The Canadian Pacific liner *Empress of Scotland*,
formerly Hamburg Amerika Line's *Kaiserin Augusta
Viktoria*, returns to Southampton after a round-the-
world cruise, April 1926. (Right) Aerial view of
the *Empress of Australia*, 21,860 tons, built as the
Hamburg Amerika *Tirpitz*. The Kaiser had wanted
her as his personal yacht on a planned victory
cruise at the end of World War I.

Die Kaiserinnen

(Links) Die *Empress of Scotland* der Canadian Pacific,
die zuvor für die Hamburg-Amerika-Linie als *Kaiserin
Augusta Viktoria* gefahren war, kommt im April 1926
nach einer Weltreise wieder in Southampton an.
(Rechts) Eine Luftaufnahme der *Empress of Australia*,
der ehemaligen *Tirpitz* der Hamburg-Amerika-Linie.
Kaiser Wilhelm hatte den 21 860-Tonner bereits zur
kaiserlichen Jacht für seine Triumphfahrt nach dem
gewonnenen Weltkrieg bestimmt.

Les « impératrices »

L'*Empress of Scotland* (l'ancien *Kaiserin Augusta
Viktoria* de la Hamburg Amerika Linie) revient à
Southampton en avril 1926 après une croisière autour
du monde sous les couleurs de la Canadian Pacific
(à gauche). (À droite) Vue aérienne de l'*Empress of
Australia* (21 860 tonneaux) construit sous le nom de
Tirpitz pour le compte de la Hamburg Amerika. Le
Kaiser avait prévu d'en faire son yacht personnel pour
effectuer une croisière de victoire à l'issue de la
Première Guerre mondiale ; elle n'eût jamais lieu !

The Duchesses

(Left) The Canadian Pacific *Duchess of Bedford*, 20,123 tons, decorated overall with flags for her maiden voyage from Liverpool across the Atlantic, 2 June 1928. She was renamed *Empress of France*. (Right) The *Duchess of Richmond*, 20,022 tons (later *Empress of Canada*), at her launch at Clydebank, 19 June 1922. (Below right) Shopping at the souvenir kiosk on the *Duchess of Bedford*, May 1928.

Die Herzoginnen

(Links) Die *Duchess of Bedford* der Canadian Pacific, 20 123 Tonnen, mit Wimpeln geschmückt für ihre Jungfernfahrt über den Atlantik, zu der sie am 2. Juni 1928 auslief. Später fuhr sie unter dem Namen *Empress of France*. (Rechts) Die *Duchess of Richmond* (später *Empress of Canada*), 20 022 Tonnen, beim Stapellauf in Clydebank am 19. Juni 1922. (Unten rechts) Am Souvenirkiosk der *Duchess of Bedford*, Mai 1928.

Les « duchesses »

(À gauche) Le *Duchess of Bedford* (20 123 tonneaux) de la Canadian Pacific – rebaptisé *Empress of France* – arbore le grand pavois à l'occasion de son voyage inaugural transatlantique au départ de Liverpool, le 2 juin 1928. Le *Duchess of Richmond* (20 022 tonneaux), futur *Empress of Canada*, lors de son lancement à Clydebank, le 19 juin 1922 (à droite). (En bas, à droite) Achats à la boutique de souvenirs du *Duchess of Bedford*, en mai 1928.

Sporting challenge

(Above) Female first-class passengers in a fiercely contested egg-and-spoon race aboard Union Castle's *Durham Castle*, August 1928. (Top right) First-class males try to knock each other off the bolster bar. (Far right) A man plays at 'marking the pig's eye' in third class. (Below near right) The impromptu nursery for junior first-class travellers. (Below far right) Parade of children for the third-class fancy-dress competition.

Sportliche Herausforderungen

(Oben) Die Damen der Ersten Klasse beim erbitterten Wett-streit im Eierlaufen im August 1928 an Bord der *Durham Castle* der Union Castle Line. Die Herren der Ersten Klasse versuchen derweil, sich vom Balken zu stoßen (oben Mitte), während in der Dritten Klasse »Das Auge des Schweins« getroffen werden muß (oben rechts). (Unten Mitte) Ein improvisierter Kinder-garten für die Jüngsten der Ersten Klasse und ein Kostüm-wettbewerb für die Kleinen der Dritten (unten rechts).

Défis sportifs

Ces passagères de première classe disputent une course à la cuillère sur le pont du *Durham Castle* (appartenant à la Union Castle), en août 1928. Les passagers des premières s'affrontent à la poutre (en haut, à droite). Un homme joue à « marquer l'œil du porc » en troisième classe (à l'extrême droite). Nursery improvisée pour les jeunes passagers de première classe (en bas, à droite). Les enfants de troisième classe posent lors d'un concours de déguisement (en bas, à l'extrême droite).

157

Panorama

Southampton docks, 5 January 1928. The liners, from left to right, are the Canadian Pacific *Empress of Scotland*, 24,581 tons, until then the largest ship to have passed through the Panama Canal; next to her, the single-stack *Alaunia*. Behind her, one of the great four-stackers, the White Star RMS *Olympic*. Alongside her (foreground) RMS *Almanzora*. The large two-stacker (right background) is White Star Line's *Homeric*.

Hafenpanorama

Die Docks von Southampton, 5. Januar 1928. Von links nach rechts zeigt das Bild die *Empress of Scotland* der Canadian Pacific, mit 24 581 Tonnen damals das größte Schiff, das je durch den Panamakanal gefahren war; neben ihr, mit einem Schornstein, die *Alaunia*. Dahinter eines der großen »Vier-Schornstein-Schiffe«, die RMS *Olympic* der White Star Line. Längsseits im Vordergrund die RMS *Almanzora* und rechts hinten mit zwei Schornsteinen die *Homeric* der White Star Line.

Panorama

Les docks de Southampton, le 5 janvier 1928. On reconnaît, de gauche à droite : l'*Empress of Scotland* (24 581 tonneaux) de la Canadian Pacific, alors le plus grand navire à avoir franchi le canal de Panama ; près de lui, l'*Alaunia*, à une cheminée ; derrière, l'un des grands « quatre cheminées » de l'époque, le RMS *Olympic* de la White Star ; puis le RMS *Almanzora* (au premier plan) et l'*Homeric*, le grand « deux cheminées » de la White Star Line (au fond, à droite).

3

Travel, Tourism and Luxury: The Thirties

In 1933 Sir Harold Keates Hales, MP, presented a suitably ornate trophy for the fastest ship across the Atlantic. The Hales Trophy had a rather brutal tradition: successful owners would remove the names and images of immediate predecessors from its base. Today the names of only three ships remain, the *Great Western*, the *Normandie* and the *United States*. By a supreme irony the name of the first ship to win it, the *Rex* of the Italian Line, the first ship actually to fly a Blue Riband when she took the prize in 1933, was removed. In 1990 the trophy was awarded not to a conventional passenger liner but to a wave-piercing catamaran, the Hoverspeed *Great Britain*, for a crossing of 3 days 7 hours 54 minutes, at an average speed of 36.97 knots. In 1998 it was won by the *Cat-Link V*, a powerboat, in 2 days 20 hours and 9 minutes, with an average of 41.28 knots.

By the Thirties passenger services criss-crossed the world, and new liners were built for numerous far-flung destinations. All this was achieved against a background of recession and slump. The shipyards were hardest hit; in Scotland and northern England unemployment in the yards reached 60 per cent at the beginning of the decade.

In Italy the government backed the Italian Line, newly formed to build two super-liners. The intention was to capture the Blue Riband and the plaudits Mussolini so craved for all things Fascist. In 1932 the 48,502-ton *Conte di Savoia* was built at Trieste and her sister, the 51,062-ton *Rex*, at the Ansaldo yard in Genoa. Both liners had a distinctly difficult beginning. At the start of her maiden voyage the *Rex* suffered engine failure and had to put into Gibraltar for repairs. The *Conte di Savoia* fared even worse, when a blockage in a safety valve some 900 miles east of New York caused a hole to be blown in the hull. The day was saved by a volunteer going below to plug the hole with cement, a wheeze which proved brilliantly successful.

Both the *Conte* and the *Rex* were resorts in their own right, offering as much holiday recreation on their decks as could be found ashore. The Atlantic voyager tasted a touch of the Venice Lido. Waiters dressed as gondoliers served passengers reclining under striped sun umbrellas and, to add to the effect, real sand was scattered across the decks round the swimming-pools. The passenger lists of the *Rex* and her sister marked a major change in transatlantic travel. The *Rex* had berths for 410 tourist-class passengers: the age of the cruise had arrived.

The era of mass migration closed suddenly when the United States introduced a new law in 1924 restricting immigration to a quota based on the census of 1910. The voyage to America remained a dream, an enduring part of national culture and mythology in Europe north and south. The great liners were cast in a magical aura, an image beautifully evoked by Federico Fellini in his depiction of the ghostly liner in his movie masterpiece *Amarcord*, based on his childhood memories of the port of Rimini.

The greatest coup was executed by the French Line. Since 1930 it had been known that Cunard was planning a regular service of three crossings a fortnight to and from New York. They were commissioning two new 80,000-ton liners, the *Queen Mary* and *Queen Elizabeth*, to make the passage in five days in normal conditions. The French replied with a mysterious project known as 'T6'. In 1935 this 82,799-ton liner was commissioned as the *Normandie*, one of the most original creations of maritime commerce of any era.

The *Normandie* made huge publicity waves from the moment she was launched. As she slid down the slipway she created an enormous surge, chucking dozens of spectators into the seething waters of the Loire. The genius behind her design was a Russian exile, Vladimir Yourkevitch, who before the war had designed warships for the Russian Imperial Navy. He first offered his plans for a new super-liner to Cunard, but they were rejected as too avant-garde and quirky. The French snapped them up after testing them with scale models.

The hull shape of the *Normandie* was unusual, nipped at the waist and bulging below the waterline, with a bulbous bow similar to that of the *Bremen* and *Europa*. This made her bow silhouette one of the most distinctive in the history of navigation. It provided the image for perhaps the most famous poster of its day, the epitome of Art Deco style. It was matched by the sheer verve of the interior styling, the light fittings, tall Art Deco columns by Lalique, huge dining rooms and the panelled Grande Allée. 'The whole place is like the setting for a ballet,' remarked the British diplomat and essayist Harold Nicolson. 'Choruses of stewards, sailors, firemen, stewardesses, engineers, and passengers. There are also some fifty liftiers in bright scarlet who look like the petals of salvias flying about these golden corridors. That is the essential effect, gold, Lalique glass and scarlet.'

The *Normandie* was the toast of film stars, entertainers, politicians and gangsters. But for all the extravagance, she proved to have one big weakness, one that she shared with the *Queen Mary*: at speed she vibrated. Within a month she took

moment the main deck was ablaze, and under the weight of water from the fire hoses she rolled on to her side in the dock. The hull was eventually found to be too damaged to be worth repairing, and after the war she was scrapped.

The Atlantic trade was only a proportion of the global passenger traffic by sea. Numerous lines and vessels plied the long-haul routes to the Pacific, Australasia, India, the Far East and South Africa. The vessels may have been less spectacular than the greyhounds of the New York run, but they were immensely successful. Typical of the P & O line was the 16,619-ton *Rawalpindi*, introduced in 1925 to the London–Bombay route, which plied at a steady 17 knots. She came to a dramatic end, torpedoed by a U-boat in the North Atlantic on 23 November 1939 with a loss of 270 lives, including her captain. Many other ships on the India and Australia route proved particularly long-lasting. The *Rangititiki*, 16,755 tons, entered the London–New Zealand service via the Panama Canal in 1928; she carried up to 598 passengers at a stately 15 knots. She was finally scrapped in 1962, having worn remarkably well, considering she worked seven hard years between 1940 and 1947 as a troopship.

This was the first great era of passenger cruising. Hitler's Third Reich commissioned vessels for the purpose of direct political indoctrination. In 1934 the KdF (*Kraft durch Freude*, 'Strength through Joy') cruises were started by the German Workers' Front for faithful party members and workers. En route they received lectures on politics and the programmes of Hitler's New Order. Two ships, the 27,822-ton *Robert Ley* (named after the KdF's founder) and the 25,484-ton *Wilhelm Gustloff* (named after the Swiss leader of the Workers' Front), were commissioned for the cruises. The *Gustloff* was sunk by a Soviet submarine in the Baltic on 30 January 1945. This ranks as the worst tragedy in maritime history, with the loss of some 5,200 lives and only 904 saved. The *Robert Ley* caught fire in the devastating bombing raid on Hamburg docks on 24 March 1945; the hull was later towed to the breakers' yard in Britain in 1947.

One of the concluding episodes of this era of cruise voyages has become the stuff of literature. Hundreds of Jewish refugees set out from Germany aboard the liner *St Louis* to seek asylum in the Americas. They were supposed to go ashore at Havana but spent months confined aboard the ship before their release. The voyage has been celebrated most prominently in the movie *The Voyage of the Damned*.

the Blue Riband with a record speed of 29.98 knots for a west-bound voyage, completed in 4 days 3 hours and 2 minutes on 3 June 1935. After her initial voyages she was drydocked and her three blade screws replaced by four. A new tourist-class lounge was added, rather cluttering the beautiful lines of her super-structure but considerably increasing her tonnage. By 1940 her life of carefree luxury was over. With the fall of France she was seized by the US authorities, who designated her as the troop carrier USS *Lafayette*. During conversion, in 1942, a spark from an acetylene torch ignited a bundle of life-preservers. In a

Left: A party of 1,200 passengers at the end of a five-day trip to Gibraltar and back aboard one of the Cunard favourites, the *Aquitania*, May 1932.
Above: Heavy cargo! Elephants of the Olympia Circus board the Atlantic Transport Line SS *Minnetonka*, 21,998 tons, at London docks to start a US tour in New York, March 1930.

Links: 1200 Passagiere der *Aquitania* krönen eine Fünf-Tages-Kreuzfahrt nach Gibraltar mit einem Bordfest, aufgenommen im Mai 1932. Die *Aquitania* zählte zu den beliebtesten Cunard-Schiffen.
Oben: Schwere Ladung! Elefanten des Zirkus Olympia gehen im März 1930 in den Londoner Docks zu einer Amerikatournee an Bord des 21 998-Tonners SS *Minnetonka* der Atlantic Transport Line.

À gauche : Une « garden-party » est organisée pour les 1 200 passagers de l'*Aquitania*, l'un des navires favoris de la Cunard, à la fin d'une croisière de cinq jours à Gibraltar et retour en mai 1932.
Ci-dessus : Du fret de poids ! Les éléphants de l'Olympia Circus embarquent sur le SS *Minnetonka* (21 998 tonneaux), de l'Atlantic Transport Line, amarré en mars 1930 aux docks de Londres avant de partir dans une nouvelle tournée aux États-Unis.

Reisen im Luxus:
Die dreißiger Jahre

Adolf Hitler launches the *Wilhelm Gustloff*, one of the 'Strength through Joy' liners for Nazi workers' organizations, 6 May 1937. She was sunk by Soviet submarine on 30 January 1945, with up to 5,200 lost.

6. Mai 1937: Adolf Hitler tauft die *Wilhelm Gustloff*, eines der »Kraft durch Freude«-Schiffe der nationalsozialistischen Deutschen Arbeitsfront. Das Schiff wurde am 30. Januar 1945 von einem sowjetischen U-Boot versenkt, über 5200 Menschen fanden den Tod.

Le 6 mai 1937, Adolf Hitler lance le *Wilhelm Gustloff*, l'un des paquebots affrétés par le Front allemand du Travail pour les croisières de propagande de « la Force par la Joie ». Coulé par un sous-marin soviétique le 30 janvier 1945, son naufrage fera 5200 victimes.

Der britische Parlamentsabgeordnete Sir Harold Keates Hales stiftete 1933 einen angemessen prachtvollen Pokal für das schnellste Schiff auf dem Atlantik. Die Sitten bei der Hales Trophy waren recht rauh: Wer die Trophäe erhielt, konnte vom Sockel Namen und Bild des unmittelbaren Vorgängers entfernen. Heute sind nur noch drei Schiffe darauf verewigt, die *Great Western*, die *Normandie* und die *United States*. Es ist ein Hohn, daß gerade die erste Gewinnerin getilgt wurde, die *Rex* der Italia-Linie; sie war das erste Schiff, das tatsächlich ein Blaues Band wehen ließ, als sie im Jahre 1933 den Pokal errang. Heute geht der Pokal längst nicht mehr an Passagierschiffe; 1990 errang ihn ein Katamaran, die *Great Britain* von Hoverspeed, die in 3 Tagen, 7 Stunden und 54 Minuten mit einer Durchschnittsgeschwindigkeit von 36,97 Knoten über die Wellen ritt. 1998 ging er an das Schnellboot *Cat-Link V*, das die Überfahrt in 2 Tagen, 20 Stunden und 9 Minuten mit einer Geschwindigkeit von 41,28 Knoten bewältigte.

In den dreißiger Jahren überzogen Passagierlinien den Erdball, und neue entstanden zu den entlegensten Zielen. Doch dieser Siegeszug entfaltete sich vor einem Hintergrund von Wirtschaftskrise und Arbeitslosigkeit. Am schlimmsten traf es die Werften; in Schottland und Nordengland waren zu Beginn des Jahrzehnts 60 Prozent der Werftarbeiter arbeitslos.

In Italien, wo Mussolini mit allen Mitteln nach Anerkennung für sein Land und die faschistische Partei strebte, stand die Regierung hinter der Italia-Linie, eigens gegründet, um mit zwei neuen Passagierschiffen das Blaue Band zu erringen. 1932 lief in Triest der 48 502-Tonner *Conte di Savoia* vom Stapel, das Schwesterschiff *Rex* mit 51 062 Bruttoregistertonnen entstand bei Ansaldo in Genua. Bei beiden Schiffen gelangen die ersten Fahrten nicht so spektakulär wie erhofft. Die *Rex* erlitt gleich zu Beginn ihrer Jungfernfahrt einen Maschinenschaden und mußte zur Reparatur in Gibraltar anlegen. Der *Conte di Savoia* erging es noch schlechter, denn etwa 900 Meilen vor New York riß ein defektes Sicherheitsventil ein Loch in die Schiffsrumpf. Größeres Unglück verhinderte ein Freiwilliger, der bereit war, hinabzusteigen und das Leck mit Zement zu stopfen – ein Notbehelf, der sich als äußerst erfolgreich erwies.

Die *Conte* und die *Rex* waren schwimmende Urlaubshotels, auf denen die Reisenden an Bord nicht weniger Zerstreuung als an Land fanden – ein Ozeandampfer mit einem Hauch des Lido von Venedig. Als Gondolieri gekleidete Kellner bedienten

Gäste, die unter gestreiften Sonnenschirmen saßen, und um die Illusion perfekt zu machen, wurde auf den Decks um die Swimmingpools echter Sand ausgestreut. Die Passagierlisten der *Rex* und ihrer Schwester kündeten von einer bedeutenden Veränderung im Transatlantikverkehr. Die *Rex* verfügte über 410 Betten der Touristenklasse – die Zeit der Vergnügungsfahrten hatte begonnen.

Ein anderes Zeitalter, das der Massenemigration, ging 1924 unvermittelt zu Ende, als die Vereinigten Staaten die Einwanderung auf bestimmte Quoten beschränkten, basierend auf einer Volkszählung von 1910. Die Reise nach Amerika lebte in Nord- wie in Südeuropa als Traum und Mythos weiter, in Geschichte und Kultur der Länder fest verankert. Die Ozeanriesen umgab nun eine magische Aura, wie Federico Fellini sie großartig in der Darstellung des geisterhaften Dampfers in seinem Meisterwerk *Amarcord* eingefangen hat, ein Film, in dem er Kindheitserinnerungen aus der Hafenstadt Rimini wiederaufleben läßt.

Den größten Coup landete die Compagnie Générale Transatlantique/French Line. Seit 1930 war bekannt, daß Cunard einen Liniendienst von und nach New York mit drei Überfahrten in 14 Tage plante. Die beiden im Bau befindlichen 80 000-Tonnen-Dampfer *Queen Mary* und *Queen Elizabeth* sollten bei normalen Witterungsbedingungen die Strecke in fünf Tagen zurücklegen. Die Franzosen antworteten darauf mit einem geheimnisvollen Projekt namens »T6«. 1935 wurde der 82 799-Tonner unter dem Namen *Normandie* in Dienst gestellt, eines der bemerkenswertesten Schiffe, die je die Weltmeere befuhren.

Schon beim Stapellauf hatte die *Normandie* für Schlagzeilen gesorgt. Als sie die Helling hinabglitt, entstand ein solcher Sog, daß Dutzende von Zuschauern in die wirbelnden Wasser der Loire gerissen wurden. Der geniale Konstrukteur dieses Schiffes, der Exilrusse Wladimir Yourkewitsch, hatte vor dem Weltkrieg für die Marine des Zaren Kriegsschiffe entworfen. Er hatte seine Pläne für ein neues Luxusschiff zuerst Cunard angeboten, wo sie jedoch als zu eigenwillig und avantgardistisch abgelehnt wurden. Nach Experimenten mit maßstabgetreuen Modellen gaben die Franzosen ihm grünes Licht.

Der Schiffskörper der *Normandie* war ungewöhnlich geformt, schmal in der Flanke, doch breiter unterhalb der Wasserlinie und mit einem Bugwulst in der Art der *Bremen* und der *Europa*. Selten hat es ein Schiff mit einer so unverwechselbaren Vorderansicht gegeben, und das Plakat, das davon entstand, war vielleicht das berühmteste seiner Zeit, ein Inbegriff des Art déco. Nicht minder schwungvoll war die Innenausstattung, mit Lampen und hohen glasverkleideten Art-déco-Säulen von Lalique, gewaltigen Speisesälen und einer holzgetäfelten Grande Allée. »Man kommt sich vor wie im Bühnenbild zu einem Ballett«, meinte der britische Diplomat und Essayist Harold Nicolson dazu. »Truppen von Stewards, Seeleuten, Feuerwehrleuten, Serviererinnen, Mechanikern und Passagieren. Dazu an die 50 Pagen in scharlachroten Uniformen, die wie Blütenblätter durch die goldenen Korridore fluten. Das ist der Eindruck, der alles prägt: Gold, Lalique-Glas und Scharlach.«

Die *Normandie* war der Liebling der Filmstars, Entertainer, Politiker und Ganoven. Doch wie sich herausstellte, hatte sie bei aller Extravaganz einen schwachen Punkt, den sie mit der *Queen Mary* gemein hatte: unter Volldampf vibrierte sie. Schon im ersten Monat errang sie das Blaue Band, als sie am 3. Juni 1935 nach 4 Tagen, 3 Stunden und 2 Minuten New York erreichte, was bei Reisen gen Westen der Rekordgeschwindigkeit von durchschnittlich 29,98 Knoten entsprach. Nach wenigen Fahrten kam sie ins Trockendock, und die dreiflügeligen Schiffsschrauben wurden durch vierflügelige ersetzt. Ein Salon für die Touristenklasse kam hinzu, der zwar die eleganten Linien des Aufbaus empfindlich störte, jedoch die Tonnage noch einmal ein gutes Stück erhöhte. Schon fünf Jahre darauf war es mit dem sorglosen Luxusleben vorbei. Nach dem Zusammenbruch Frankreichs requirierten die US-Behörden die *Normandie* und bestimmten sie unter dem Namen USS *Lafayette* zum Truppentransporter. Während der Umbauarbeiten im Jahre 1942 geriet beim Schweißen ein Stapel mit Rettungswesten in Brand. Binnen kurzem stand das gesamte Hauptdeck in Flammen, und die Löschboote pumpten soviel Wasser hinein, daß sie schließlich im Dock kenterte. Der Schaden war so groß, daß eine Reparatur sich nicht lohnte, und nach dem Krieg wurde das Schiff abgewrackt.

Nicht nur auf dem Atlantik, sondern auch auf anderen Meeren blühte der Passagierverkehr. Zahlreiche Linien und Schiffe bedienten die Langstreckenrouten zum Pazifik, nach Australien, Asien, Indien, in den Fernen Osten und nach Südafrika. Die Schiffe waren zwar weniger spektakulär als die Schaustücke der New-York-Route, doch überaus erfolgreich. Ein typisches Schiff der P & O-Linie war mit 16 619 Tonnen die

Rawalpindi, die seit 1925 die Route London–Bombay befuhr und eine Durchschnittsgeschwindigkeit von 17 Knoten erreichte. Ihr Ende war tragisch: Am 23. November 1939 wurde sie von einem deutschen U-Boot im Nordatlantik versenkt, 270 Menschen kamen um, darunter der Kapitän. Anderen Dampfern auf der Indien- und Australienroute war ein längeres Leben beschieden. Die *Rangititiki*, 16 755 Tonnen, nahm den Liniendienst London–Neuseeland durch den Panamakanal im Jahre 1928 auf; sie beförderte bis zu 598 Passagiere im gemächlichen Tempo von 15 Knoten. Als sie 1962 abgebrochen wurde, war sie noch immer in bemerkenswert gutem Zustand, zumal sie von 1940 bis 1947 sieben harte Jahre im Militärdienst verbracht hatte.

Die dreißiger Jahre waren das erste große Jahrzehnt der Ausflugsfahrten. In Deutschland entstanden im Dritten Reich Schiffe ausdrücklich für die politische Erziehung. Von 1934 an betrieb die Deutsche Arbeitsfront ihre »Kraft durch Freude«-Reisen für Arbeiter und treue Parteimitglieder. An Bord gab es Vorträge über die neue Welt, die unter Hitlers Führerschaft entstehen sollte. Zwei Schiffe wurden speziell für diese KdF-Fahrten gebaut, der nach dem Gründer der Bewegung benannte 27 822-Tonner *Robert Ley* und der 25 484-Tonner *Wilhelm Gustloff*, der den Namen des aus der Schweiz stammenden Führers der Arbeitsfront trug. Die Versenkung der *Gustloff* durch ein sowjetisches U-Boot am 30. Januar 1945 in der Ostsee gilt als die größte Tragödie in der Geschichte der Seefahrt. An die 5200 Menschen ließen ihr Leben, nur 904 wurden gerettet. Die *Robert Ley* brannte bei dem verheerenden Bombenangriff auf den Hamburger Hafen am 24. März 1945 aus; das Wrack wurde 1947 nach Großbritannien geschleppt und dort verschrottet.

Ein Ereignis aus den letzten Tagen dieser Ära der Ozeandampfer ist durch den Film *Reise der Verdammten* bekannt geworden. Hunderte jüdischer Flüchtlinge brachen in der Hoffnung auf Zuflucht in Amerika von Hamburg aus mit der *St. Louis* auf. Sie sollten in Havanna an Land gehen, doch dort saßen sie monatelang auf ihrem Schiff fest, bis ihre Einreise schließlich genehmigt wurde.

The prize for the fastest ship completing the crossing of the Atlantic both ways, presented by the British MP Harold Keates Hales in 1933. Cunard refused it for the *Queen Mary*, saying they believed in safety above speed.

Die Trophäe für die schnellste Atlantiküberfahrt in beiden Richtungen, gestiftet 1933 von dem britischen Parlamentsabgeordneten Harold Keates Hales. Als Cunard den Preis für die *Queen Mary* erhalten sollte, lehnte die Reederei mit dem Argument ab, Sicherheit gehe ihr über Geschwindigkeit.

Ce trophée fut offert en 1933 au navire le plus rapide dans la traversée de l'Atlantique dans les deux sens par le député britannique Harold Keates Hales. La Cunard le refusa pour le *Queen Mary*, disant préférer la sécurité à la vitesse.

En 1933, sir Harold Keates Hales, membre du parlement britannique, met en jeu un magnifique trophée, attribué au navire ayant effectué la traversée la plus rapide de l'Atlantique. La règle du trophée voulant que le vainqueur bénéficie du privilège d'effacer du socle le nom et la silhouette du précédent lauréat, seuls sont restés aujourd'hui dans les annales les noms de trois paquebots : le *Great Western*, le *Normandie* et le *United States*. Ironie suprême, le nom du premier navire à gagner ce trophée – le *Rex*, de la ligne Italia (d'ailleurs également le premier à arborer déjà le Ruban bleu lorsqu'il emporte le trophée en 1933) – a disparu. En 1990, le trophée est attribué non à un navire passager traditionnel mais à un catamaran, l'Hoverspeed *Great Britain*, qui réalise la traversée en 3 jours 7 heures et 54 minutes à la vitesse moyenne de 36,97 nœuds ; en 1998, le *Cat-Link V*, un navire offshore, obtient la palme sur le même trajet, accompli en 2 jours 20 heures et 9 minutes, soit une moyenne de 41,28 nœuds.

Dans les années 1930, la création d'innombrables routes maritimes sillonnant les océans du monde vers des destinations lointaines entraîne la construction de nouveaux paquebots malgré la récession et la crise économique. Les chantiers navals sont les plus durement touchés ; au début de la décennie, le chômage atteint près de 60 pour cent de la population travaillant sur les chantiers navals en Écosse et dans le nord de l'Angleterre.

En Italie, le gouvernement subventionne la ligne Italia, nouvellement créée pour la construction de deux super paquebots dans l'intention avouée de remporter le Ruban bleu et de mettre en avant la réussite du régime fasciste de Mussolini. Le *Conte di Savoia* (48502 tonneaux) est ainsi construit à Trieste en 1932 et le *Rex* (51062 tonneaux) au chantier Ansaldo de Gênes. Ces deux paquebots ont des débuts particulièrement difficiles : lors de son voyage inaugural, le *Rex* subit une avarie de moteur et doit faire escale à Gibraltar pour être réparé ; le *Conte di Savoia* connaît pire encore lorsqu'un blocage d'une vanne de sécurité à près de 900 milles à l'est de New York provoque un trou dans la coque sous la ligne de flottaison, qu'un marin volontaire parvint heureusement à colmater de l'extérieur par un bouchon de ciment.

Le *Conte di Savoia* et le *Rex* sont de véritables hôtels flottants, qui offrent autant de loisirs sur leurs ponts qu'on peut en trouver à terre et où le passager transatlantique connaît un peu de l'atmosphère du Lido de Venise. Les passagers, installés sous des parasols à rayures, sont servis par des garçons de cabine en costume de gondolier et peuvent s'allonger autour des piscines sur du vrai sable. En proposant une classe touriste pour 410 passagers, le *Rex* et son «sister-ship» marquent un changement majeur dans le mode de voyage transatlantique : la croisière.

L'époque des migrations de masse s'achève brusquement en 1924 lorsque les États-Unis promulguent une nouvelle loi limitant l'immigration selon un quota basé sur un recensement de l'année 1910. Le voyage en Amérique reste cependant un rêve, ancré durablement dans la culture nationale et la mythologie des pays d'Europe, du Nord comme du Sud. Les grands paquebots sont alors parés d'une aura magique, magnifiquement évoquée par Federico Fellini lorsqu'il décrit le paquebot fantôme dans son chef-d'œuvre cinématographique *Amarcord*, basé sur ses souvenirs d'enfance dans le port de Rimini.

C'est la Compagnie Générale Transatlantique/French Line qui réussit le plus grand coup dans la course au gigantisme. La Cunard, qui envisage depuis 1930 de mettre en place un service régulier de trois traversées transatlantiques par quinzaine à destination et au départ de New York, commande deux nouveaux paquebots de 80000 tonnes, le *Queen Mary* et le *Queen Elizabeth*, capables d'effectuer la traversée en cinq jours dans des conditions de navigation normales. Les Français répliquent aussitôt en lançant un mystérieux projet de navire, désigné par le sigle « T6 », qui donnera naissance, en 1935, au *Normandie*. Ce dernier, avec 82799 tonneaux, est l'une des créations les plus originales de la marine marchande, toute époque confondue.

Dès son lancement, ce paquebot fait la une des journaux. Lorsqu'il glisse avec son ber dans les eaux de la Loire, il crée une vague si énorme qu'elle balaie des dizaines de spectateurs massés sur les quais. Ce navire est l'œuvre géniale d'un Russe exilé, Vladimir Yourkevitch, qui a autrefois dessiné des bâtiments de guerre pour la Marine impériale russe. Il propose d'abord les plans de ce « super paquebot » à la Cunard mais celle-ci les refuse comme étant trop originaux et avant-gardistes. Les Français profitent de l'occasion et s'arrogent le projet après avoir testé le paquebot en modèle réduit.

La coque du *Normandie*, pincée au vibord et bombée sous la ligne d'eau, avec sa proue à bulbe comme le *Bremen* et l'*Europa*, présente une ligne inhabituelle. Cela confère à sa

The cleaning gang stepping ashore after a hard day's work aboard the Orient liner *Orion* as she waits to sail again from Tilbury docks in June 1936.

Juni 1936: Die Putzkolonne geht nach einem harten Arbeitstag von Bord des Orient-Liners *Orion*, der in den Londoner Tilbury Docks auf seine nächste Überfahrt wartet.

L'équipe de nettoyage redescend à terre après avoir passé une longue journée à remettre en état l'*Orion*, de la compagnie Orient, à quai aux Tilbury docks en juin 1936.

proue l'une des silhouettes les plus particulières de l'histoire de la navigation et fait d'elle le plus célèbre et le plus bel exemple de style Art déco. L'intérieur est tout aussi extraordinaire, avec ses grandes colonnes créées par Lalique, ses vastes salles à manger et sa Grande Allée, ornée de magnifiques panneaux d'art. « L'ensemble évoque un décor de ballet, remarque le diplomate et essayiste britannique Harold Nicolson, où circulent des théories de stewards, de marins, de pompiers, de serveuses, d'ingénieurs et de passagers. On y rencontre également près de cinquante garçons de cabine, que leur tenue écarlate fait ressembler à des pétales de sauge voletant dans les couloirs dorés. C'est cela l'impression générale : or, Lalique et rouge. »

Si le *Normandie* devient rapidement la coqueluche des stars du cinéma, des artistes, des hommes politiques et même des gangsters, il montre également les qualités d'un puissant coursier puisqu'il remporte le Ruban bleu un mois après son lancement, le 3 juin 1935, en effectuant la traversée de l'Atlantique d'est en ouest en 4 jours 3 heures et 2 minutes à la vitesse record de 29,98 nœuds. Malgré sa conception novatrice, le navire révélera ses limites en montrant des vibrations à vitesse élevée, maladie dont souffrira d'ailleurs aussi le *Queen Mary* et à laquelle il sera remédié après ses premiers voyages en remplaçant ses hélices à trois pales par des quatre pales. On profite également de cette occasion pour ajouter un nouveau salon à la classe touriste, ce qui alourdira quelque peu les lignes magnifiques de sa superstructure mais augmentera aussi considérablement son tonnage. Cette vie de luxe s'achève brutalement en 1940. Saisi par les autorités américaines, lors de l'effondrement de la France, il est rebaptisé USS *Lafayette* et affecté au transport de troupes. C'est lors de sa transformation, en 1942, qu'une étincelle d'un poste de soudure à acétylène met le feu à un tas de gilets de sauvetage ; l'incendie embrase rapidement le pont principal du paquebot qui, sous les tonnes d'eau des pompiers, chavire à quai en quelques heures. L'épave, jugée trop endommagée pour valoir un renflouement, le paquebot est mis à la ferraille après la guerre.

Le trafic transatlantique ne représente qu'une partie des relations maritimes internationales. D'innombrables compagnies et navires sillonnent les océans pour desservir le Pacifique, l'Australasie, l'Inde, l'Extrême-Orient et l'Afrique du Sud. Si les paquebots sont sans doute moins spectaculaires que les lévriers transatlantiques, ils ont cependant beaucoup

de succès. Le *Rawalpindi* (16619 tonneaux), un navire caractéristique de la compagnie P & O, est ainsi mis en service en 1925 sur la route Londres-Bombay, qu'il parcourt à 17 nœuds en vitesse de croisière. Torpillé par un U-boot dans l'Atlantique Nord le 23 novembre 1939, son naufrage fera 270 victimes, dont son commandant. D'autres navires vont assurer plus longuement les relations avec l'Inde et l'Australie. Le *Rangititiki* (16755 tonneaux), mis en service en 1928 sur la route Londres–Nouvelle-Zélande via le canal de Panama, transporte 598 passagers à 15 nœuds de moyenne. Il est envoyé à la ferraille en 1962, ayant remarquablement bien vieilli si l'on considère qu'il a servi sept ans de transport de troupes entre 1940 et 1947.

Les années 1930 sont la première grande époque des croisières. En 1934, le Troisième Reich, sous l'impulsion de Adolf Hitler, affrète ainsi deux navires – le *Robert Ley* (un paquebot de 27822 tonneaux portant le nom du fondateur des KdF) et le *Wilhelm Gustloff* (25484 tonneaux, du nom du dirigeant suisse du Front du travail) – pour des croisières de propagande « Kraft durch Freude » (« la Force par la Joie ») destinées aux membres du Deutsche Arbeitsfront (Front allemand du Travail) et des ouvriers les plus fidèles, au cours desquelles sont données des conférences sur la politique et le programme du Nouvel ordre hitlérien. Le naufrage du *Gustloff*, coulé le 30 janvier 1945 en mer Baltique par un sous-marin soviétique, est l'une des pires tragédies de l'histoire maritime avec près de 5200 victimes, seuls 904 passagers ayant pu être sauvés. Quant au *Robert Ley*, il est dévasté par un incendie lors des bombardements du port de Hambourg, le 24 mars 1945 et son épave est remorquée dans les chantiers des ferrailleurs britanniques en 1947.

Les derniers épisodes de cette époque appartiennent désormais à la littérature. L'histoire des centaines de réfugiés juifs qui ont fui l'Allemagne à bord du paquebot *St Louis* pour chercher refuge en Amérique mais qui, sensés débarquer à La Havane, passèrent des mois confinés à bord du navire avant d'être libérés, a été magistralement célébrée dans un film : *Le Voyage des Damnés*.

Two of the Jewish refugees aboard the *St Louis* arriving in Antwerp, 17 June 1939. They had already sailed across the Atlantic, to be refused entry to Miami and Havana.

Zwei jüdische Flüchtlingskinder auf der *St. Louis*, die am 17. Juni 1939 in Antwerpen eintraf. Den Flüchtlingen war in Miami und Havanna die Landung verwehrt worden, und so kehrten sie mit ihrem Schiff nach Europa zurück.

Deux petits réfugiés juifs arrivent à Anvers le 17 juin 1939 à bord du *St Louis*. Après avoir traversé l'Atlantique une première fois, ils se sont vu refouler à Miami et à La Havane.

Speed, power and grace
Two of the great Italian liners of the Thirties. (Left) *Conte di Savoia*, 48,502 tons, built at Trieste in 1932. Here she is alongside in Naples in 1935, the epitome of elegance. (Above) *Rex*, 51,062 tons, dressed overall as she enters service, September 1932. She held the Blue Riband from 1933 to 1935, and was the flagship of the Italian Line.

Geschwindigkeit, Kraft und Anmut
Zwei große italienische Passagier- dampfer der dreißiger Jahre. (Links) Die *Conte di Savoia*, 48502 Tonnen, 1932 in Triest erbaut. Hier liegt sie in ihrer ganzen Pracht im Jahre 1935 in Neapel am Kai. (Oben) Die *Rex*, 51062 Tonnen, läuft fahnen- geschmückt zur Jungfernfahrt aus, im September 1932. Das Flaggschiff der Italia-Linie war 1933 bis 1935 Inhaberin des Blauen Bandes.

Vitesse, puissance et grâce
Deux des grands paquebots italiens des années 1930. Le *Conte di Savoia* (48502 tonneaux), construit à Trieste en 1932 et visible ici à Naples en 1935 (à gauche), était un modèle d'élégance. (Ci-dessus) Le *Rex* (51062 tonneaux), navire amiral de la ligne Italia, ici entièrement pavoisé lors de sa mise en service en septembre 1932, a conservé le Ruban bleu de 1933 à 1935.

Deck games

Shovelboard or shuffleboard was a favourite deck sport
throughout the Twenties and Thirties. (Right) The game played
aboard the Canadian Pacific liner *Duchess of Bedford*, 20,123
tons, December 1931. (Above) A stranger game aboard another
CPR liner, the *Duchess of Richmond*, 20,222 tons, also in
December 1931.

Zerstreuung an Deck

Shuffleboard war ein beliebtes Deckspiel der zwanziger und
dreißiger Jahre. (Rechts) Eine Partie an Deck des 20 123-
Tonners *Duchess of Bedford* der Canadian Pacific im
Dezember 1931. (Oben) Ein noch eigenartiges Spiel an Bord
eines anderen CPR-Liners, des 20 222-Tonners *Duchess of
Richmond*, ebenfalls im Dezember 1931.

Jeux de pont

Le jeu de palets était une des distractions favorites des
passagers des années 1920 et 1930, comme ici, en décembre
1931, à bord du *Duchess of Bedford* (20 123 tonneaux, à droite),
de la Canadian Pacific. (Ci-dessus) Un autre jeu insolite à
bord d'un autre paquebot de la CPR, le *Duchess of Richmond*
(20 222 tonneaux), également en décembre 1931.

Exercise and relaxation

(Top left) A rigged canvas swimming-pool aboard the *Duchess of Richmond*, 1931. (Below left) A riding machine in the gym; (top right) a work-out with clubs and rings; (below right and right) a banjo player competes with the wind; serried ranks of sunbathers, all aboard the *Duchess of Bedford*, 1931.

Sport und Entspannung

(Oben links) Ein aus Leinwänden aufgebautes Schwimmbecken an Bord der *Duchess of Richmond*, 1931. Die Reitmaschine im Turnsaal (links unten), sportliche Übungen mit Keulen und Ringen (rechts oben), ein Banjospieler, der sich gegen den Wind behaupten muß (rechts unten) und Erholung auf dem Sonnendeck (rechts), alles an Bord der *Duchess of Bedford*, 1931.

Exercices et détente

Une piscine de toile a été montée sur le pont du *Duchess of Richmond* (en haut, à gauche) tandis que le *Duchess of Bedford* dispose, en 1931, d'un gymnase avec vélo d'exercice (en bas, à gauche), agrès et espalier (en haut, à droite). Un banjoïste joue contre le vent (en bas, à droite), peut-être pour le plus grand plaisir des passagers prenant leur bain de soleil en rangs serrés (à droite).

Sprucing up

The RMS *Mauretania* returns to Southampton for her annual
overhaul, autumn 1932 (above). The *Mauretania* was the
first to be pulled out of the summer schedule for repairs.
(Right) Being towed out of Southampton dock for a voyage
to New York on her 26th anniversary of service in 1933,
sporting her new all-white livery. From 1930 she had been
used mainly as a cruise ship.

Großreinemachen

Die RMS *Mauretania* läuft zur jährlichen Überholung in
Southampton ein, Herbst 1932 (oben). Die *Mauretania* war
die erste, die am Ende der Sommersaison ins Dock kam.
(Rechts) Mit neuem weißem Anstrich kehrt sie 1933 zurück,
bereit für die Fahrt nach New York zum 26. Jubiläum
ihres Dienstantritts. Seit 1930 fuhr sie hauptsächlich
als Kreuzfahrtschiff.

Sur son trente-et-un

Le RMS *Mauretania* revient à Southampton à l'automne 1932
pour son carénage annuel (ci-dessus). Ce paquebot fut le
premier à être retiré du service d'été pour réparations.
(À droite) Arborant une toute nouvelle livrée blanche à
l'occasion de son 26e anniversaire de service, en 1933, il
quitte le port de Southampton pour effectuer sa traversée
vers New York. Depuis 1930, il est affété essentiellement
pour la croisière.

The end of the line
(Left) The *Mauretania* being painted white, May 1933.
(Above) An inventory being compiled in her elegant A-
deck reading room and saloon before the liner is broken
up, May 1935. (Right) The catalogue of the lifeboats and
deck fittings being drawn up before their sale at auction.

Am Ende ihrer langen Fahrt
(Links) Die *Mauretania* erhält ihren weißen Anstrich,
Mai 1933. (Oben) Inventarlisten werden im eleganten
Lesesaal und Salon des A-Decks erstellt, als das Schiff
im Mai 1935 außer Dienst gestellt wird. (Rechts)
Rettungsboote und Aufbauten werden für die
Versteigerung katalogisiert.

La fin d'un paquebot
Le *Mauretania* est repeint en blanc en mai 1933
(à gauche). Deux ans plus tard, des commissaires
dressent l'inventaire dans la salle de lecture élégante du
pont A avant le désarmement du paquebot (ci-dessus),
d'autres inspectent les canots de sauvetage et l'acca-
stillage du pont avant leur vente aux enchères (à droite).

Last rites

(Left) The great funnels of the old *Mauretania* being dismantled and cut up for scrap in the breakers' yard, Rosyth, September 1935. (Above) The ornamental grille from the top deck being removed to be packed and sold, June 1935. (Right) What's in a name? The nameplate being stripped of its lettering.

Das letzte Stündlein

Auf der Abbruchwerft in Rosyth, September 1935. (Links) Die großen Schornsteine der alten *Mauretania* werden abgenommen und zum Verschrotten zerlegt. (Oben) Das schmiedeeiserne Gitter vom Oberdeck kommt zum Verkauf, Juni 1935. (Rechts) Nicht einmal die Buchstaben ihres Namensschildes haben Bestand.

Les derniers sacrements

(À gauche) Les grandes cheminées du vieux *Mauretania* sont démontées et découpées sur le chantier du ferrailleur à Rosyth, en septembre 1935. (Ci-dessus) Des ouvriers emportent la grille en fer forgé du pont supérieur pour l'emmener à la vente (juin 1935). (À droite) Qu'est-ce qu'un nom ? Quelques lettres que l'on retire d'un panneau de métal !

Four great liners

The inauguration of the new dock at Southampton, May 1934: (from left to right) *Homeric*, 34,351 tons, *Mauretania*, 31,938 tons, *Columbus*, 32,581 tons, and *Empress of Britain*, 42,348 tons. Confusingly, both *Homeric* and *Columbus* sailed at different times as *Columbus* for Norddeutscher Lloyd. The second *Columbus* was sunk by her crew in the Atlantic rather than fall into the hands of the British, 19 December 1939.

Parade der Ozeanriesen

Einweihung des neuen Docks in Southampton im Mai 1934: (Von links nach rechts) *Homeric*, 34 351 Tonnen, *Mauretania*, 31 938 Tonnen, *Columbus*, 32 581 Tonnen, und *Empress of Britain*, 42 348 Tonnen. Verwirrenderweise fuhren sowohl die *Homeric* als auch die *Columbus* zu verschiedenen Zeiten unter dem Namen *Columbus* für den Norddeutschen Lloyd. Die zweite *Columbus* wurde von ihrer Mannschaft am 19. Dezember 1939 auf dem Atlantik versenkt, damit sie nicht in britische Hände fiel.

Quatre grands paquebots

L'inauguration d'un nouveau quai de Southampton, en mai 1934 : (de gauche à droite) l'*Homéric* (34 351 tonneaux), le *Mauretania* (31 938 tonneaux), le *Columbus* (32 581 tonneaux) et l'*Empress of Britain* (42 348 tonneaux). Étrangement, l'*Homeric* et le *Columbus* ont tous deux navigué aux couleurs de la Norddeutscher Lloyd, toutefois à des époques différentes, sous le même nom de *Columbus*. Le second *Columbus* fut sabordé par son équipage dans l'Atlantique le 19 décembre 1939 pour éviter qu'il ne tombe aux mains des Britanniques.

Top jobs
Overhauling the Canadian Pacific *Empress of Britain* at
Southampton, November 1931. (Above) An inspection of the
interior of a stack. (Right) Preparing a funnel for a repaint.
The 42,348-ton liner was the largest to ply between
Commonwealth ports, and boasted the largest swimming-
pool of any liner of the time.

In schwindelnder Höhe
Überholung des Canadian-Pacific-Liners *Empress of Britain*
in Southampton, November 1931. (Oben) Das Innere des
Schornsteins wird inspiziert. (Rechts) Vorbereitungen für
den neuen Anstrich. Der 42348-Tonner war das größte Schiff,
das zwischen den Commonwealth-Häfen verkehrte, und hatte
unter allen Passagierschiffen damals den größten
Swimmingpool.

Des travaux en hauteur
Des ouvriers inspectent l'intérieur d'une cheminée (ci-dessus)
de l'*Empress of Britain*, de la Canadian Pacific, en radoub à
Southampton, en novembre 1931. D'autres se préparent à la
repeindre (à droite). Ce paquebot de 42348 tonneaux, le plus
grand à desservir les ports du Commonwealth, possédait
la plus grande piscine installée à l'époque à bord d'un navire.

The art and craft of shipbuilding

(Left) John Bart, a veteran of 14 years in the shipyards, riveting plates. Bart had survived the worst years of depression in the British yards. (Right) Shipbuilders laying out plywood according to the designer's plans. (Opposite, left and right) Hammering links of sea chain at the Pontypridd Chain Works, Wales, and some of the 700 tons of chain being loaded for the new Orient liner *Orcades*, 23,456 tons.

Kunst und Handwerk des Schiffsbauers

(Links) John Bart, seit 14 Jahren Werftarbeiter, nietet Stahlplatten zusammen. Bart hatte die schlimmsten Krisenjahre des britischen Schiffsbaus überstanden. (Rechts) Werftarbeiter verlegen einen Holzfußboden nach den Plänen des Architekten. (Gegenüber, links und rechts) Ankerketten werden in den Pontypridd Chain Works in Wales geschmiedet; einige der insgesamt 700 Tonnen Ketten, mit denen der neue 23456-Tonnen-Liner *Orcades* der Orient Line ausgerüstet war, werden verladen.

Arts et métiers de la construction navale

John Bart, un ouvrier ayant travaillé 14 ans dans les chantiers navals – et survécu aux pires années de la dépression de la construction navale, est en train de riveter des plaques de la coque (à gauche). Des ouvriers assemblent des panneaux de contreplaqué (à droite); d'autres, travaillant aux Pontypridd Chain Works (Pays de Galles), martèlent les maillons d'une chaîne qui sera chargée (700 tonnes) à bord du paquebot *Orcades* (23456 tonneaux) de la compagnie Orient (ci-contre, à gauche et à droite).

Clean up and running repair
(Left) Overhaul of the screws of SS *Belpareil* of Norway
in Birkenhead docks as she prepares for a voyage to
China in 1936. (Right) Lifting out sections of one of
the funnels of the P & O *Ranpura*, 16,585 tons, at the
Royal Albert Docks, London, November 1933.

Instandhaltung und Inspektion
(Links) Die Schiffsschrauben des norwegischen
Dampfers SS *Belpareil* werden vor der Überfahrt nach
China im Jahre 1936 im englischen Birkenhead überholt.
(Rechts) Dem 16585-Tonner *Ranpura* der P & O wird im
November 1933 in den Londoner Royal Albert Docks ein
Teil eines Schornsteins abgenommen.

Nettoyage et remise en état
Révision des hélices du SS *Belpareil* de la Norvège,
amarré en 1936 aux quais de Birkenhead, avant son
départ vers la Chine (à gauche). Extraction d'un
tronçon de la cheminée du *Ranpura* (16585 tonneaux),
de la P & O, aux Royal Albert Docks de Londres, en
novembre 1933 (à droite).

Africa-bound

(Left) The new Union Castle *Pretoria Castle*, 17,392 tons, built for the round-Africa route. In 1939–42 she was an armed merchant cruiser, and was then converted to an aircraft carrier. She was rebuilt as the *Warwick Castle* in 1946, and was eventually scrapped in 1962. (Right) Tug of war aboard a Union Castle ship heading south for the Equator from Madeira, June 1939.

Auf nach Afrika

(Links) Die neue *Pretoria Castle* der Union Castle Line, 17 392 Tonnen, war für den Dienst rund um Afrika gedacht. Von 1939 bis 1942 war sie als bewaffnetes Hilfs-schiff im Einsatz, dann wurde sie zum Flugzeugträger umgebaut. Nach dem Krieg restauriert, ging sie von 1946 an als *Warwick Castle* auf Fahrt und blieb noch bis 1962 im Dienst. (Rechts) Tauziehen auf einem Schiff der Union Castle Line auf dem Weg von Madeira südwärts zum Äquator, Juni 1939.

En route pour l'Afrique

Le nouveau *Pretoria Castle* (17 392 tonneaux), de la Union Castle, est construit pour faire le tour de l'Afrique (à gauche). Transformé en navire de commerce armé entre 1939 et 1942, il fut aménagé en porte-avions puis reconstruit sous le nom de *Warwick Castle* en 1946, avant d'être envoyé à la ferraille en 1962. Une séance de tir à la corde à bord d'un des navires de la Union Castle en route vers l'Équateur au départ de Madère, en juin 1939 (à droite).

Farewells

(Left) Streamers thrown from the decks of the Orient Line *Orcades*, 23,456 tons, as she leaves Sydney harbour for London, 1939. She was to be sunk off the Cape of Good Hope on 10 October 1942, with the loss of 48 lives. (Right) Waving farewell to the Orient liner *Orontes*, 19,970 tons, as she sets out for Australia with the England cricket team under Douglas Jardine on their controversial tour of 1932.

Abschiedsgrüße

(Links) Luftschlangen wehen von Deck, als die *Orcades* der Orient Line, 23456 Tonnen, 1939 im Hafen von Sydney nach London ablegt. Am 10. Oktober 1942 wurde sie am Kap der Guten Hoffnung versenkt, 48 Menschen kamen um. (Rechts) Zaungäste winken dem 19970-Tonner *Orontes* der Orient Line auf dem Weg nach Australien zu. An Bord ist die englische Cricketmannschaft unter Douglas Jardine, unterwegs zu ihrer umstrittenen Tour des Jahres 1932.

Les adieux

(À gauche) Les passagers lancent des serpentins des ponts de l'*Orcades* (23456 tonneaux), de l'Orient Line, au moment de son départ de Sydney pour Londres, en 1939. Son naufrage au large du cap de Bonne-Espérance, le 10 octobre 1942, allait faire 48 disparus. (À droite) Les adieux d'une famille au paquebot *Orontes* (19970 tonneaux), de la même compagnie, lors de son appareillage pour l'Australie avec l'équipe de cricket d'Angleterre dirigée par Douglas Jardine lors de leur tournée controversée de 1932.

Splash

Enjoying the swimming-pool (above) on the upper decks of *Orontes*, 1932. *Orontes* remained in service until 1962. (Right) The Orient Line *Orion*, 23,371 tons, at the moment of launch, 7 December 1934; the bottle had been released when the Duke of Gloucester pressed a switch 12,000 miles away in Brisbane.

Platsch!

Badevergnügen im Swimmingpool auf dem Oberdeck der *Orontes*, 1932 (oben). Die *Orontes* blieb noch bis 1962 im Dienst. (Rechts) Die *Orion* der Orient Line, 23 371 Tonnen, im Augenblick des Stapellaufs am 7. Dezember 1934; die Flasche für die Schiffstaufe löste der Herzog von Gloucester im 12 000 Meilen entfernten Brisbane per Knopfdruck.

Plongeons

Les passagers de l'*Orontes* profitent des joies de la piscine du pont supérieur, en 1932 (ci-dessus). Ce paquebot restera en service jusqu'en 1962. (À droite) L'*Orion* (23 371 tonneaux), de la Orient Line, au moment de son lancement, le 7 décembre 1934 ; la bouteille a été libérée à distance par le duc de Gloucester, alors à Brisbane, à 12 000 milles de là.

Style-setter

Views of the fabulous *Normandie*, the most fashionable
liner of her day. (Above) The 82,799-ton liner won the
Blue Riband on her first transatlantic voyage in 1935.
(Right) The famous tear-drop shape of the *Normandie*'s
funnels, and her waisted silhouette from the bows (far
right) as she leaves harbour, 1935.

Trendsetter

Ansichten der fabelhaften *Normandie*, des extravagan-
testen Ozeanliners seiner Zeit. (Oben) Der 82 799-Tonner
errang das Blaue Band schon bei der ersten Atlantiküberquerung 1935. (Rechts) Die berühmten tropfen-
förmigen Schornsteine der *Normandie* und die schlanke
Silhouette in der Vorderansicht (ganz rechts) beim
Auslaufen 1935.

Un modèle

(Ci-dessus) Le fabuleux *Normandie* (82 799 tonneaux),
le paquebot le plus élégant de son époque, remporta le
Ruban bleu en 1935 lors de son premier voyage transatlantique. La forme en goutte d'eau des cheminées (à
droite) et la silhouette cintrée de sa proue (à l'extrême
droite, lors de l'appareillage du navire en 1935) sont
caractéristiques du *Normandie*.

Blue Riband winner
The *Normandie* being fitted out at the yards of Chantiers de l'Atlantique at Saint-Nazaire in 1932. After her triumph in 1935, she lost the Blue Riband to the *Queen Mary* the next year, regained it in 1937 and then lost it again.

Gewinner des Blauen Bandes
Die *Normandie* im Ausrüstungsdock der Chantiers de l'Atlantique in Saint-Nazaire, 1932. Nach ihrem Triumph im Jahre 1935 mußte sie das Blaue Band im folgenden Jahr an die *Queen Mary* abtreten, errang es 1937 zurück und verlor es danach von neuem.

Vainqueur du Ruban bleu
Le *Normandie* en cours d'armement aux Chantiers de l'Atlantique de Saint-Nazaire en 1932. Après son triomphe de 1935, il perdit le Ruban bleu l'année suivante au bénéfice du *Queen Mary*, le reprit en 1937 et le perdit de nouveau.

Fitting out

(Previous pages) The giant rudder of the *Normandie* being prepared in a Skoda factory. (Above) Fitting out the decks, 1934, with the CGT SS *Espagne* being dismantled on the other side of the basin. (Right) The *Normandie* in dry dock as her screws are fitted and the final coat of paint is applied.

Sie nimmt Formen an

(Vorherige Doppelseite) Das gewaltige Ruder der *Normandie* wurde von den Skoda-Werken gebaut. (Oben) Ausstattung der Decks, 1934; auf der anderen Seite des Werftbeckens wird der Dampfer SS *Espagne* der Compagnie Générale Transatlantique (CGT) abgebrochen. (Rechts) Die *Normandie* im Trockendock zur Montage der Schiffsschrauben und zum letzten Anstrich.

L'armement

Le gouvernail géant du *Normandie* en phase de finition à l'usine Skoda (pages précédentes). Les ponts sont aménagés en 1934 tandis que le SS *Espagne*, de la Compagnie Générale Transatlantique (CGT), est en cours de désarmement de l'autre côté du bassin (ci-dessus). Le *Normandie* sur son dock flottant lors du remontage de ses hélices et l'application des dernières couches de peinture (à droite).

Reception

(Above) The welcome at New York as the *Normandie* arrives
for the first time at CGT's pier 48, June 1935. (Right) A sailor
operates an engine-room telegraph from the spacious bridge.

Der Empfang

(Oben) Schaulustige haben sich in New York am Pier 48,
der Anlegestelle der CGT, versammelt, als die *Normandie*
im Juni 1935 nach ihrer ersten Atlantiküberquerung einläuft.
(Rechts) Ein Matrose bedient auf der weitläufigen Brücke
den Telegrafen zum Maschinenraum.

Réception chaleureuse

L'accueil du *Normandie* à New York lors de sa première
arrivée au pier 48 de la CGT, en juin 1935. Un marin utilise
le transmetteur d'ordres de la vaste passerelle du *Normandie*
(à droite).

Art Deco glory

(Above) The doors, panelling and mural between the smoking room and grand saloon of the *Normandie*. This design was a complete break with the past, and though often imitated it was never to be surpassed. (Right) The Lalique 'columns of light' and ceiling lights in the first-class Café Grill.

Pracht des Art déco

(Oben) Türen, Vertäfelung und Wandbild zwischen Rauchersalon und Großem Salon der *Normandie*. Die gesamte Gestaltung brach mit aller Tradition und sollte, wenn auch oft imitiert, unübertroffen bleiben. (Rechts) Die »Lichtsäulen« und Deckenlampen von Lalique im Café Grill der Ersten Klasse.

Splendeur de l'Art déco

(Ci-dessus) Portes, panneaux et décors muraux agrémentent le passage entre le fumoir et le grand salon du *Normandie*. Cette décoration est une rupture complète avec le passé et bien que souvent imitée, ne fut jamais dépassée. (À droite) Les colonnes de lumière de Lalique et les éclairages en plafond du Café Grill des première classe.

Grand luxe
Fixtures and fittings aboard the *Normandie.*
(Top left) One of the four bedrooms of the Trouville Suite;
(top right) promenade deck cabin with private verandah;
(below) the dining-room and living room, with floor-to-ceiling
mirror and grand piano, of the Caen Suite. (Right) The
Lalique-panelled first-class dining-room.

Grand luxe
Einrichtung und Ausstattung der *Normandie.* (Oben links)
Eines von vier Schlafzimmern der Trouville-Suite; (oben
rechts) Kabine auf dem Promenadendeck mit eigener Veranda;
(unten) Wohnzimmer und Speisezimmer der Caen-Suite
mit Spiegelwänden und eigenem Piano. (Rechts) Der mit
Lalique-Glas getäfelte Speisesaal der Ersten Klasse.

Grand luxe
Le mobilier et les accessoires à bord du *Normandie.* L'une
des quatre chambres de la suite Trouville (en haut, à gauche) ;
une cabine du pont promenade avec sa véranda particulière
(en haut, à droite) ; la salle à manger et le salon de la suite
Caen (ci-dessous), avec son miroir pleine hauteur et un grand
piano. La grande salle à manger des première classe était
entièrement décorée de panneaux dus à Lalique (à droite).

207

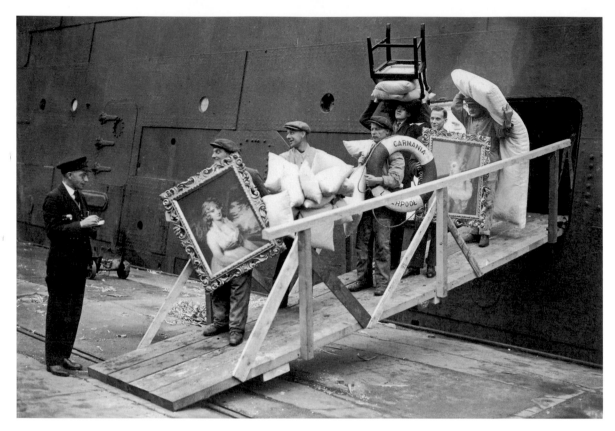

Selling up

Pictures, mattresses, memorabilia being removed from the Cunard liner *Carmania* at Tilbury Dock before she is scrapped. (Right) The 19,524-ton *Carmania* alongside at Tilbury, November 1931. On 14 September 1914 she sank the German armed merchant cruiser *Cap Trafalgar* off Trinidad; 16 died.

Ausverkauf

Bilder, Matratzen und Erinnerungsstücke werden am Londoner Tilbury Dock von Bord des Cunard-Liners *Carmania* geholt, der zum Verschrotten geht. (Rechts) Die *Carmania*, 19524 Tonnen, am Kai in Tilbury, November 1931. Am 14. September 1914 versenkte sie den deutschen Hilfskreuzer *Cap Trafalgar* vor Trinidad; 16 Menschen kamen um.

Vendu

Tableaux, coussins et souvenirs sont déménagés du paquebot *Carmania*, de la Cunard, amarré au Tilbury Dock, avant qu'il ne parte à la ferraille. Le *Carmania* (19524 tonneaux) à quai à Tilbury, en novembre 1931 (à droite). Le 14 septembre 1914, il coula le croiseur marchand armé allemand *Cap Trafalgar* au large de Trinidad, faisant 16 morts.

Pride of New York

(Left) The USS *Manhattan*, 24,289 tons, is welcomed by fireboats on her maiden arrival at her home port, 1932. (Right) Four of 250 Jewish refugees being carried by the *Manhattan* from Germany to Southampton. (Bottom right) Jesse Owens practising on the *Manhattan*, en route for the Berlin Olympics of 1936, where he was to win four gold medals. The *Manhattan* was to serve as the troopship USS *Wakefield*; she suffered a damaging fire in 1942, but was rebuilt and left service in 1964.

Der Stolz von New York

(Links) Feuerlöschboote begrüßen 1932 die USS *Manhattan*, 24 289 Tonnen, als sie von ihrer Jungfernfahrt in den Heimathafen zurückkehrt. (Rechts) Vier von 250 jüdischen Flüchtlingen, die mit der *Manhattan* aus Deutschland nach Southampton kommen. (Unten rechts) Jesse Owens hält sich auf der *Manhattan* fit, unterwegs zu den Berliner Olympischen Spielen von 1936, bei denen er vier Goldmedaillen errang. Im Krieg diente die *Manhattan* unter dem Namen USS *Wakefield* als Truppentransporter und wurde 1942 durch einen Brand beschädigt; wiederhergestellt, blieb sie noch bis 1964 im Dienst.

La fierté de New York

Le USS *Manhattan* (24 289 tonneaux) est accueilli par les bateaux-pompes du port de New York lors de son retour de voyage inaugural à son port d'attache, en 1932 (à gauche). Quatre des 250 réfugiés juifs qui ont été transportés d'Allemagne à Southampton par le *Manhattan* (à droite). Jesse Owens s'entraîne à bord du *Manhattan* qui l'emmène aux olympiades de 1936 à Berlin, où il allait remporter quatre médailles d'or (en bas, à droite). Ce paquebot allait servir de transport de troupes pendant la guerre sous le nom de USS *Wakefield* ; ravagé par un incendie en 1942, il fut reconstruit et resta en service jusqu'en 1964.

Phoenix

(Right) The second *Mauretania* is launched from the Cammell Laird yard, Birkenhead, July 1938. The 35,738-ton liner served throughout the Second World War as a troopship, returning to the North Atlantic route in 1947, where she served until 1965. (Above) The liner is towed by the tug *Thistle Cock* from the fitting-out basin across the Mersey to Gladstone graving dock: her first voyage, 14 May 1939.

Ein Phönix

(Rechts) Die neue *Mauretania*, das zweite Schiff dieses Namens, läuft im Juli 1938 in der Cammell-Laird-Werft in Birkenhead vom Stapel. Der 35738-Tonner diente im Zweiten Weltkrieg als Truppentransporter und kehrte 1947 auf die Nordatlantikroute zurück, wo er bis 1965 fuhr. (Oben) Der Schlepper *Thistle Cock* bringt den Liner vom Ausrüstungsdock zum Gladstone-Trockendock auf der anderen Seite des Mersey – die erste Fahrt der neuen *Mauretania* am 14. Mai 1939.

Un phœnix

(À droite) Le second *Mauretania* est lancé en juillet 1938 aux chantiers Cammell Laird de Birkenhead. Ce paquebot de 35738 tonneaux sert de transport de troupes pendant toute la Seconde Guerre mondiale, puis reprit son service commercial sur l'Atlantique Nord de 1947 à 1965. (Ci-dessus) Le paquebot est remorqué par le *Thistle Cock* entre son bassin d'armement sur la Mersey et le bassin de radoub de Gladstone : son premier voyage, le 14 mai 1939.

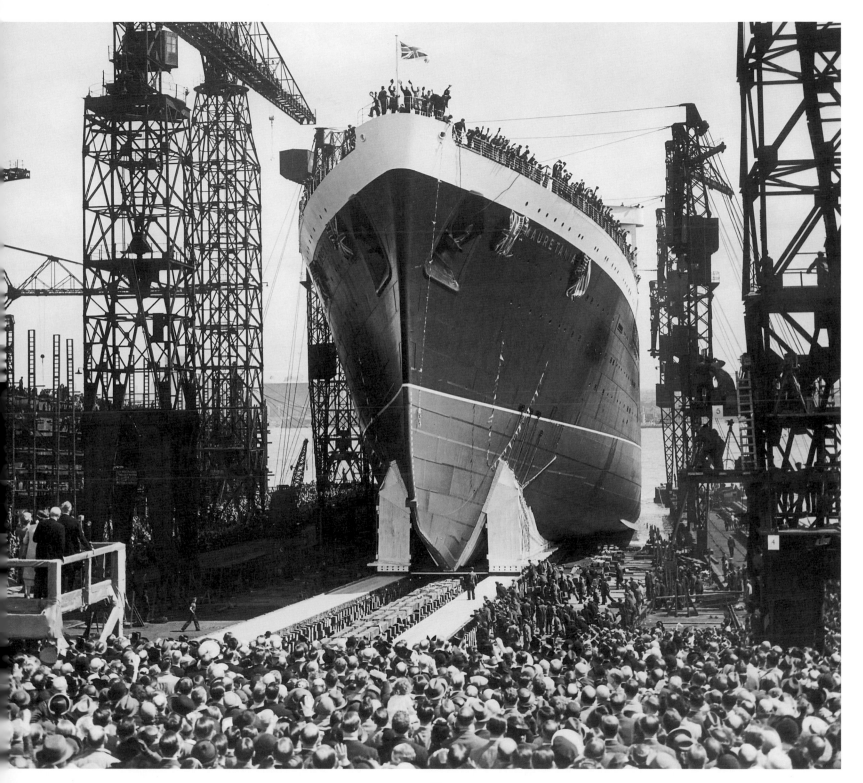

Nuts and bolts
(Above) Hammering down rivets inside the hull of
the new *Mauretania* at the Cammell Laird yard.
(Right) Preparation of the main ducts leading to the
four main boilers: these will be concealed in the
larger of her two funnels, aft.

Grob- und Feinarbeit
(Oben) Auf der Cammell-Laird-Werft werden Nieten in
den Rumpf der neuen *Mauretania* gehämmert. (Rechts)
Die Auslässe der vier Haupt-Dampfkessel sind später
im größeren ihrer beiden Schornsteine verborgen.

Le travail de finition
(Ci-dessus) Un ouvrier pose les rivets maintenant les
panneaux de la coque du nouveau *Mauretania* aux
chantiers Cammell Laird. Les conduits des quatre
chaudières principales seront ensuite dissimulés
par une grande cheminée (à droite).

(Above) Fitting 'Leo', one of the engraved glass astrological panels in first-class accommodation, and (left) fitting the bulbs in an uplight in the cabin-class (tourist) restaurant.

(Oben) Der Löwe, ein Motiv aus einer Serie von Ätzglasscheiben mit Abbildungen von Tierkreiszeichen, wird an seinen Platz in einer Erster-Klasse-Kabine angebracht, und die Lampen im Speisesaal der Kabinen-(Touristen-)Klasse werden mit Glühbirnen versehen (links).

(Ci-dessus) Le « Lion », l'un des panneaux de verre gravé représentant les signes astrologiques décorant les appartements des première classe, et le remplacement d'une ampoule d'une des grandes lampes du restaurant de la classe touriste (à gauche).

Disaster

(Above) The 34,569-ton CGT/French Line *Paris* caught fire and rolled over at Le Havre, 13 April 1939 – a fate similar to the *Normandie*'s. (Right) Crowds turn out at Ashbury Park, New Jersey, 1934, to see the charred *Morro Castle*, which had mysteriously caught fire with the loss of 134 lives.

Katastrophen

(Oben) Der 34,569-Tonner *Paris* der französischen CGT geriet am 13. April 1939 in Le Havre in Brand und kenterte – ein ähnliches Schicksal sollte die *Normandie* ereilen. (Rechts) Eine Menschenmenge ist 1934 in Ashbury Park (New Jersey) zusammengekommen, um die *Morro Castle* zu betrachten; aus ungeklärter Ursache hatte sie Feuer gefangen, und 134 Menschen verloren ihr Leben.

Désastre

Le *Paris*, un paquebot de 34,569 tonneaux appartenant à la CGT, prend feu et s'incline sur le flanc au Havre, le 13 avril 1939 (ci-dessus) – un destin semblable à celui du *Normandie*. La foule se presse à Ashbury Park (New Jersey) en 1934 pour voir passer la coque carbonisée du *Morro Castle*, dévasté après un incendie inexpliqué qui fit 134 morts (à droite).

Roll of honour

(Left) Great ships alongside the piers at New York, March 1939: the liners are, from foreground, *Hamburg, Bremen, Columbus, De Grasse, Normandie, Britannic, Aquitania, Conte di Savoia, Fort Townsend* and *Monarch of Bermuda*. (Right) The same setting, 16 September 1939: from foreground to distance, the liners are *Île de France, Normandie, Queen Mary*, already in her wartime grey, *Aquitania, Rex* and *Monarch of Bermuda*.

Eine prachtvolle Parade

(Links) Ozeanriesen an ihren Piers in New York, März 1939: (von vorn nach hinten) *Hamburg, Bremen, Columbus, De Grasse, Normandie, Britannic, Aquitania, Conte di Savoia, Fort Townsend* und *Monarch of Bermuda*. (Rechts) Der gleiche Ort mit der Belegung vom 16. September 1939: (von vorn) *Île de France, Normandie, Queen Mary* (schon in grauem Kriegsanstrich), *Aquitania, Rex* und *Monarch of Bermuda*.

Tableau d'honneur

En mars 1939, les grands paquebots sont alignés le long des quais de New York (à gauche). Il s'agit, en partant du premier plan, des *Hamburg, Bremen, Columbus, De Grasse, Normandie, Britannic, Aquitania, Conte di Savoia, Fort Townsend* et *Monarch of Bermuda*. Le 16 septembre 1939, au même endroit (à droite), ce sont l'*Île de France*, le *Normandie*, le *Queen Mary* (déjà dans sa livrée militaire grise), l'*Aquitania*, le *Rex* et le *Monarch of Bermuda*.

Great liner, great day

(Above) Haymaking by the Clyde with the *Queen Elizabeth* on the stocks at the John Brown yard a month before her launch, August 1938. (Right) The world's largest liner slips gracefully to the sea at the John Brown yard, launched by her namesake Queen Elizabeth, 27 September 1938.

Ein großes Schiff, ein großer Tag

(Oben) Heuernte am Clyde, im Hintergrund die *Queen Elizabeth* auf der John-Brown-Werft. Das Bild entstand im August 1938, einen Monat vor Stapellauf. (Rechts) 27. September 1938: Der größte Passagierdampfer der Welt gleitet auf der John-Brown-Werft elegant ins Wasser, vom Stapel gelassen von seiner Namenspatronin Königin Elizabeth.

Le grand jour d'un grand paquebot

En août 1938, les paysans de la Clyde font les foins avec pour horizon la haute silhouette du *Queen Elizabeth*, reposant sur son ber des chantiers John Brown, un mois avant son lancement (ci-dessus). Le plus grand paquebot du monde glisse doucement vers la mer (à droite) après avoir été lancé par son homonyme la reine Elizabeth, le 27 septembre 1938.

Secret mission to completion

Glaswegians watch as the *Queen Elizabeth*, now in battleship grey, slips out of the Clyde at Gourock on 3 March 1940 to be completed in America (above), enthusiastically welcomed as she sails into New York on 7 March (right). She symbolized the new chapter in the story of the great liners.

In geheimer Mission

Einwohner von Glasgow sehen zu, als die *Queen Elizabeth*, nun in Schlachtschiffgrau, am 3. März 1940 bei Gourock die Clydemündung verläßt und zur Fertigstellung nach Amerika aufbricht (oben), wo ihr bei der Ankunft in New York am 7. März ein großer Empfang bereitet wird (rechts). Das Schiff sollte ein neues Kapitel im Buch der Ozeanriesen aufschlagen.

En mission de guerre

Ce 3 mars 1940, les habitants de Glasgow regardent le *Queen Elizabeth*, dans sa livrée militaire grise, descendre la Clyde à Gourock pour gagner les États-Unis (ci-dessus), où il sera réaménagé. Accueilli avec enthousiasme à New York le 7 mars (à droite), le navire ouvre une nouvelle page de l'histoire des grands paquebots.

4

Queen Mary: The Passengers' Favourite

For the best part of two years from the end of 1931 the huge rust-brown hull of Job Number 534 in the John Brown shipyard on Clydeside was the most famous symbol in Britain of the economic Depression. The keel was laid during December 1930, and all work was suspended exactly a year later. The hull was well advanced, and the knife-edge soaring bows and the huge length of riveted steel dominated the Clydeside skyline.

It took that time for David Kirkwood, the MP for Clydeside, to persuade the government to rescue the great ship, and with it the economy of the Clyde yards and the pride of Britain's merchant marine. In 1933 the Board of Trade agreed a strict set of terms. A sum of £3 million was to be made available to finish the ship, with a further £5 million to build her sister ship. There was one major condition for Cunard. It was to merge with the ailing White Star Line, whose fleet was in need of modernization. The descendants of Samuel Cunard had to accept alliance with their Atlantic rivals.

Quite early on it was decided that the new ship should be a sovereign, a queen of the seas, and the name most mentioned in the Cunard boardroom was Victoria. The launch was to be an important national occasion, so King George V was invited well ahead and was told, cryptically, that the ship would be named after a great queen. In his acceptance he said that he was delighted the ship was to be named after his wife, Queen Mary.

On the day of the launch, 26 September 1934, squalls of rain came beating up the Clyde. The Queen released an oversized bottle of Australian white wine on the bow, and in christening her namesake *Queen Mary* uttered the 28 words of the only speech she ever gave in public as consort. Never one for exaggerating great occasions, she recorded in her diary that night, 'Launched the world's largest ship today. Too bad it rained.' The King was more gracious, and in his speech summed up the nation's relief that the ship was being launched at last. 'Now, with the hope of better trade on both sides of the Atlantic, let us look forward to her playing a great part in the revival of international commerce. It has been the nation's will that she should be completed, and today we can send her forth . . . alive with beauty, energy and strength.'

In war and peace the new liner was to have her fair share of collisions and other troubles, but she was a remarkably fortunate ship, and is the only one of the great liners which remains in something like her original form to this day. She had noth-

ing of the extravagant chic of the *Normandie*. Her decor and furnishings were even described as dowdy. Today, though, they appear the epitome of the Art Deco style. Particularly fine was the inlay work and panelling. One set of panels and screens, rather ominously and prophetically, depicted commercial aircraft crossing the Atlantic, the great flying boats and biplanes whose successors were to put the liners out of business.

The *Queen Mary* proved a huge favourite with transatlantic travellers of all kinds. Most were prepared to forgive her obvious flaws, the cloud of ash blowing from her funnels on to the aft decks, the vibrations and a notorious roll which according to one of her crew 'would roll the milk out of a cup of tea'. She sailed from Southampton on her maiden voyage on 27 May 1936, a Royal Marine band playing 'Rule Britannia' on the quayside. She took the Blue Riband on 31 August with a crossing of 3 days, 20 hours and 42 minutes eastbound at a speed of 31.69 knots: the first commercial crossing under four days.

In October 1936 she encountered her first major Atlantic storm. A stewardess recalled, 'She suddenly started to go and she went, so slowly, down and down and down. I was thrown out of my bunk and thought she was never coming back... Slowly she righted herself and then began a horrible corkscrew motion that went on and on, even after the sea had become calm.' The *Queen Mary*'s roll, according to her last captain, J. Treasure-Jones, made her 'the nearest ship ever to a living being'. Extensive modifications to her screws were carried out to correct the vibrations, and stabilizer fins were added in the 1950s.

Unlike the *Normandie*, whose passengers were often overawed by her grandeur, the *Queen Mary*'s homely charms made money for her owners. Her statistics were listed in her publicity, 4 million rivets, 600 clocks, 56 kinds of decorative woods, an overall length more than the height of the Eiffel Tower. At 1,018 feet she was just 11 feet short of the French liner, but some 1,744 gross tons heavier. Both had four screws, the *Queen Mary* driven by steam turbine, and the *Normandie* by steam turbo-electric propulsion.

On 30 August 1939 she set sail from Southampton with 2,332 passengers, a record. By the time she arrived at New York Britain was at war. She stayed at her usual pier for most of the winter, being prepared for war service: grey paint, anti-mine devices, and anti-aircraft guns on the upper decks. In March she was joined by her new sister, the *Queen Elizabeth*, already painted battleship grey.

The war record of the two *Queens* is unassailable. Winston Churchill said they may have shortened the war in Europe by a year because between them they could move more than 15,000 troops across the Atlantic in five days. The *Queen Mary* was faster than almost any warship afloat, and could easily outstrip any marauding U-boat.

War service was not without mishap. On a run from New York in 1942 she picked up her regular escort of a light cruiser, HMS *Curacoa*, with six destroyers as she came into hostile waters around Scotland. The *Curacoa* was four knots slower than the liner and had no chance of matching her as she executed precautionary zigzags. The *Curacoa* had tried to keep ahead but at 1.30 pm on 2 October 1942, in clear visibility, the *Queen Mary* struck the cruiser amidships. The warship sank in five minutes and 329 out of its company of 450 were lost. The *Queen Mary*'s captain, Commodore Sir Gordon Illingworth, decided that with 10,398 American troops aboard he could not risk stopping to help. The incident was kept secret at the time. The judgement, on 21 January 1947, held the *Curacoa* entirely to blame, but a later judgement apportioned one third of the responsibility to the look-outs of the *Queen Mary*.

At the end of the war, the *Queen Mary* carried more than 22,000 GI brides and their children to new lives in the US and Canada between February and September 1946. On 27 September she docked at Southampton and two days later she was decommissioned as a troop carrier; her war service was over.

Immediately a team of 1,500 dockyard workers was dispatched to return the *Queen Mary* to her civilian guise. Old works were restored and embellished and new pieces were added, most notably a long frieze in pear and sycamore by the artist Bainbridge Copnall. The famous shopping arcade was restored, but the installation of fluorescent lighting was heavily criticized.

The Forties and early Fifties were highly successful for the *Queen Mary* and the *Queen Elizabeth*, and possibly they represented the most successful passenger liner partnership ever. Cunard exploited the gentle rivalry between the two and their crews with great acumen. The *Queen Mary* was a great favourite with royalty, nobility, the wealthy and the stars. But the time came to consider replacing the two *Queens*, and the *Queen Elizabeth 2* eventually made her debut.

The reflected majesty of the *Queen Mary* as she sits in Southampton's dry dock, January 1938. Later that year she was to regain the Blue Riband from her great rival the *Normandie*, and hold it until 1952.

Das majestätische Spiegelbild der *Queen Mary* im Trockendock in Southampton, Januar 1938. Einige Monate später jagte sie ihrer großen Rivalin, der *Normandie*, das Blaue Band wieder ab und behielt es bis 1952.

Le *Queen Mary*, en cale sèche à Southampton en janvier 1938, dans toute sa majesté. Cette même année, le paquebot va reprendre le Ruban bleu à son grand rival le *Normandie* et le conserver jusqu'en 1952.

At the end of September 1967 the *Queen Mary* completed her last run across the Atlantic to New York, her thousandth voyage. Her next and last trip was a difficult passage round Cape Horn, with 1,000 passengers and ill-tempered under-strength crew. In December she arrived off Long Beach, California, and the British Consul-General removed her officially from the Register of Ships. She had been bought by the municipality of Long Beach for $3.45 million. At precisely 12.07 pm Pacific time on 9 December 1967 Captain Treasure-Jones signalled 'finished with engines' for the last time.

Of all the great liners the *Queen Mary* survives and is enjoyed in something like her old glory. Today she is an hotel, museum and conference centre. But then she was designed to be the most accommodating floating hotel of her day.

Fast zwei Jahre lang, vom Ende des Jahres 1931 an, war der rostbraune Schiffsleib, Auftragsnummer 534 der John-Brown-Werft am Clyde, in Großbritannien das augenfälligste Symbol der Wirtschaftskrise. Das Schiff wurde im Dezember 1930 auf Kiel gelegt, und Ende des folgenden Jahres kamen sämtliche Arbeiten daran zum Erliegen. Damals waren die Arbeiten am Schiffskörper schon weit fortgeschritten, und der turmhohe messerscharfe Bug und die gewaltigen genieteten Stahlflächen beherrschten das Panorama am Clyde.

Diese zwei Jahre brauchte David Kirkwood, der Parlamentsabgeordnete für Clydeside, bis er die Regierung überreden konnte, das große Schiff zu retten und mit ihm die Arbeitsplätze in den Werften am Clyde und die Ehre der britischen Handelsmarine. 1933 erklärte sich das Handelsministerium unter streng festgelegten Bedingungen zur Hilfe bereit. Drei Millionen Pfund wurden für die Fertigstellung zur Verfügung gestellt, weitere fünf Millionen für den Bau eines Schwesterschiffes. Jedoch war der Kredit für Cunard an eine Bedingung geknüpft: die Fusion mit der angeschlagenen White Star Line, deren Flotte dringend modernisierungsbedürftig war. Die Nachfahren Samuel Cunards mußten sich mit ihren Rivalen im Atlantikverkehr zusammentun.

Schon zu Beginn stand fest, daß das neue Schiff eine Königin der Meere werden sollte, und der Name, der in den Chefetagen von Cunard am häufigsten zu hören war, war »Victoria«. Der Stapellauf war ein Staatsereignis, und schon lange im voraus wurde König Georg V. dazu geladen; im Schreiben hieß es, das Schiff werde nach einer großen Königin benannt. Der König nahm die Einladung an und antwortete, er sei hocherfreut, daß das Schiff den Namen seiner Gemahlin tragen solle, Queen Mary.

Am Tag der Schiffstaufe, dem 26. September 1934, goß es am Clyde in Strömen. Die Königin ließ eine Magnumflasche australischen Weißweins am Bug zerschellen und taufte das Schiff nach ihrem Namen *Queen Mary*. Die 28 Worte, die sie dabei sprach, waren die einzige offizielle Rede, die sie in ihrer Zeit als Gemahlin Georgs V. hielt. Wortkarg, wie sie war, schrieb sie am Abend in ihr Tagebuch: »Größtes Schiff der Welt getauft. Leider schwerer Regen.« Der Monarch war großzügiger mit seinen Worten und hielt eine Ansprache, in der er die Erleichterung der ganzen Nation zum Ausdruck brachte, daß das Schiff nun endlich vom Stapel lief. »Nun wo wir beiderseits des Atlantiks auf bessere Wirtschafts-

bedingungen hoffen dürfen, wollen wir ihr wünschen, daß sie einen großen Beitrag zum Aufschwung des Handels leisten wird. Es war der Wille des Volkes, daß dieses Schiff vollendet wird, und heute können wir es auf den Weg schicken – ein Schiff voller Schönheit, Energie und Stärke.«

In Kriegs- wie in Friedenszeiten hatte die *Queen Mary* ihre Last zu tragen, aber sie war ein Glücksschiff, das alle Krisen und Kollisionen überstand, und ist der einzige unter den klassischen Ozeandampfern, der heute noch weitgehend in Originalform erhalten ist. Auf ihr fand sich nichts vom extravaganten Schick der *Normandie* – Dekor und Ausstattung galten sogar als billig. Heute jedoch erscheinen sie uns als klassisches Werk des Art déco, und besonders bemerkenswert sind die Einlegearbeiten und Vertäfelungen. Ein Satz dieser Paneelen zeigt wie ein böses Omen die Verkehrsflugzeuge über dem Atlantik, die großen Flugboote und Doppeldecker, deren Nachfolger schon bald die Ozeanriesen von den Meeren vertreiben sollten.

Die *Queen Mary* erwies sich bei Reisenden jeglicher Couleur als äußerst beliebt. Die meisten vergaben ihr ihre offensichtlichen Schwächen, den Ruß, der aus den Schornsteinen auf die Achterdecks regnete, die Vibrationen und das berüchtigte Schlingern, das, wie einer ihrer Seeleute sagte, »die Milch aus den Teetassen schaukelte«. Als sie am 27. Mai 1936 in Southampton zur Jungfernfahrt ablegte, spielte eine Kapelle der königlichen Marine am Kai »Rule Britannia«. Am 31. August errang sie mit einer Fahrtzeit von 3 Tagen, 20 Stunden und 42 Minuten und einer Geschwindigkeit von 31,69 Knoten das Blaue Band – die erste Passagierüberfahrt in weniger als vier Tagen.

Im Oktober 1936 erlebte sie ihren ersten Atlantiksturm. »Plötzlich tauchte sie ein«, erinnert sich eine Stewardeß. »Ganz langsam, tiefer und immer tiefer. Ich fiel aus der Koje und dachte, jetzt ist es aus. Doch allmählich richtete sie sich wieder auf, und dann begann sie entsetzlich zu rollen und rollte immer noch weiter, als die See längst wieder ruhig war.« »Kein anderes Schiff hat so viel von einem lebendigen Wesen gehabt«, meinte ihr letzter Kapitän J. Treasure-Jones einmal zum Schlingern der *Queen Mary*. Änderungen an den Schiffsschrauben verringerten die Vibrationen, und in den fünfziger Jahren wurde sie noch mit Stabilisatoren ausgestattet.

Anders als die *Normandie*, die mit ihrer Pracht manche Reisenden verschreckte, fuhr die *Queen Mary* mit ihrer

The third of four screws for the new *Queen Mary* is lowered on to the quayside at the John Brown yard. Together they weighed 105 tons.

Die dritte von vier Schiffsschrauben für die neue Queen Mary wird auf den Kai der John-Brown-Werft gehievt. Zusammen wogen die Schrauben 105 Tonnen.

La troisième nouvelle hélice du nouveau *Queen Mary* est posée sur le quai des chantiers John Brown. Les quatre hélices pèsent ensemble 105 tonnes.

anheimelnden Art schon bald Gewinne ein. Die Prospekte warben mit ihrer Größe – 4 Millionen Nieten waren verbaut worden, 600 Uhren tickten an Bord, sie war mit 56 verschiedenen Edelhölzern ausgestattet, und in ihrer Gesamtlänge übertraf sie die Höhe des Eiffelturms. Mit 310,30 Metern war sie zwar gut 3 Meter kürzer als ihre französische Konkurrentin, übertraf diese jedoch um 1744 Tonnen in der Tonnage. Beide waren mit vier Schrauben ausgestattet, die *Queen Mary* wurde direkt von einer Dampfturbine angetrieben, die Maschine der *Normandie* arbeitete turbo-elektrisch.

Am 30. August 1939 stach die *Queen Mary* von Southampton mit der Rekordzahl von 2332 Passagieren in See. Als sie in New York ankam, war der Krieg ausgebrochen. Den Winter über blieb sie an ihrem üblichen Pier und wurde mit einem grauen Anstrich und dem Einbau von Minenabwehrvorrichtungen und Flugabwehrgeschützen auf dem obersten Deck für den Kriegseinsatz vorbereitet. Im März traf ihr neues Schwesterschiff *Queen Elizabeth* ein, das schon mit grauem Militäranstrich aus der Werft gekommen war.

Der Nutzen der beiden *Queens* im Zweiten Weltkrieg war unschätzbar. Sie konnten mehr als 15000 Mann binnen fünf Tagen über den Atlantik bringen, und nach einer Aussage von Winston Churchill dürften sie den Krieg in Europa um ein ganzes Jahr verkürzt haben. Die *Queen Mary* war schneller als fast jedes Kriegsschiff und dampfte angreifenden U-Booten einfach davon.

Doch der Kriegsdienst verlief nicht ohne Unglück. Als sie 1942, von New York kommend, in die unsicheren Gewässer rings um Schottland kam, bekam sie wie üblich einen leichten Kreuzer zur Eskorte, die HMS *Curacoa*, dazu sechs Zerstörer. Die *Curacoa* war etwa vier Knoten langsamer als der Ozeandampfer und hatte keine Chance mitzuhalten, als dieser, um sich vor Angreifern zu schützen, einen Zickzackkurs fuhr. Die *Curacoa* mühte sich, stets voraus zu bleiben, doch am 2. Oktober 1942, um 13 Uhr 30 geriet der Kreuzer bei klarer Sicht der *Queen Mary* vor den Bug, und sie rammte ihn mittschiffs. Der Kreuzer sank binnen fünf Minuten, und 329 der 450 Mann Besatzung kamen um. Der Kapitän der *Queen Mary*, Commodore Sir Gordon Illingworth, entschied, daß er mit 10398 amerikanischen Soldaten an Bord nicht riskieren konnte, zur Bergung zu stoppen. Der Vorfall wurde seinerzeit vertuscht; ein Urteil des Kriegsgerichts vom 21. Januar 1947 gab der *Curacoa* die volle Schuld, doch bei einer späteren Revision wurde die Schuld am Unglück zu einem Drittel dem Beobachtungspersonal der *Queen Mary* angelastet.

Nach Kriegsende brachte die *Queen Mary* zwischen Februar und September 1946 mehr als 22000 GI-Bräute und deren Kinder zu einem neuen Leben in die Vereinigten Staaten und nach Kanada. Zwei Tage nachdem sie am 27. September in Southampton angelegt hatte, wurde sie offiziell als Truppentransporter außer Dienst gestellt – ihr Kriegseinsatz war vorüber.

Sogleich machten sich 1500 Werftarbeiter ans Werk, die *Queen Mary* wieder für den Passagierverkehr herzurichten. Die alte Ausstattung wurde restauriert und neu verziert, und Neues kam hinzu; am auffälligsten war ein großer Fries des Künstlers Bainbridge Copnall in Birnbaum- und Ahornholz. Die berühmte Einkaufsstraße entstand neu, wobei die Ausstattung mit Neonröhren heftige Kritik erntete.

Die vierziger und frühen fünfziger Jahre waren die beste Zeit der *Queen Mary* und der *Queen Elizabeth*, und man darf die beiden gewiß das erfolgreichste Passagierdampfer-Duo aller Zeiten nennen. Cunard nutzte die freundschaftliche Rivalität der beiden Schiffe und ihrer Mannschaften geschickt für die Werbung. Gekrönte Häupter, die Aristokratie, Geldadel und Filmstars fuhren auf der *Queen Mary*. Doch die Zeit kam, als an die Nachfolge der beiden *Queens* gedacht werden mußte, und so reiften die Pläne für die *Queen Elizabeth 2* heran.

Ende September 1967 unternahm die *Queen Mary* ihre letzte Atlantikfahrt nach New York, die tausendste Überfahrt. Als nächste und letzte Fahrt folgte die schwierige Umschiffung von Kap Horn mit 1000 Passagieren und einer gereizten, unterbesetzten Mannschaft. Im Dezember machte sie vor Long Beach in Kalifornien fest, und der britische Generalkonsul strich sie offiziell aus dem Schiffsregister. Die Stadt Long Beach hatte sie für 3,45 Millionen Dollar erworben. Am 9. Dezember 1967 um 12.07 Uhr pazifischer Zeit gab Kapitän Treasure-Jones zum letzten Mal das Kommando »Maschinen Stopp«.

Als einzige aus der großen Zeit der Ozeanliner existiert die *Queen Mary* auch heute noch weitgehend unverändert, nun als Hotel, Museum und Konferenzzentrum. Und als das beste schwimmende Hotel ihrer Zeit war sie schließlich von Anfang an gedacht gewesen.

Royal Navy helicopters give a farewell salute to the *Queen Mary* for her last voyage, to Long Beach, California, 1 November 1967.

Hubschrauber der Royal Navy verabschieden die *Queen Mary* mit einem Formationsflug, als sie am 1. November 1967 zur letzten Fahrt ablegt, zu ihrem Ruheplatz im kalifornischen Long Beach.

Les hélicoptères de la Royal Navy saluent le *Queen Mary* lors de son dernier voyage vers Long Beach (Californie), le 1er novembre 1967.

La vaste carène brune du « Job Number 534 », qui s'élève au-dessus des chantiers John Brown de Clydeside pendant pratiquement deux ans à partir de la fin de l'année 1931, fut le plus célèbre symbole de la dépression économique en Grande-Bretagne. C'est en effet en décembre 1930, exactement un an après la pose de la quille, et alors que la construction de la coque, en plaques d'acier rivetées, est déjà bien avancée, que le chantier s'arrête.

La proue en lame de couteau du navire domine silencieusement l'horizon de Clydeside jusqu'à ce que David Kirkwood, le député de Clydeside, parvienne à persuader le gouvernement de sauver le grand navire et, avec lui, les chantiers de la Clyde et la fierté de la marine marchande britannique. En 1933, le ministre du Commerce accepte finalement de débloquer trois millions de livres pour achever la construction du navire, plus cinq autres millions pour celle d'un second exemplaire à la stricte condition que la compagnie Cunard fusionne avec la White Star Line, en perte de vitesse et dont la flotte a besoin d'être modernisée. Les descendants de Samuel Cunard doivent s'allier avec leurs anciens rivaux de l'Atlantique.

On décida assez rapidement que le nouveau navire serait un souverain des mers, une reine des océans (les navires sont de genre féminin en Grande-Bretagne) et le nom le plus souvent mentionné à la Cunard est alors Victoria. Le lancement devant être un événement d'importance nationale, le roi George V fut approché pour présider à la cérémonie et, lorsqu'on lui confia, en secret, que le navire devrait porter le nom d'une grande reine, il accepta en se disant ravi que le navire porte le nom de sa femme, la reine Mary (c'est-à-dire *Queen Mary*).

Le jour du lancement, le 26 septembre 1934, la pluie tombe en rafales sur le chantier de la Clyde. Lorsque la reine lâche une bouteille de vin blanc australien sur la proue du navire pour baptiser son homonyme *Queen Mary*, elle prononce les 28 mots du seul discours qu'elle ait jamais fait en public au titre de princesse consort. Le soir même, peu encline à exagérer les grands événements, elle écrira dans son journal : « Baptisé aujourd'hui le plus grand navire du monde. Dommage qu'il ait plu. » Le roi est plus disert et son discours exprime le soulagement de toute la nation que le navire ait finalement pu être lancé. « Aujourd'hui, avec l'espoir de meilleures relations commerciales de part et d'autre de l'Atlantique, nous pouvons croire qu'il jouera un grand rôle dans la renaissance du commerce international. Achevé par la volonté de la nation, nous pouvons aujourd'hui l'envoyer aux lointains … beau, plein de vie, d'énergie et de puissance. »

Si le nouveau paquebot subit, en temps de guerre comme en période de paix, son content de collisions et autres problèmes, il reste un navire remarquablement chanceux. C'est d'ailleurs le seul des grands paquebots d'autrefois qui ait conservé jusqu'à aujourd'hui quelque chose de sa silhouette originelle. Certes, il n'a rien du chic extravagant du *Normandie*, et sa décoration et son mobilier sont même décrits à l'époque comme démodés. Il est pourtant considéré aujourd'hui comme le prototype du style Art déco grâce à ses remarquables décors, notamment un ensemble de panneaux muraux et d'écrans, d'aspect prophétique, qui représente des avions – ces biplans et ces grands hydravions dont les successeurs allaient détrôner les paquebots – franchissant l'Atlantique.

Le *Queen Mary* devient rapidement l'un des paquebots préférés des voyageurs transatlantiques de toutes sortes. La plupart sont prêts à lui pardonner ses évidents défauts, par exemple ces nuages de scories échappés de ses cheminées qui noircissent les ponts arrière, ou ces vibrations et ce roulis célèbres qui, d'après l'un des membres de l'équipage, « auraient pu faire tourner du lait dans une tasse de thé ». Le *Queen Mary* part de Southampton pour son voyage inaugural le 27 mai 1936, aux accents du « Rule Britannia » que joue une fanfare du Royal Marine alignée sur le quai. Le paquebot remporte le Ruban bleu le 31 août en réalisant la traversée de l'Atlantique d'ouest en est en 3 jours 20 heures et 42 minutes à la vitesse moyenne de 31,69 nœuds : la première traversée commerciale sous la barre des quatre jours.

En octobre 1936, le *Queen Mary* connaît sa première grande tempête dans l'Atlantique. Une hôtesse raconte : « Il a commencé à s'enfoncer lentement, très lentement, et de plus en plus profondément. J'ai été projetée hors de ma couchette et j'ai pensé qu'il n'allait jamais remonter … Et puis, il s'est redressé tout aussi lentement en entamant un éprouvant mouvement de torsion, qui s'est poursuivi même une fois la mer calmée. » Le roulis du *Queen Mary*, d'après son dernier commandant, J. Treasure-Jones, en faisait « un navire très proche d'un être vivant ». Dans les années 1950, d'importantes modifications sont apportées à ses hélices pour réduire les vibrations tandis qu'on lui ajoute des ailerons stabilisateurs.

Contrairement au *Normandie*, dont la majesté impressionne souvent les passagers, les charmes domestiques du *Queen*

Mary font gagner de l'argent à son armateur. Ses caractéristiques enrichissent la publicité : 4 millions de rivets, 600 horloges, une décoration réalisée dans 56 espèces différentes de bois, une longueur totale supérieure à la hauteur de la tour Eiffel. Avec ses 310 mètres, il reste plus petit que le paquebot français de 3,30 mètres seulement, mais a une jauge brute supérieure de 1774 tonneaux. Tous deux sont propulsés par quatre hélices, mues par une turbine à vapeur pour le *Queen Mary* et par un système turbo-électrique pour le *Normandie*.

Le *Queen Mary* part le 30 août 1939 de Southampton avec 2332 passagers à bord – un record. Lorsqu'il arrive à New York, la Grande-Bretagne est entrée en guerre et il doit rester à quai pendant la plus grande partie de l'hiver, afin d'être aménagé pour son service militaire : peinture grise, équipement anti-mines et canons anti-aériens sur les ponts supérieurs. En mars, il est rejoint par son nouveau frère d'armement, le *Queen Elizabeth*, déjà repeint en gris.

Les états de service des deux *Queens* pendant la guerre sont remarquables. Winston Churchill a dit qu'ils auraient pu réduire d'un an la durée de la guerre parce qu'à eux deux ils auraient pu faire traverser l'Atlantique à plus de 15000 hommes en cinq jours. Le *Queen Mary* est en effet plus rapide que n'importe quel autre bâtiment militaire et peut facilement échapper à un U-boot en maraude.

Ce « service militaire » ne se déroule pas sans mésaventures. Lors d'un voyage vers New York, en 1942, il est accompagné par un croiseur léger, le HMS *Curacoa*, et six destroyers à son entrée dans les eaux hostiles autour de l'Écosse. Le *Curacoa* a une vitesse inférieure de quatre nœuds à celle du paquebot et ne peut donc pas vraiment l'escorter tandis qu'il exécute des zigzags prudents. Le *Curacoa* s'efforce cependant de rester en tête du convoi lorsque, à 1 h 30 du matin, le 2 octobre 1942, par grande visibilité, le *Queen Mary* éperonne le croiseur par le milieu et le coule en cinq minutes, faisant 329 victimes sur les 450 membres de l'équipage. Le commandant du *Queen Mary*, le commodore Sir Gordon Illingworth, juge qu'avec les 10398 militaires américains qu'il a à bord, il ne peut pas courir le risque de stopper pour porter secours aux naufragés. L'incident fut tenu secret jusqu'au procès, le 21 janvier 1947, qui déclara le *Curacoa* entièrement responsable ; un autre jugement attribua cependant un tiers de la responsabilité aux vigies du *Queen Mary*.

À la fin de la guerre, entre février et septembre 1946, le *Queen Mary* amène plus de 22000 épouses de GI et leurs enfants aux États-Unis et au Canada. Le 27 septembre, il s'amarre à un quai de Southampton et est « démobilisé » deux jours plus tard. Près de 1500 ouvriers sont aussitôt embauchés pour rendre au *Queen Mary* son costume civil. Les anciens ouvrages sont restaurés et embellis, de nouveaux éléments de décor ajoutés, notamment une longue frise en poirier et sycomore due à l'artiste Bainbridge Copnall, et la célèbre galerie marchande restaurée (l'installation d'un éclairage fluorescent est cependant très critiqué).

Les années 1940 et le début des années 1950 sont marquées par le succès croissant du *Queen Mary* et du *Queen Elizabeth*, tous deux formant sans aucun doute le couple de navires le plus réussi de tous les temps. La Cunard exploite d'ailleurs intelligemment l'aimable rivalité entre les deux navires et leurs équipages. Le *Queen Mary* remporte ainsi un plus grand succès auprès des familles royales, de la noblesse, des gens fortunés et des stars. Mais, il faut bientôt se résoudre à remplacer les deux *Queens* vieillissantes et le projet qui conduira à la naissance du *Queen Elizabeth 2* (le 2 indique qu'il s'agit du second paquebot de la série des *Queen Elizabeth* et non pas du nom de la reine actuelle) est lancé.

Après avoir effectué sa dernière traversée de l'Atlantique, la millième de sa carrière, à la fin de septembre 1967, l'ultime voyage du *Queen Mary* l'entraîne dans le Pacifique. Il passe le cap Horn avec 1000 passagers à bord et un équipage réduit et d'humeur maussade. Il arrive en décembre à Long Beach, en Californie. Le consul général britannique raye officiellement le *Queen Mary* des registres maritimes. Il a été acquis par la municipalité de Long Beach pour 3,45 millions de dollars. Le 9 décembre 1967, à 12 h 07 (heure du Pacifique), le commandant Treasure-Jones signale pour la dernière fois « Machines arrêtées ».

Seul survivant de l'époque des grands paquebots transatlantiques, le *Queen Mary* jouit encore aujourd'hui de son ancienne gloire. Il est désormais un hôtel, musée et centre de conférences. En effet, il a été conçu, pour être l'hôtel flottant le plus agréable de son époque.

Where are we now? Passengers look at one of the maps of the internal decks of the *Queen Mary*.

Wo sind wir denn gerade? Passagiere der *Queen Mary* studieren eine der Karten, die unter Deck aufgehängt waren.

Où sommes-nous ? Ces passagers étudient le plan des ponts du *Queen Mary* affiché dans une coursive.

Before the launch
Gathering the oats harvest (above) beside the Clyde with the hull of 'Liner 534' dominating the skyline, 27 August 1934. Within a month she would be launched as the *Queen Mary*. (Right) Dock workers shoring up the cradle round the bows of the liner to prepare for her launch.

Kurz vor Stapellauf
Haferernte am Clyde am 27. August 1934 (oben). »Liner 534« beherrscht den Horizont – einen knappen Monat später sollte er als *Queen Mary* vom Stapel laufen. (Rechts) Werftarbeiter bereiten den Schlitten unter dem Rumpf vor, auf dem sie ablaufen soll.

*

Avant le lancement
Ce 27 août 1934, les champs d'avoine des bords de la Clyde sont dominés par la gigantesque coque du « Liner 534 » (ci-dessus). Ce navire sera lancé le mois suivant sous le nom de *Queen Mary*. Entre-temps, les ouvriers ont étayé les accores avant soutenant la coque du paquebot (à droite).

Work for all

(Above) The last of the four great
screws is hoisted aboard the
freighter *Bradda* at London docks,
bound for Glasgow. The bronze
screw, made by J. Stone & Co.
of Deptford, weighed 35 tons.
(Right) A piece of steel frame about
to be loaded from the Darlington
Forge for transport to the John
Brown yard. Building the *Queen
Mary* brought employment to
60 British cities.

Arbeit für alle

(Oben) Die letzte der vier großen
Schiffsschrauben wird in den Lon-
doner Docks an Bord des Frachters
Bradda gehievt, Zielhafen Glasgow.
Die Schraube, die von J. Stone &
Co. in Deptford hergestellt wurde,
bestand aus Bronze, und wog 35
Tonnen. (Rechts) In der Darlington-
Schmiede wird ein großes Rumpf-
teil aus Gußstahl zum Transport in
die John-Brown-Werft verladen.
Der Bau der *Queen Mary* schuf
Arbeitsplätze in 60 britischen
Städten.

Du travail pour tous

La dernière des quatre grandes
hélices est montée à bord du cargo
Bradda, amarré aux docks de
Londres en partance pour Glasgow.
L'hélice de bronze, réalisée par la
société J. Stone & Co., de Deptford,
pesait 35 tonnes (ci-dessus). Cette
pièce d'acier du gouvernail, réalisée
par les forges de Darlington, est
prête à être chargée et transportée
aux chantiers John Brown
(à droite). La construction du
Queen Mary a fourni du travail aux
ouvriers de 60 villes britanniques.

CAST STEEL STERN FRAME
FOR NEW CUNARD LINER
Approx. Wt. 190 Tons.
MADE BY ~
THE DARLINGTON FORGE LP.

Casing and rivets
(Left) Work on the casing of the
mast in the John Brown yard
during fitting out. (Above) Riveters
working on the decks of the liner on
the same chilly day, 10 March 1935.

Rohre und Nieten
(Links) Arbeit an der Außenhülle
des Mastes im Ausrüstungsdock der
John-Brown-Werft. (Oben) Niet-
schläger an Deck des Schiffes,
aufgenommen am selben kühlen
Tag, dem 10. März 1935.

Montage et rivets
Une équipe finit la préparation d'un
mât du paquebot aux chantiers
John Brown (à gauche) tandis que
les riveteurs s'affairent au rivetage
sur les ponts, en cette journée
froide du 10 mars 1935 (ci-dessus).

Building the hull
Work on the bows of 'Liner 534' in 1934, as she
towers above two warships under construction
in the Clydebank yard of John Brown.

Bau des Schiffrumpfes
Arbeiten am Bug, 1934. Die beiden Kriegsschiffe
im Vordergrund, die ebenfalls in Clydebank in der
John-Brown-Werft gebaut werden, wirken schmächtig
im Vergleich zum turmhohen »Liner 534«.

La construction de la coque
En 1934, la coque du « Liner 534 » domine déjà deux
bâtiments de guerre en construction dans les chantiers
John Brown de Clydebank.

Launch of a *Queen*

(Above) 'Liner 534' the day before she is to be christened by her namesake, the austere Queen Mary, who was to perform one of the few public ceremonies in the reign of her husband, King George V. (Right) The moment of launch as the *Queen Mary* hits the water.

Geburt einer Königin

(Oben) »Liner 534« einen Tag bevor sie von ihrer Namenspatronin, der wortkargen Queen Mary, getauft werden sollte – einer der wenigen öffentlichen Anlässe, an denen sie während der Regierungszeit ihres Gatten Georg V. teilnahm. (Rechts) Der Augenblick, in dem die *Queen Mary* ins Wasser gleitet.

Le lancement d'une « reine »

(Ci-dessus) On voit ici le « Liner 534 » la veille d'être baptisé par son homonyme, l'austère reine Mary, au cours d'une des rares cérémonies publiques à laquelle elle assistera sous le règne de son mari, le roi George V. (À droite) Le *Queen Mary*, glissant sur son ber, pénètre dans les flots.

The *Queen's* rainy day

Spectators on the opposite bank of the Clyde put up umbrellas as they watch the *Queen Mary*, 81,235 tons, splashing into the waters of the estuary, 26 September 1934. The launch of the new liner was celebrated throughout the shipbuilding industry in Britain as a sign that the economic depression might be coming to an end.

Triumph im Regen

Neugierige verfolgen vom gegenüberliegenden Clyde-Ufer unter Regenschirmen, wie die *Queen Mary* mit ihren 81 235 Tonnen ins Wasser der Flußmündung gleitet, am 26. September 1934. Die Schiffsbauindustrie überall in Großbritannien wertete den Stapellauf des neuen Passagierdampfers als Zeichen dafür, daß es nach der Wirtschaftskrise allmählich wieder aufwärts ging.

Jour pluvieux pour la « reine »

Les spectateurs massés sur la rive opposée de la Clyde assistent, parapluies ouverts, au premier contact du *Queen Mary* (81 235 tonnes) avec les eaux de l'estuaire, le 26 septembre 1934. Le lancement de ce nouveau paquebot fut salué dans toute l'industrie navale britannique comme un signe de la fin de la récession économique.

A king on the *Queen*
A day shift of fitters (above) during the later phases of the
liner's completion in 1935. (Right) Workers and families greet
the new King Edward VIII as he visits the liner in March 1936.
Though the liner was to sail into a glorious career, his reign
was not: he abdicated later the same year.

Ein König an Bord der *Queen*
Die Tagschicht der Monteure (oben) rückt zur Arbeit an. Zu
diesem Zeitpunkt im Jahr 1935 nähert sich das Schiff der
Vollendung. (Rechts) Arbeiter und Angehörige begrüßen den
neuen König Edward VIII., als er dem Schiff im März 1936
einen Besuch abstattet. Die *Queen Mary* fuhr einer goldenen
Zukunft entgegen, doch die Aussichten des Königs waren
weniger glücklich; noch im selben Jahr dankte er ab.

Le roi visite la *Queen*
Un bataillon d'ouvriers embarque sur le paquebot au petit
matin pour en achever la construction, en 1935 (ci-dessus). En
mars 1936, ils viendront avec leur famille saluer le nouveau roi
Edouard VIII, venu visiter le navire (à droite). Si le *Queen
Mary* connut une glorieuse carrière, il n'en fut pas de même
du roi, qui abdiqua quelques mois plus tard.

'Liner 534' becomes the *Queen Mary*
(Above) Two views of the bows of the liner
as they ride above the cranes at the John
Brown yard, late August 1934, just a month
before her launch. (Right) Two views of the
last phase of the fitting-out in the dry dock
at the John Brown yard. Screws and hull are
checked just days before the maiden voyage
in May 1936.

Vom »Liner 534« zur *Queen Mary*
(Oben) Zwei Ansichten des Buges, wie er
Ende August 1934, nur einen Monat vor dem
Stapellauf, hoch über die Kräne der John-
Brown-Werft ragt. (Rechts) Die letzte Phase
der Ausrüstung im Trockendock der Werft.
Schrauben und Rumpf werden noch einmal
überprüft, nur wenige Tage vor der Jung-
fernfahrt im Mai 1936.

Le « Liner 534 » devient le *Queen Mary*
(Ci-dessus) La proue du paquebot domine
déjà les grues des chantiers John Brown
à la fin août 1934, soit un mois avant son
lancement. (À droite) La poupe et la proue du
Queen Mary en fin d'armement en cale sèche
aux chantiers John Brown. Les hélices et la
coque ne seront vérifiées que quelques jours
seulement avant son voyage inaugural, en
mai 1936.

All lit up and ready to go!
(Above) The liner is a blaze of light as
she prepares for her first sea trials to the
Isle of Arran, March 1936. On 14 May she
sailed on a two-day cruise in the English
Channel before her maiden voyage across
the Atlantic. (Right) Cheers for the first
glimpse of her as a complete liner,
25 March 1936. She was to remain popular
with her British and American public even
in retirement.

Die Fahrt kann beginnen!
(Oben) Die *Queen Mary* erstrahlt im Licht
all ihrer Lampen, während die Vorbereitungen zur ersten Probefahrt, im März 1936
zur Insel Arran laufen. Am 14. Mai unternahm sie noch eine zweitägige Reise in
den Ärmelkanal, dann war sie bereit zur
Jungfernfahrt über den Atlantik. (Rechts)
Zuschauer winken, als sie am 25. März
1936 nach Abschluß der Ausrüstungs-
arbeiten das Dock verläßt. Die Beliebtheit
bei ihrem britischen und amerikanischen
Publikum sollte sie nie verlieren, nicht
einmal nach Ende ihrer Dienstzeit.

Tous feux allumés et prêt à appareiller !
Le *Queen Mary* entièrement éclairé peu de
temps avant ses premiers essais en mer
au large de l'île d'Arran, en mars 1936
(ci-dessus). Le 14 mai, il partait faire une
croisière de deux jours dans la Manche
avant d'effectuer son voyage inaugural à
travers l'Atlantique. (À droite) Les curieux
saluent la première apparition du navire
devenu paquebot, le 25 mars 1936. Il allait
conserver sa popularité auprès du public
britannique et américain même à la fin de
son service.

Maiden embarkation

(Above) An elegant limousine being hoisted aboard at
Southampton docks as she prepares to depart on her maiden
crossing, 27 May 1936. (Right) Passengers, carrying their
own bags in third class, board for the same departure.
A close encounter with fog prevented the *Queen Mary* from
gaining the Blue Riband on this occasion.

Einsteigen zur ersten Reise

(Oben) Kurz vor dem Ablegen zur Jungfernfahrt am 27. Mai
1936 wird am Kai in Southampton noch eine elegante
Limousine verladen. (Rechts) Passagiere, die in der Dritten
Klasse ihre Koffer selbst tragen müssen, gehen an Bord. Nebel
verhinderte, daß die *Queen Mary* schon auf dieser ersten Fahrt
das Blaue Band errang.

Premiers embarquements

(Ci-dessus) Une élégante limousine est grutée à bord
du navire, amarré au quai de Southampton peu avant
l'appareillage pour son voyage inaugural, le 27 mai 1936.
(À droite) Les passagers de troisième classe, portant eux-
mêmes leurs bagages, embarquent le même jour. Le brouillard
empêcha le *Queen Mary* de remporter le Ruban bleu lors de
cette traversée.

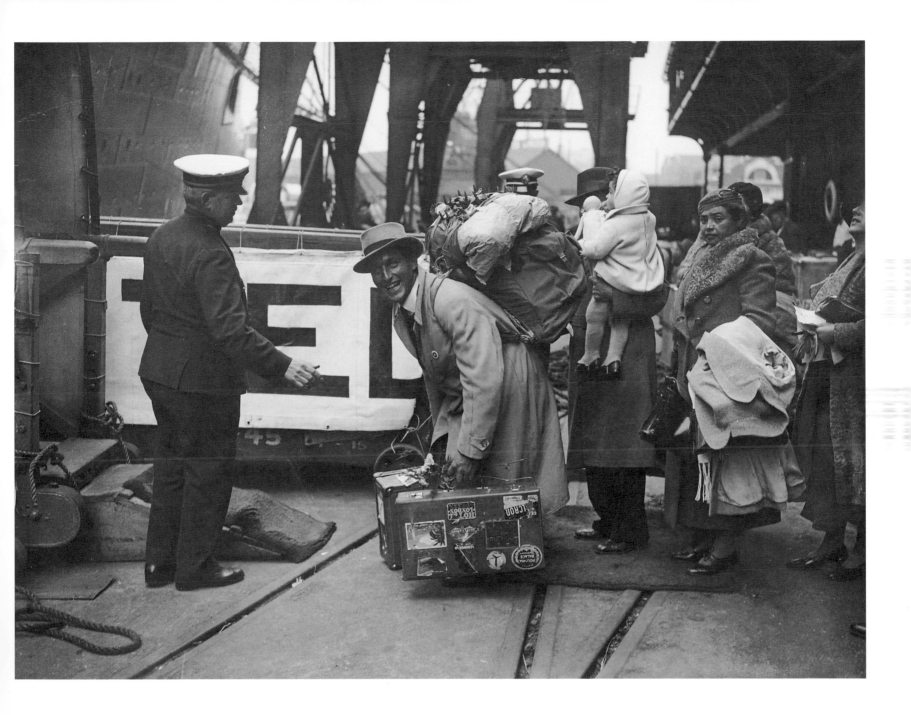

First departure

(Left) The first lifeboat drill on the maiden voyage of
the *Queen Mary* to New York, and the crowded decks
as the liner pulls away from Southampton docks (right).
(Opposite) The same occasion viewed from the docks.

Leinen los!

(Links) Die erste Rettungsübung auf der Jungfernfahrt der
Queen Mary nach New York; Reisende drängen sich an der
Reling, als das Schiff im Hafen von Southampton ablegt (rechts).
(Gegenüber) Derselbe Augenblick, vom Kai aus gesehen.

Premier départ

Le premier exercice de sauvetage lors du voyage inaugural du
Queen Mary vers New York (à gauche). La foule se rassemble
sur les ponts au moment du départ de Southampton, vue
depuis le navire (à droite) et depuis les quais (ci-contre).

Ocean Liner Deco
(Above) The cocktail bar and observation lounge, furnished in fine Thirties style. The bar is made of Macassar ebony, and the mural behind it, entitled 'Royal Jubilee Week', is by Alfred R. Thomson. (Right) Passengers crowd the main hall on her maiden voyage.

Dampferstil
(Oben) Cocktailbar und Salon auf dem Oberdeck, im schönsten Stil der dreißiger Jahre gestaltet. Die Bar ist aus Makassar-Ebenholz, und das Wandbild dahinter mit dem Titel »Royal Jubilee Week« stammt von Alfred R. Thomson. (Rechts) Reisende der Jungfernfahrt haben sich im Großen Saal versammelt.

Le style « paquebot océanique »
(Ci-dessus) Le bar et le salon panoramique du *Queen Mary*, meublés dans le style des années 1930. Le panneau mural qui décore le bar, réalisé en ébène de Madagascar, est intitulé « Royal Jubilee Week » et dû à Alfred R. Thomson. (À droite) Les passagers envahissent le hall principal lors du voyage inaugural.

Passengers and crew

(Above) The famous illuminated map in the cabin-class dining room: the light pinpointed the ship's position in the Atlantic. (Right, above) Cooks and crew line up for safety drills; bellhops undergoing an inspection. (Right, below) Bellhops deliver flowers; cabin-class passengers are served afternoon tea on the promenade deck.

Passagiere und Mannschaft

(Oben) Die berühmte beleuchtete Landkarte im Speisesaal der Kabinenklasse: das Licht zeigt die jeweilige Position des Schiffes im Atlantik. (Rechts, obere Reihe) Köche und Personal sind zur Seenotübung angetreten; Pagen werden inspiziert. (Rechts, untere Reihe) Blumen, von Pagen überbracht; den Passagieren der Kabinenklasse wird der Nachmittagstee auf dem Promenadendeck serviert.

Passagers et équipage

(Ci-dessus) La célèbre carte lumineuse de la salle à manger de la classe touriste : le point lumineux signale la position du navire dans l'Atlantique. (Ci-contre, en haut) Les cuisiniers et l'équipage s'alignent pour un exercice de sauvetage tandis que les garçons de cabine subissent une inspection. (Ci-contre, en bas) Les chasseurs livrent des fleurs ; les passagers de la classe touriste au moment du thé sur le pont promenade.

Last days of peace
(Above and right) Passengers greet
the dawn as the liner slips into
New York, 12 August 1939. Within
a month Britain would be at war
and the liner would be conscripted
for troopship duties.

Die letzten Friedenstage
(Oben und rechts) Passagiere
begrüßen den Morgen des
12. August 1939, als der Dampfer
in New York einläuft. Binnen eines
Monats sollte Großbritannien in
den Krieg eingetreten sein und
die *Queen Mary* als Truppentransporter fahren.

Derniers jours de tranquillité
Les passagers saluent l'aube au
moment où le paquebot pénètre
dans le port de New York, le
12 août 1939 (ci-dessus et à droite).
Un mois plus tard, la Grande-
Bretagne entrera en guerre et
le paquebot sera réquisitionné
comme transport de troupes.

Troopship

(Top, left and right) GIs asleep on the main deck; being shipped out to the liner, in her wartime grey, 1944.
(Above) The dining rooms had to operate constantly when carrying thousands of troops. Crowded mess decks caused great discomfort. (Opposite) The *Queen Mary* alongside with the *Normandie*, watched by New York policemen, 1942.

Kriegseinsatz

(Ganz oben, links und rechts) GIs schlafen auf dem Haupt-deck; Soldaten setzen zu dem Schiff in seinem militärgrauen Anstrich über, 1944. (Oben, links und rechts) Mit Tausenden von Männern an Bord wurde der Speisesaal rund um die Uhr gebraucht. Das Gedränge auf den Mannschaftsdecks war eine Strapaze. (Gegenüber) Die *Queen Mary* neben der *Normandie*, von New Yorker Polizisten bewacht, 1942.

Transport de troupes

(En haut, à gauche et à droite) Quelques GI se sont endormis sur le pont principal, en attendant d'être débarqués du navire, en tenue militaire grise, en 1944. (Ci-dessus) Les salles à manger devaient fonctionner en permanence pour nourrir les milliers de soldats embarqués qui encombraient les ponts. Le manque de confort est flagrant. (Ci-contre) En 1942, le *Queen Mary* se trouve bord à bord avec le *Normandie*, sous la surveillance de policiers new-yorkais.

—— 5 ——
Devastation and Recovery:
The Forties

Devastation and Recovery:
The Forties

On 3 September 1939, the 13,500-ton liner *Athenia*, outward bound from her home port of Glasgow for Montreal, was torpedoed and sunk in the mid-Atlantic. The war between Britain and Germany was barely three hours old. Aboard were 1,418, of which 300 were citizens of the United States. The British immediately exploited the disaster for the same propaganda purposes as they had the torpedoing of the *Lusitania* in 1915. It was an ominous prelude to a global war at sea: more than 2,000 merchant ships would be lost, and one fifth of the world's liners would be sunk, destroyed or damaged beyond repair in the six years of hostilities.

The *Bremen*, gutted by fire in 1941, sank in the river Weser. Her sister ship, *Europa*, survived until 1945 when she was seized by American forces for use as a troopship. In 1946 she was given to the French as a replacement for the *Normandie*. Renamed the *Liberté*, she was badly damaged in port at Le Havre, but miraculously her fortunes revived and she served through the last great era of scheduled liner travel in the Fifties. In 1962 she was dismantled in an Italian breakers' yard. Of the two Italian greyhounds, the Germans bombed the *Conte di Savoia* at Venice on 11 September 1943 in order to deny her to the Allies, while the following year the *Rex* was specifically targeted in a raid by RAF Beaufighters.

The loss of life was huge and frequently horrific. By one calculation one in 33 of all men of the American merchant marine called up for war service became a casualty. At the height of the Battle of the Atlantic the German Navy alone had some 1,000 U-boats capable of offensive operations. Some of the most devastating attacks were in coastal waters from aerial bombing, strafing and rockets. During the evacuation of British troops from France on 17 June 1940, the 16,200-ton Cunard *Lancastria* was attacked by dive-bombers as she was embarking troops at Saint-Nazaire. One bomb went off amidships; more than half of the 6,000 soldiers already aboard perished, and the ship sank within 20 minutes. On 2 November 1943 the Dutch motor-liner *Zaandam*, 10,500 tons, was hit by two torpedoes 400 miles off the coast of Brazil, and went down within ten minutes. Some 80 days later three survivors were picked up by a US navy warship, the longest anyone had survived in the open sea.

On 3 May 1945 the 27,560-ton *Cap Arcona* was embarking some 5,000 concentration camp victims and 1,000 guards in Lübecker Bay, North Germany, when she was attacked with rockets by British fighter-bombers. She and a small freighter caught fire and more than 5,000 aboard the two ships died in 20 minutes. Controversy surrounds the attack, which came only two days before Germany surrendered. But Himmler had ordered that the concentration camp victims should not be allowed to fall into enemy hands; many had been shot on the beaches and it is thought the rest were due to be killed.

Three quarters of the shipping sunk in the war was lost in the Atlantic, but the Pacific proved a vast naval battlefield as well, particularly for submarines and marine air operations. The Japanese company NYK (Nippon Yusen Kaisha) lost most of its principal ships. The *Nitta Maru*, 17,150 tons, was completed in 1940 for the trans-Pacific run from Yokohama to San Francisco, but by the end of the year America and Japan were at war, and she and her sister ships were converted into aircraft carriers. On 4 December 1943 she was sunk by torpedoes from the American submarine USS *Archerfish*. Her two sisters suffered a similar fate.

The biggest casualty of the great liners on the Allied side was the 42,348-ton *Empress of Britain*, built for Canadian Pacific's Southampton–Quebec service. She was attacked by German bombers on 26 September 1940, and sunk by U-boat two days later, with a loss of 49 of her company.

Convoying to avoid submarine and air attack proved particularly hazardous for the big liners: many of them were faster than most of the ships in their escort. This makes more impressive the epic voyage of the *Queen Mary* and other great liners from Suez to Australia in 1943. They were taking 31,000 Australian soldiers to defend their homeland from a feared Japanese invasion. The convoy was a roll of honour of some of the greatest pre-war liners, the *Aquitania* and *Île de France*, the Holland America Line's *Nieuw-Amsterdam*, and the Furness-Bermuda Line's *Queen of Bermuda*. This last could make only 18 knots, a little over half the *Queen Mary*'s top steaming speed. It was an astonishingly lucky convoy. Hitler had put up a bounty of about $250,000 for the U-boat captain who sank a major vessel, preferably the *Queen Mary*. Aboard was more than one third of the entire Australian expeditionary force.

The story of the largest grey-funnel liner proved the stuff of epic. On 27 September 1938 the consort of King George VI (now the Queen Mother) launched the liner that bore her name, Cunard's RMS *Queen Elizabeth*. At 83,673 gross tons and 1,031 feet long, she is still the largest ocean liner ever constructed for point-to-point voyages (there are bigger cruise liners). She nearly did not become a liner at all. Completion was delayed

with the onset of the war, and at one time the British Admiralty considered converting her into a fleet aircraft carrier. Work resumed in 1939, and on 3 March 1940, with a crew of only 230, Captain John Townley put to sea on 'a dangerous secret mission'. Once out in the Clyde he opened his sealed orders, which told him to sail for New York with all possible speed.

The Germans had expected the huge liner to be fitted out near Southampton, and bombers were despatched on regular reconnaissance patrols to spot her coming up the Channel and then sink her. The deception proved brilliantly successful, and the *Queen Elizabeth*, half finished and in flat livery of battleship grey, completed the dash across the Atlantic in four days.

By the summer of 1945 she had covered more than half a million miles as a troopship, and must have carried something like 750,000 passengers. Between them the two great Cunard *Queens* are believed to have carried at least one million combat troops to war. The *Queen Elizabeth* marks the change from wartime to civilian passenger service in the mid-Forties. She had survived unscathed, though had one narrow escape. In November 1942 Josef Goebbels himself reported on German radio that the *Queen Elizabeth* had been sunk by U-boat 704. The liner then made a serious breach of security rules, to radio that she had been briefly stationary in the general area of the reported incident but was safe.

She sailed back to the Clyde in March 1946 to be repainted in the Cunard livery, the style for which she was intended, and to have her machinery overhauled. Her maiden voyage as a passenger liner was on 16 October 1946, at least six years, one war, and 500,000 miles of steaming late. She was done out in the homely 'Liner Art Deco' fashion already deployed with such acumen in the *Queen Mary*. It was a mixture of the Art Deco of the Thirties and the 'English country house' style.

The aftermath of war brought a new era of migration. Ships carried Europeans to Australia and Canada, and brought immigrants to Britain and Holland from the Caribbean, the Indian sub-continent and Indonesia. Many of the passages were heavily subsidized; later on the Australian government was to offer immigration for a £10 voucher. Britain was desperate for labour from the Commonwealth and Empire and southern Europe to rebuild its industries. Conditions aboard the migration ships were spartan, to put it mildly. One of P & O's elderly ships, the *Ranchi*, broke down with 900 migrants aboard in the middle of the Suez Canal. It caused a massive blockage of 82 ships, still believed to be the greatest traffic jam in the canal's history.

At the war's end the major lines prepared to invest in the new market of popular, economy tourism. In 1948 Cunard launched the 34,100-ton *Caronia*, custom-built for cruises (when she carried about 600), though she did work on some scheduled routes (her total capacity was 930). The aim was to offer a country hotel or club holiday afloat. Once seen she was never to be forgotten; she was painted in four shades of green, which earned her the title of the 'green goddess'.

Am 3. September 1939 wurde der 13500-Tonnen-Dampfer *Athenia* auf der Fahrt von seinem Heimathafen Glasgow nach Montreal auf hoher See von einem Torpedo getroffen und sank. Der Krieg zwischen Deutschland und Großbritannien war noch nicht einmal drei Stunden alt. 300 der 1418 Menschen an Bord waren Bürger der Vereinigten Staaten, und Großbritannien machte sich den Vorfall sogleich für Propagandazwecke zunutze, nach dem gleichen Muster, nach dem man 1915 die Versenkung der *Lusitania* genutzt hatte. Es war ein grimmiger Auftakt zu einem weltweiten Krieg auf See: Über 2000 Handelsschiffe gingen verloren, und ein Fünftel der Passagierdampferflotte wurde in dem sechsjährigen Krieg versenkt, zerstört oder so schwer beschädigt, daß die Schiffe nicht mehr zu retten waren.

Die *Bremen*, 1941 ausgebrannt, sank in der Weser. Ihr Schwesterschiff *Europa* überstand den Krieg und wurde 1945 zunächst von den Amerikanern als Truppentransporter eingesetzt. 1946 ging sie als Reparationsleistung für die *Normandie* an Frankreich und erhielt den neuen Namen *Liberté*. Bei einer Havarie im Hafen von Le Havre wurde sie schwer beschädigt, doch von da an wendete sich ihr Glück, und sie blieb die fünfziger Jahre hindurch im Dienst, im letzten großen Jahrzehnt der Ozeanriesen. 1962 wurde sie in Italien abgewrackt. Auch die beiden italienischen Schnellschiffe überlebten den Krieg nicht; am 11. September 1943 bombardierten die Deutschen die *Conte di Savoia* in Venedig, damit sie nicht in die Hände der Alliierten kam, und im folgenden Jahr fiel die *Rex* einem Angriff britischer Beaufighter-Jäger zum Opfer.

Die Zahl der Todesopfer war gewaltig, und viele kamen qualvoll um. Jeder 33. Matrose der amerikanischen Handelsmarine, der zum Kriegsdienst eingezogen wurde, kehrte nicht zurück. Auf dem Höhepunkt der Atlantikschlacht hatte allein die deutsche Marine fast 1000 U-Boote im Einsatz. Besonders schwere Schäden richteten Boden-, Luft- und Raketenangriffe in Küstennähe an. Der Cunard-16200-Tonner *Lancastria* wurde von Sturzbombern angegriffen, als er am 17. Juni 1940 im französischen Saint-Nazaire rückkehrende britische Truppen an Bord nahm. Eine der Bomben schlug mittschiffs ein; mehr als die Hälfte der 6000 Soldaten, die bereits an Bord waren, kam um, und das Schiff sank binnen 20 Minuten. Am 2. November 1943 wurde das holländische Motorschiff *Zaandam*, 10500 Tonnen, 400 Meilen vor der brasilianischen Küste von zwei Torpedos getroffen und sank in wenigen Minuten. Etwa 80 Tage darauf nahm ein Schiff der US-Kriegsmarine drei Überlebende auf – die längste Zeit, die jemals Schiffbrüchige auf offener See überstanden haben.

Am 3. Mai 1945 hatten an die 5000 Insassen von Konzentrationslagern und 1000 Mann Wachpersonal in der Lübecker Bucht den 27560-Tonner *Cap Arcona* bestiegen, als der Angriff britischer Jagdbomber erfolgte. Die *Arcona* und ein kleinerer Frachter gerieten in Brand, und binnen 20 Minuten waren auf den beiden Schiffen 5000 Menschen umgekommen. Noch heute ist der Angriff nur zwei Tage vor Kriegsende umstritten. Doch Himmler hatte angeordnet, daß die KZ-Insassen nicht in Feindeshand gelangen durften; viele waren schon am Ufer erschossen worden, und die übrigen sollten vermutlich mit dem Schiff versenkt werden.

Drei Viertel der Schiffe, die im Krieg verlorengingen, wurden im Atlantik zerstört, doch auch der Pazifik war ein einziges Kampffeld der Seeschlachten, besonders der U-Boot- und Luftangriffe. Die japanische NYK-Reederei (Nippon Yusen Kaisha) verlor den Großteil ihrer Schiffe. Der 17150-Tonner *Nitta Maru* wurde 1940 für die Pazifiklinie Jokohama–San Francisco in Dienst gestellt, doch schon am Ende des Jahres lagen Japan und die Vereinigten Staaten im Krieg, und aus der *Nitta Maru* und ihren Schwesterschiffen wurden Flugzeugträger. Am 4. Dezember 1943 wurde sie von den Torpedos des amerikanischen U-Bootes USS *Archerfish* versenkt, und ihren beiden Schwestern erging es nicht besser.

Der größte Passagierdampfer, der auf alliierter Seite verlorenging, war mit 42348 Tonnen die *Empress of Britain*, die für die Canadian Pacific die Route Southampton–Québec befuhr. Deutsche Bomber flogen ihren Angriff am 26. September 1940, und zwei Tage darauf versenkte ein U-Boot das Schiff; 49 Seeleute ließen ihr Leben.

Um sie vor den Angriffen der Unterseeboote zu bewahren, erhielten die Ozeanriesen Geleitschutz, doch diese Konvoifahrten erwiesen sich als gefährlich, denn viele Passagierschiffe waren schneller als ihre militärische Eskorte. Um so erstaunlicher ist die legendäre Fahrt der *Queen Mary* und einer Reihe weiterer großer Dampfer von Suez nach Australien im Jahre 1943. Sie brachten 31000 australische Soldaten in die Heimat zurück, wo man mit einer japanischen Invasion rechnete. Der Konvoi war eine Parade der großen Ozeanriesen der Vorkriegszeit mit der *Aquitania* und der *Île de*

France, der *Nieuw-Amsterdam* der Holland-Amerika-Linie und der *Queen of Bermuda* der Furness-Bermuda-Linie. Letztere war maximal 18 Knoten schnell, kaum halb so schnell wie die *Queen Mary* unter Volldampf. Die Nazis hatten einen Preis von umgerechnet $250000 für den U-Boot-Kapitän ausgesetzt, dem es gelang, eines der großen Schiffe zu versenken – am liebsten natürlich die *Queen Mary*, die mehr als ein Drittel des gesamten australischen Expeditionskorps an Bord hatte –, aber die Fahrt blieb von allem Unglück verschont.

Auch die Geschichte des größten Cunard-Liners ist Legende. Am 27. September 1938 taufte die Gemahlin König Georg VI. (die heutige »Queen Mum«) das Schiff auf ihren Namen, RMS *Queen Elizabeth*. Mit 83673 Bruttoregistertonnen und einer Länge von 314 Metern sollte sie der größte Ozeandampfer bleiben, der je für den Liniendienst gebaut wurde (es gibt größere Kreuzfahrtschiffe). Beinahe wäre sie ihrer Bestimmung gar nicht zugekommen, denn der Kriegsbeginn verzögerte die Fertigstellung, und die britische Admiralität trug sich mit dem Gedanken, sie zum Flugzeugträger umzubauen. Doch noch 1939 wurde der Bau wiederaufgenommen, und am 3. März 1940 stach Kapitän John Townley mit nur 230 Mann Besatzung zu einer »gefährlichen Geheimmission« in See. Als er die Mündung des Clyde hinter sich hatte, öffnete er den versiegelten Umschlag und fand die Order, mit größtmöglicher Geschwindigkeit New York zu erreichen.

Die Deutschen hatten damit gerechnet, daß das gewaltige Schiff zur Fertigstellung nach Southampton kommen würde, und Bomber flogen regelmäßig zu Erkundungsflügen aus, um es schon bei der Einfahrt in den Ärmelkanal zu sichten und zu versenken. Die Kriegslist war ein voller Erfolg, und die halbfertige *Queen Elizabeth* erreichte in ihrem unauffälligen Schlachtschiffgrau schon nach vier Tagen ihr Ziel jenseits des Atlantiks.

Als der Sommer 1945 kam, hatte sie als Truppentransporter über eine halbe Million Meilen zurückgelegt und etwa 750000 Mann befördert. Man schätzt, daß die beiden Cunard-*Queens* gemeinsam im Laufe des Krieges mehr als eine Million Soldaten transportierten. Mit Kriegsende durfte die *Queen Elizabeth* ins zivile Leben zurückkehren. Sie hatte den Krieg unbeschadet überstanden, auch wenn sie einmal nur mit knapper Not davongekommen war: Im November 1942 gab Joseph Goebbels höchstpersönlich im deutschen Rundfunk bekannt, daß die *Queen Elizabeth* vom U-Boot 704 versenkt

worden sei. Das Schiff funkte daraufhin – ein ernster Verstoß gegen die Sicherheitsregeln –, daß man zwar im Bereich der angeblichen Versenkung kurz habe stoppen müssen, daß jedoch alle wohlauf seien.

Im März 1946 kehrte sie in die Werft am Clyde zurück und erhielt den Anstrich in den Cunard-Farben, für den sie bestimmt gewesen war. Mit überholten Maschinen lief sie am 16. Oktober 1946 zu ihrer Jungfernfahrt als Passagierdampfer aus, gut sechs Jahre, einen Krieg und 500000 Seemeilen nach Fertigstellung. Sie war im prachtvollen Art-déco-Stil der dreißiger Jahre ausgestattet, der schon bei der *Queen Mary* so gut angekommen war, hier noch im englischen Landhausstil verschönert.

In der Folge des Krieges kam eine neue Auswanderungswelle. Schiffe brachten Europäer nach Australien und Kanada und Immigranten aus der Karibik, vom indischen Subkontinent und aus Indonesien nach Großbritannien und Holland. Vieles wurde staatlich subventioniert; zeitweilig bot die australische Regierung Einwanderern die Überfahrt für £10 an. Großbritannien war auf Arbeitskräfte aus dem Commonwealth und dem Empire angewiesen, um die im Krieg zerstörte Wirtschaft wieder aufzubauen. Diese Immigranten fuhren auf Schiffen, deren Zustand oft desolat war. Einmal erlitt ein altersschwacher Dampfer der P & O, die *Ranchi*, mit 900 Einwanderern an Bord mitten im Suezkanal einen Maschinenschaden. 82 Schiffe stauten sich, was bis heute als größter Stau in der Geschichte des Kanals gilt.

Nach Kriegsende investierten alle großen Gesellschaften in den zukunftsträchtigen Zweig des Massentourismus. 1948 ließ Cunard den 34100-Tonner *Caronia* vom Stapel laufen, der ausdrücklich als Kreuzfahrtschiff gebaut war (mit einer Kapazität von 600 Passagieren), obwohl er auch im Liniendienst (930 Passagiere) zum Einsatz kam. Der Dampfer sollte den Standard eines Clubs oder vornehmen Landhotels haben, nur eben zu Wasser. Der Anblick der *Caronia* war unvergeßlich, denn sie war in vier verschiedenen Grüntönen gestrichen, was ihr den Spitznamen »Grüne Göttin« einbrachte.

A seaman cleans the radar before the maiden voyage of the Union Castle *Edinburgh Castle*, 28,700 tons, to South Africa, December 1948.

Letzte Wartung der Radarantenne, bevor der 28700-Tonner *Edinburgh Castle* der Union Castle Line im Dezember 1948 zur Jungfernfahrt nach Südafrika aufbricht.

Un matelot nettoie le radar de l'*Edinburgh Castle* (28700 tonneaux), de la Union Castle, avant son voyage inaugural vers l'Afrique du Sud, en décembre 1948.

Le 3 septembre 1939, le paquebot *Athenia* (13500 tonneaux), parti de son port d'attache de Glasgow pour rejoindre Montréal, est torpillé et coulé au milieu de l'Atlantique. À bord se trouvaient 1418 passagers, dont 300 étaient citoyens des États-Unis. La Grande-Bretagne, qui a déclaré la guerre à l'Allemagne à peine trois heures plus tôt, exploite aussitôt ce désastre comme elle l'avait déjà fait en 1915 après le torpillage du *Lusitania*. Ce naufrage prélude dramatiquement à une guerre maritime globale, qui se déroulera pendant les six années du conflit et au cours de laquelle plus de 2000 navires marchands disparaîtront, et où un cinquième des paquebots du monde entier sera coulé, détruit ou endommagé irrémédiablement.

Si le *Bremen* coule dans la Weser à la suite d'un incendie en 1941, son « sister-ship », l'*Europa*, parvient à franchir la guerre sans encombre jusqu'en 1945, époque à laquelle il fut saisi par les Américains pour assurer le transport de troupes, puis il est offert à la France en 1946 pour remplacer le *Normandie*. Rebaptisé *Liberté*, il est gravement endommagé dans le port du Havre mais, bénéficiant d'une chance miraculeuse, peut continuer d'effectuer un service régulier pendant toutes les années 1950, la dernière grande époque des voyages en paquebot. Désarmé en 1962, il finit chez un ferrailleur italien. Quant aux deux lévriers des mers italiens, les Allemands bombardent le *Conte di Savoia* à Venise le 11 septembre 1943 pour en priver les Alliés, tandis que l'année suivante le *Rex* est explicitement visé par un raid de Beaufighters de la Royal Air Force.

Les pertes en vies humaines sont souvent dramatiques et importantes (on a calculé qu'un marin de la marine marchande américaine sur 33 appelés a été condamné). Au plus fort de la Bataille de l'Atlantique, la Marine allemande disposait à elle seule de 1000 sous-marins d'attaque. Les offensives les plus dévastatrices pour les navires se déroulent cependant à proximité des côtes lors de bombardements aériens, de mitraillages au sol et de tirs de roquettes. Lors de l'évacuation des troupes britanniques de Saint-Nazaire, le 17 juin 1940, le *Lancastria*, un navire de 16200 tonneaux appartenant à la Cunard, est attaqué par des bombardiers en piqué ; une des bombes, explosant par le milieu du navire, tue plus de la moitié des 6000 soldats déjà à bord et fait couler le navire en 20 minutes. Le 2 novembre 1943, le paquebot hollandais *Zaandam* (10500 tonneaux) est touché par deux torpilles à 400 milles

au large du Brésil et coule en dix minutes. Deux mois et demi plus tard, un bâtiment de guerre de la US Navy repêche trois naufragés, un record de survie en pleine mer.

Le 3 mai 1945, le *Cap Arcona* (27560 tonneaux) embarque 5000 victimes des camps de concentration et 1000 gardes dans la baie de Lübeck, au nord de l'Allemagne, lorsqu'il est attaqué à la roquette par des chasseurs bombardiers britanniques. Le navire, ainsi qu'un petit cargo voisin, prennent feu, provoquant en 20 minutes la mort de plus de 5000 passagers. Cette attaque, qui n'eut lieu que deux jours avant la reddition de l'Allemagne, fit l'objet d'une controverse, l'un des arguments évoqués pour la défendre étant que Himmler avait ordonné qu'aucune victime des camps de concentration ne tombe aux mains de l'ennemi ; beaucoup avaient été tués sur les plages et on pense que les autres auraient subi le même sort.

Si les trois quarts des navires ayant sombré pendant la guerre ont fait naufrage dans l'Atlantique, le Pacifique est également le théâtre de grandes batailles navales, surtout dans le domaine des opérations sous-marines et aéronavales, au cours desquelles la compagnie maritime japonaise NYK (Nippon Yusen Kaisha) perd notamment la plupart de ses grands navires. Achevé en 1940 pour assurer la ligne transpacifique entre Yokohama et San Francisco, son *Nitta Maru* (17150 tonneaux) et ses « sister ship » sont aussitôt transformés en porte-avions vers la fin de l'année, lorsque les États-Unis et le Japon entrent en guerre. Le 4 décembre 1943, il est coulé par le sous-marin américain USS *Archerfish*. Ses deux frères d'armement subiront le même sort.

En ce qui concerne les grands paquebots, la plus grosse perte subie du côté allié est l'*Empress of Britain*, un navire de 42348 tonneaux construit par la Canadian Pacific pour assurer la ligne Southampton-Québec. Attaqué par des bombardiers allemands le 26 septembre 1940, il est coulé deux jours plus tard par un U-boot. Cette tragédie coûta la mort de 49 marins.

Les convois mis en place pour pallier les attaques sous-marines et aériennes se révèlent particulièrement périlleux pour les grands paquebots, qui sont souvent plus rapides que la plupart des bâtiments de leur escorte. Cela rend plus impressionnant encore le voyage épique effectué en 1943 de Suez à l'Australie par le *Queen Mary* et quelques autres grands paquebots. Ils transportent 31000 soldats australiens revenant défendre leur pays du risque d'invasion japonaise. Ce convoi rassemble le « gotha » des plus grands paquebots d'avant-guerre : l'*Aquitania* et l'*Île de France*, le *Nieuw-Amsterdam* (Holland America Line) et le *Queen of Bermuda* (Furness-Bermuda Line). Ce dernier ne peut avancer qu'à 18 nœuds, soit à peine plus de la moitié de la vitesse maximum du *Queen Mary*. Le convoi bénéficie cependant d'une chance extra-ordinaire. Hitler a en effet offert une récompense de près de 250 000 $ au commandant de U-boot qui coulerait un de ces navires, de préférence le *Queen Mary* à bord duquel se trouve près du tiers de la force expéditionnaire australienne.

L'histoire du *Queen Elizabeth*, de la Cunard, n'est pas moins épique. Lorsque l'épouse du roi George VI (aujourd'hui la reine mère) lance, le 27 septembre 1938, le paquebot qui porte son nom, le RMS *Queen Elizabeth*, ce navire de 83 673 tonneaux et de 314 mètres de long est le plus grand paquebot jamais construit pour des traversées océaniques (il existe toutefois des paquebots de croisière plus importants encore). Ce navire a bien failli ne pas devenir un paquebot. En effet, la déclaration de guerre retarde son achèvement et l'Amirauté britannique envisage même de le transformer en porte-avions. Le travail reprend heureusement en 1939 et, le 3 mars 1940, le commandant John Townley appareille avec un équipage de 230 hommes seulement pour une « mission secrète et dangereuse ». Ce n'est qu'une fois sorti de la Clyde qu'il rompt les sceaux de son ordre de mission et apprend qu'il doit rallier New York le plus rapidement possible.

Les Allemands, qui avaient espéré que le paquebot géant serait armé près de Southampton, envoient régulièrement des bombardiers effectuer des patrouilles de reconnaissance pour le repérer dans la descente de la Manche et l'y couler. La supercherie réussit brillamment et le *Queen Elizabeth*, à moitié terminé et dans la livrée grise d'un navire de guerre, réalise la traversée de l'Atlantique en quatre jours.

À l'été 1945, il a parcouru plus d'un demi-million de milles en tant que transport de troupes et convoyé près de 750 000 passagers. On a calculé que les deux *Queens* de la Cunard auraient transporté à eux deux au moins un million de soldats. A la fin de la guerre, le *Queen Elizabeth* retourne à la vie civile. Si le *Queen Elizabeth* subit les années de guerre sans incident majeur, il échappe toutefois de peu au sort de nombre d'autres navires lors d'une attaque sous-marine. En novembre 1942, lorsque Josef Goebbels annonce à la radio allemande que le *Queen Elizabeth* a été coulé par le U-boot 704, le commandant du paquebot fait une grave entorse aux règles de sécurité pour indiquer par radio que, s'il est resté quelque

temps en panne dans la zone signalée, il n'a subi aucun dommage important.

Le *Queen Elizabeth* revient dans la Clyde en mars 1946 pour être repeint aux couleurs de la Cunard et subir une révision de ses machines. Le navire effectue son voyage inaugural en tant que paquebot le 16 octobre 1946, c'est-à-dire six ans, une guerre et 500 000 milles plus tard. Il reçoit également sa décoration intérieure, réalisée dans le style « Art déco pour paquebots » confortable et domestique adopté déjà avec quelque bonheur sur le *Queen Mary*. Il s'agit d'un mélange habile des styles « English country house » et Art déco des années 1930.

Les séquelles de la guerre entraînent une nouvelle vague de migrations. Les navires transportent alors des Européens vers l'Australie et le Canada, et ramènent des immigrants des Caraïbes, du sous-continent indien et d'Indonésie en Grande-Bretagne et aux Pays-Bas. Nombre des passagers ont reçu un important pécule de leur pays, comme le gouvernement australien qui leur proposera un voucher de 10 £. La Grande-Bretagne a effectivement un besoin pressant de main-d'œuvre, qu'elle trouve dans son Empire, le Commonwealth et même en Europe du Sud, pour reconstruire son industrie. Les conditions de vie à bord des navires d'immigrants sont pour le moins spartiates. L'un des plus anciens navires de la P & O, le *Ranchi*, tombe en panne au milieu du canal de Suez avec 900 migrants à bord. Son épave bloque alors 82 navires, dans ce qui doit être encore le plus gros embouteillage de toute l'histoire du canal.

Dès la fin de la guerre, les grandes compagnies maritimes se préparent à investir dans le nouveau marché du tourisme populaire et économique. En 1948, la Cunard lance le *Caronia* (34 100 tonneaux), un paquebot de 600 passagers spécialement conçu pour la croisière (il est également mis en service sur certaines lignes régulières, transportant alors 930 passagers), qui offre tout le confort d'un hôtel ou d'un club de vacances flottant. On ne pouvait l'oublier après l'avoir vu : il était peint en quatre tons de vert, ce qui lui valut le titre de « déesse verte ».

Helping a young passenger aboard the Orient liner *Orcades* with her life-jacket. She was one of a group of emigrants to Australia.

Ein galanter Matrose hilft einer jungen Australien-Emigrantin beim Anlegen der Schwimmweste an Bord des Orient-Liners *Orcades*.

Un marin aide un jeune passager de l'*Orcades* (compagnie Orient) à enfiler son gilet de sauvetage. L'enfant fait partie d'un groupe d'émigrants allant s'installer en Australie.

Conscripted for war
(Left) US sailors on the bow of
a destroyer watch the *Empress of
Scotland*, until 1942 the *Empress
of Japan*, being eased into her
berth. (Above) The CGT/French
Line *Île de France* arriving in
San Francisco Bay, 1942, under
the flag of the British Navy,
which had commandeered her
as a troopship.

Zum Kriegsdienst eingezogen
(Links) Die *Empress of Scotland*,
bis 1942 *Empress of Japan*, wird
an ihren Liegeplatz dirigiert;
amerikanische Matrosen sehen
vom Bug eines Zerstörers zu.
(Oben) Die *Île de France* der
französischen CGT. läuft 1942
unter der Flagge der britischen
Navy in die Bucht von San
Francisco ein – die Engländer
hatten sie als Truppentransporter
requiriert.

Bon pour le service
Ces marins américains, rassemblés
à la proue d'un destroyer,
observent les manœuvres de
mouillage de l'*Empress of Scotland*,
baptisé *Empress of Japan* jusqu'en
1942 (à gauche). L'*Île de France*,
de la CGT, arrive dans la baie de
San Francisco en 1942 sous les
couleurs de la marine britannique
(ci-dessus), qui l'a réquisitionné
comme transport de troupes.

Fire aboard the *Normandie*

(Above) Fireboats try to put out the blaze which had started
on 9 February 1942 as the liner was being converted to
the troopship USS *Lafayette*. (Right) She took on so much
water that she soon rolled on to her side. Wartime censorship
has airbrushed the gun mountings on her foredeck in
this photograph.

Feuer an Bord der *Normandie*

(Oben) Feuerlöschboote mühen sich, den Brand zu löschen,
der am 9. Februar 1942 während der Umbauarbeiten zum
amerikanischen Truppentransporter USS *Lafayette* auf der
Normandie ausgebrochen war. (Rechts) Im Schiff sammelte
sich soviel Wasser, daß es bald darauf kenterte. Zensoren
retuschierten damals die Geschützstellungen, die auf dem
Vorderdeck bereits montiert waren, aus dieser Fotografie heraus.

L'incendie du *Normandie*

Les bateaux-pompes essaient d'éteindre l'incendie qui s'est
déclaré le 9 février 1942 à bord du *Normandie* lors des travaux
de transformation du paquebot en transport de troupes sous le
nom de USS *Lafayette* (ci-dessus). Il chavira bientôt sur le côté,
surchargé par les tonnés d'eau qui furent déversées à bord
(à droite). Le comité de censure a gratté de la photographie
les emplacements des canons à l'avant du navire.

Beached beauty

(Previous pages) The greatest of all the Art Deco liners, *Normandie* lies on her side at her pier in New York after the disaster which ended her days. You can see the airbrushed gun mount quite clearly on her starboard side in this shot. (Left) Dockyard workers empty more than 100,000 tons of water from the hull. (Right) Raising her hull from the Hudson river. These salvage pictures were taken a year and a half after the accident, in July and August 1943.

Ende einer Schönheit

(Vorherige Seiten) Der prachtvollste aller Art-déco-Liner, die *Normandie*, liegt gekentert am Pier in New York – das Unglück sollte das Ende eines Schiffslebens bedeuten. Die Stelle an der Steuerbordseite, wo die Geschützstellung herausretuschiert wurde, ist bei dieser Aufnahme deutlich zu erkennen. (Links) Hafenarbeiter pumpen über 100000 Tonnen Wasser aus dem Rumpf. (Rechts) Der Schiffskörper wird im Hudson River aufgerichtet. Diese beiden Aufnahmen von der Bergung entstanden anderthalb Jahre nach dem Unglück, im Juli und August 1943.

Une beauté échouée

Le *Normandie*, le plus grand de tous les paquebots Art déco, gît sur le flanc à son quai du port de New York après l'incendie qui l'a dévasté. On distingue nettement les traces de grattage à l'emplacement de l'affût de canon, côté tribord (pages précédentes). Les ouvriers des docks vident le navire des 100000 tonnes d'eau de ses cales (à gauche). Les manœuvres de renflouement de la coque, chavirée dans les eaux de l'Hudson (à droite). Ces photographies ont été prises un an et demi après l'accident, soit en juillet et août 1943.

Casualties of war

(Above) A dramatic shot of the *Dunbar Castle*, hit by a magnetic mine off the Goodwin Sands, 1940.
(Above right) Survivors of the *Laconia*, torpedoed in the Atlantic. (Below right) The Japanese *Terukuni Maru* after she hit a German mine, November 1939. (Far right) Crew abandon the *Columbus*, scuttled in the Atlantic, 19 December 1939.

Kriegsopfer

(Oben) Eine dramatische Aufnahme der *Dunbar Castle*, 1940 vor den Goodwin Sands von einer Magnetmine getroffen.
(Oben rechts) Überlebende der *Laconia*, die ein Torpedo im Atlantik versenkte. (Unten rechts) Die japanische *Terukuni Maru*, nachdem sie im November 1939 auf eine deutsche Mine gelaufen war. (Ganz rechts) Die Mannschaft verläßt die *Columbus*, die sie am 19. Dezember 1939 auf dem Atlantik in Brand gesetzt hat.

Dommages de guerre

Le *Dunbar Castle*, touché par une mine flottante au large de Goodwin Sands, en 1940, émerge encore pour quelques instants (ci-dessus). Le naufrage du *Laconia*, également torpillé dans l'Atlantique, fit cependant des survivants (ci-contre, en haut). Le navire japonais *Terukuni Maru* est abandonné après avoir heurté une mine allemande, en novembre 1939 (ci-contre, en bas). L'équipage quitte le *Columbus* qu'ils ont sabordé dans l'Atlantique le 19 décembre 1939 (à l'extrême droite).

Free and not so free

(Left) Repatriated British PoWs arrive at Leith, Scotland, aboard the Canadian Pacific liner *Empress of Russia*, October 1943. (Right) Italian PoWs from the battlefields of Sicily being landed by a British troopship. Tantalizingly, the censors would not allow the name of the ship – believed to be *Otranto* or *Orontes* of Orient Line – to be published: this was 1943. The guards face in towards their prisoners, bayonets fixed.

Frei und weniger frei

(Links) Freigekommene britische Kriegsgefangene treffen im Oktober 1943 auf der *Empress of Russia* der Canadian Pacific im schottischen Leith ein. (Rechts) Italienische Kriegsgefangene von den sizilischen Schlachtfeldern gehen von Bord eines britischen Truppentransporters. Die Zensoren ließen damals nicht zu, daß der Name des Schiffes – vermutlich die *Otranto* oder die *Orontes* der Orient Line – genannt wurde: Die Aufnahme entstand 1943. Die Wachen haben die Gefangenen umstellt, die Bajonette aufgepflanzt.

À moitié libres

Des prisonniers de guerre britanniques rapatriés arrivent à Leith (Écosse) en octobre 1943 à bord du paquebot *Empress of Russia* de la Canadian Pacific (à gauche). Les Italiens faits prisonniers en Sicile débarquent d'un transport de troupes britanniques et sont alignés face à leurs gardes, baïonnette au canon (à droite). Les censeurs n'ont pas permis que le nom du navire – probablement l'*Otranto* ou l'*Orontes* de la Orient Line – soit publié ; nous sommes en 1943.

Starry farewells

(Left) The film star James Stewart, a distinguished and decorated pilot in the US Air Force, leaves Southampton for home aboard the *Queen Elizabeth*. Crammed aboard with him are 16,000 service personnel.
(Below left) Another veteran star, Marlene Dietrich, shows a leg aboard the *Queen Elizabeth*, August 1945. She had given 500 concerts and performances to Allied troops. (Right) The send-off for the 16,000 US personnel returning home from Southampton, 27 August 1945.

Abschiedsgrüße

(Oben links) Der Filmschauspieler James Stewart, als Pilot der US Air Force ausgezeichnet, tritt in Southampton mit der *Queen Elizabeth* die Heimreise an. Insgesamt drängen sich auf dieser Fahrt 16000 Heimkehrer an Bord. (Unten links) Eine weitere Filmgröße, Marlene Dietrich, zeigt im August 1945 an Deck der *Queen Elizabeth* Bein. 500mal hatte sie für die alliierten Truppen gesungen und gespielt. (Rechts) Zuschauer winken zum Abschied, als das Schiff mit 16000 Mann amerikanischen Personals am 27. August 1945 in Southampton ablegt.

Des adieux de stars

(En haut, à gauche) La vedette de cinéma James Stewart, pilote valeureux décoré de la US Air Force, quitte Southampton à bord du *Queen Elizabeth* pour rentrer dans son pays. Il se retrouve entassé à bord avec 16000 autres soldats américains. (En bas, à gauche) En août 1945, une autre star, Marlene Dietrich, montre ses jambes à bord du *Queen Elizabeth*. Elle vient de donner 500 concerts aux troupes alliées. (À droite) Les adieux des Américains à Southampton lors de leur départ pour les États-Unis, le 27 août 1945.

American wounded wave at Manhattan

(Above) The Swedish-American liner *Gripsholm* is also
carrying 1,209 PoWs from German camps, February 1945.
From 1940 to 1946 the 17,993-ton liner served as an International
Red Cross exchange ship. (Right) A rousing homecoming
for 3,750 soldiers of the British Second Army returning from
South-East Asia aboard P & O's *Strathmore*, 23,428 tons.

Amerikanische Kriegsverletzte in Manhattan

(Oben) 1209 amerikanische Kriegsgefangene kehren im
Februar 1945 auf der *Gripsholm* der Schweden-Amerika-Linie
aus deutschen Lagern zurück. Der 17993-Tonner diente
zwischen 1940 und 1946 für den Gefangenenaustausch des
Roten Kreuzes. (Rechts) Ein Ständchen zur Begrüßung für 3750
Soldaten der britischen Zweiten Armee, die mit dem 23428-
Tonner *Strathmore* der P & O aus Südostasien zurückkehren.

Les blessés américains saluent Manhattan

Le paquebot *Gripsholm* de la ligne suédoise-américaine
ramène chez eux 1209 prisonniers de guerre libérés des
camps allemands, en février 1945 (ci-dessus). De 1940 à 1946,
ce paquebot de 17993 tonneaux servit de navire d'échange
pour la Croix Rouge Internationale. (À droite) Un accueil
vibrant est réservé aux 3750 soldats de la Deuxième Armée
britannique de retour de l'Asie du Sud-Est à bord du
Strathmore (23428 tonneaux), de la P & O.

Going home

(Above) USS *Europa*, formerly a Blue Riband winner for
Norddeutscher Lloyd, arrives at Southampton to take GIs home
in 1946. On this occasion her old German skipper Captain
Schaff was aboard. (Right) A crowded *Île de France*, still in her
wartime grey, sails from Southampton in September 1945,
passing the stern of *Europa*.

Heimkehr

(Oben) Die USS *Europa*, die einst für den Norddeutschen Lloyd
das Blaue Band errungen hatte, legt 1946 in Southampton an,
um GIs nach Hause zu bringen. Bei dieser Fahrt hatte sie ihren
alten deutschen Skipper an Bord, Kapitän Schaff. (Rechts)
Vollbepackt bricht die *Île de France*, noch in Kriegsschiffgrau,
im September 1945 von Southampton auf und fährt hier am
Heck der *Europa* vorüber.

Retour à la maison

En 1946, l'USS *Europa*, ancien lauréat du Ruban bleu
sous les couleurs de la Norddeutscher Lloyd, arrive à
Southampton pour ramener chez eux les GI (ci-dessus).
L'ancien commandant allemand du navire, le capitaine Schaff,
était d'ailleurs également à bord. L'*Île de France*, surchargé
et la coque peinte en gris, appareille de Southampton en
septembre 1945 en passant à tribord de l'*Europa* (à droite).

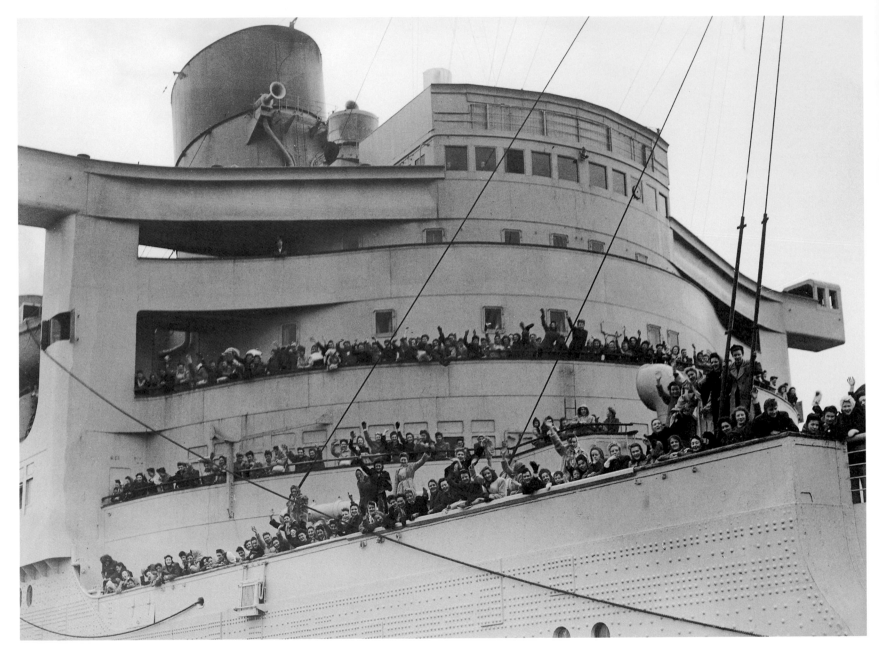

A new life after the war
(Above) GI brides on the *Queen Mary*, February 1946.
(Right above) Three British GI brides with their babies
bundled up in life-jackets, a classic *Picture Post* shot.
(Right below) Aboard the Orient liner *Ormonde*, taking
emigrants to Australia, 1947. (Far right) South Africa-bound
aboard the *Carnarvon Castle*, 1948.

Zu einem neuen Leben
(Oben) GI-Bräute an Bord der *Queen Mary*, Februar 1946.
(Oben rechts) Drei britische GI-Bräute, die ihre Babys in
Rettungswesten gesteckt haben, eine klassische Aufnahme
der *Picture Post*. (Unten rechts) Junge Emigranten auf dem
Weg nach Australien an Deck des Orient-Liners *Ormonde*,
1947. (Ganz rechts) Auf der *Carnarvon Castle* unterwegs
nach Südafrika, 1948.

Une nouvelle vie après la guerre
Des fiancées des GI à bord du *Queen Mary*, en février 1946
(ci-dessus). (En haut, à droite) Trois jeunes épouses de soldats
britanniques posent avec leurs enfants, emmaillotés dans leur
gilet de sauvetage ; une photo classique de la *Picture Post*. En
1947, le paquebot *Ormonde*, de la compagnie Orient, transporte
des émigrants vers l'Australie (en bas, à droite). Départ vers
l'Afrique du Sud à bord du *Carnavon Castle*, en 1948
(à l'extrême droite).

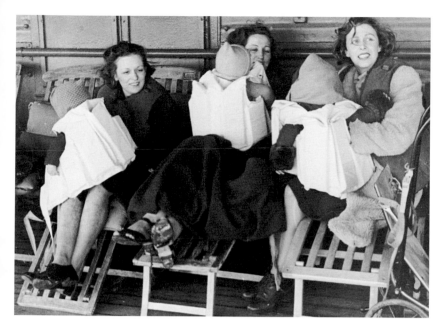

A thorough scrub for a *Queen*
(Left) Scraping and servicing the screws of the
Queen Elizabeth in Southampton dry dock, 1946.
Hurried into wartime service, she never received
full builder's trials on the Clyde. Now she is
having them, six years late! (Above) Routine
maintenance on the stern the year before,
when she was still serving as the world's
biggest troopship.

Großreinemachen bei der *Queen*
(Links) Die Schiffsschrauben der *Queen
Elizabeth* werden 1946 im Trockendock in
Southampton geschrubbt und inspiziert. Da
sie dringend für den Kriegsdienst gebraucht
wurde, hatte sie nie die Schlußinspektion
bekommen, die sonst die Werft im Clyde
durchführte. Nun wird sie nachgeholt, mit
sechs Jahren Verspätung! (Oben) Wartungsarbeiten am Heck ein Jahr zuvor, als sie noch
als größter Truppentransporter der Welt fuhr.

Une complète remise en état de la *Queen*
En 1946, les ouvriers de Southampton préparent
la révision des hélices du *Queen Elizabeth*,
presque au sec sur son dock flottant, à
Southampton (à gauche). À cause de la guerre,
il n'avait pas été possible de procéder à des
essais complets du paquebot. Six ans plus tard,
c'est enfin fait ! Un entretien de routine avait été
effectué l'année précédente, lorsque le paquebot
servait encore de transport de troupes
(ci-dessus).

In her true colours

The *Queen Elizabeth* in the red, black and white livery
of Cunard White Star at last leaves on her maiden
commercial voyage from Southampton, 16 October 1946.
From the world's largest troopship she has become the
world's largest passenger liner in service.

In angestammten Farben

Die *Queen Elizabeth* erstrahlt im Rot, Schwarz und
Weiß von Cunard White Star, als sie am 16. Oktober
1946 in Southampton endlich zu ihrer Jungfernfahrt
als Passagierdampfer ablegt. Aus dem weltgrößten
Truppentransporter ist das größte damals verkehrende
Linienschiff geworden.

Ses vraies couleurs

Le *Queen Elizabeth*, sous les couleurs rouge, noire
et blanche de la Cunard White Star, part enfin
effectuer son voyage commercial inaugural au départ
de Southampton, le 16 octobre 1946. L'ancien plus grand
transport de troupes allait devenir le plus grand
paquebot de passagers du monde en service.

Passengers' pleasure

(Above) Tea is served on the promenade deck of the
Queen Elizabeth en route for Southampton, 31 July 1948.
(Right, top) Two veteran Cunarders doze, and two young
Americans sunbathe, while (right, below) other passengers
stroll and exchange chat at the cocktail bar, a series by
the *Picture Post* master photographer Bert Hardy.

Reisevergnügen

(Oben) Teezeit auf dem Promenadendeck der *Queen Elizabeth*,
unterwegs nach Southampton am 31. Juli 1948. (Rechts, obere
Reihe) Zwei Cunard-Veteranen machen ein Nickerchen, zwei
junge Amerikaner genießen die Sonne; andere Passagiere
(rechts, untere Reihe) gehen spazieren oder unterhalten sich
angeregt an der Cocktailbar – aus einer Fotoreportage von
Bert Hardy, dem Meisterfotografen der *Picture Post*.

Le plaisir des passagers

L'heure du thé sur le pont promenade du *Queen Elizabeth* en
route pour Southampton, le 31 juillet 1948 (ci-dessus). Deux
vétérans de la Cunard ronflent paisiblement tandis que deux
jeunes Américaines profitent d'un bain de soleil (ci-contre, en
haut) et que les autres passagers se promènent et discutent au
bar (ci-contre, en bas). Ces photographies appartiennent à une
série du *Picture Post* réalisées par le grand photographe Bert
Hardy.

— 6 —
Fanfare for the Fifties

On 7 July 1952 the sleek lines of the SS *United States*, pride of the United States Lines fleet, headed past the Bishop Rock, the westernmost lighthouse in England, towards Southampton. She had cleared the Ambrose Lightship off New York only 3 days, 10 hours, and 40 minutes before. The 53,329-ton liner had smashed the record for the fastest crossing of the Atlantic on her maiden voyage, with an average speed of 35.59 knots, winning the Blue Riband and with it the Hales Trophy. She took the record for the westward route on her return journey on 15 July, at an average speed of 34.51 knots. She was to be the last great liner to achieve this accolade.

She had accomplished the feat for which she was designed, to regain the Blue Riband and challenge the dominance of the Cunard *Queens* in the Atlantic. She was designed and built under conditions of considerable secrecy, partly for commercial reasons, partly for security, and in large part from sheer American pride. She was able to carry 14,000 troops in war, while her civilian passenger capacity was 1,998, with 913 in first, 538 in cabin and 537 in tourist class. Her principal architect was William Gibbs, doyen of American marine architects, who had also designed another star of United States Lines, the *America*. He refused to take credit for the final design, with the testy disclaimer that 'about 50 per cent of the marine engineering brains of the country have been applied to the ship'. Altogether a huge $70,000,000 was invested in the project. The new ship had several revolutionary aspects that moved her a generation ahead of her great rivals the *Queen Mary* and *Queen Elizabeth*.

The *United States* was constructed with a beam width of 101 feet 6 inches, 16 feet 6 inches narrower than the *Queen Mary*, so that she could pass through the Panama Canal. She was built to the highest safety specifications, which included more watertight compartments than any other ship of the day. As she was built with war service in mind – the Americans had not enjoyed relying on British troop carriers in the recent conflict – most of her safety features were aimed at protecting against naval attack rather than the natural hazards of turbulent seas, wind, fog and ice. She had an alternative power plant, complete with its own oil-fired boiler, to drive two of her four screws in case her main turbines were damaged. Much of her superstructure was aluminium alloy, both to save weight and to minimize the hazard of explosion. Her decor, for all its modernity, did not appeal to every passenger, lacking the pol-

ished panelling and overstuffed comfort of the more traditional liners. She did gain admirers, however, among them the Duke and Duchess of Windsor, who switched their allegiance to the new American flagship.

The *United States*' partner on the scheduled run from New York to Le Havre and Southampton was the 33,961-ton *America*, built in 1940, whose standard of comfort was a remarkable testimony to the revival and adaptability of passenger liners after the war. Throughout the Fifties these two liners provided American passengers with a super 'Atlantic ferry' under their own national flag. The dazzling début of the *United States* marked the opening of the last great era of scheduled transatlantic travel by sea, the Fifties and early Sixties.

The Fifties saw a tremendous revival of the world's merchant fleets as the shipping lines refurbished their vessels after long, hard war service. The age of the tourist-class passenger dawned, and the shipping lines responded by building or reconditioning dozens of liners. The Holland-America Line halted the building of two cargo ships and had them redesigned as the tourist liners *Ryndam* and *Maasdam*. Their mould-breaking design gave the 845 tourist-class passengers the virtual run of the ship, except for a small first-class area that carried a token 39 people. The concept was so successful that other lines soon copied it – American Banner Lines with *Atlantic*, German Atlantik Line with *Hanseatic*, totally rebuilt from the former *Empress of Scotland*.

Lines serving South Africa, Australia, New Zealand and the Pacific also flourished and introduced new and distinctive designs. Union Castle, Canadian Pacific, Shaw Savill, Orient Line and Cunard all expanded, with new ships for a new clientele wanting cruising holidays. It was also a period of migration to and from Europe, to South America and Australasia. Among the famous new 'Castle' liners of Union Castle were the *Edinburgh* and *Pretoria Castles*, and others soon followed: *Bloemfontein, Rhodesia, Kenya, Braemar* and *Pendennis Castle*.

The P & O Line introduced seven new ships between 1948 and 1954. Shaw Savill's *Southern Cross* had a distinctive new silhouette resulting from her novel design: engines and funnels aft, no cargo space, and consequently huge areas, virtually the run of the ship on the upper decks, for her 1,100 tourist-class passengers. She was to be partnered by the *Dominion Monarch*, built in 1939, but which came into her own as a byword for luxury only in the Fifties.

The fastest American liner before the *United States* was the

Constitution, 30,293 tons, which entered service with American Export Lines between America and the Mediterranean in 1951. She and her sister *Independence*, also 30,293 tons, had a unique slimmed profile, tapered funnels and counter stems.

Although tourism was the coming thing, ship designs still emphasized luxury; in 1952 the French Line's new *Antilles* and *Flandre* both offered more than 400 first-class berths, though fewer than 300 for cabin and tourist class. They were followed in 1953 by Swedish American Line's *Kungsholm*, which had such a high reputation for service that she could offer off-season cruises in one class. Furness-Bermuda Line introduced a new ship, *Ocean Monarch*, to partner their *Queen of Bermuda* specifically as cruise ships in the Caribbean for half the year.

The Fifties was the last great era of the 'ship of state'. CGT/French Line introduced the *Liberté*, gloriously transformed from the pre-war German Blue Riband champion, Norddeutscher Lloyd's *Europa*; she was to partner another legend, the *Île de France*. Similarly, the brilliantly refurbished *Nieuw-Amsterdam* was the flagship of the Holland-America Line. The Germans returned to the transatlantic route, scene of so much of their maritime success, with the introduction of a new *Bremen*, built from the hull of the French troopship *Pasteur*.

The pride of the revived Italian fleet, the 29,083-ton *Andrea Doria*, was built at the Ansaldo yards in Genoa in 1953. On the evening of 25 July 1956 she was heading for New York through banks of fog off Nantucket Island, when an officer of the watch spotted the Swedish liner *Stockholm*. Inexplicably, the two ships, though mutually visible, steered towards each other. The ice-breaking bow of the *Stockholm* hit the starboard side of the *Andrea Doria* aft of the bridge at 11.10 pm. Soon she was listing so badly that it was difficult to launch the lifeboats. Shortly after 6 am on 26 July she rolled over and sank: in all 52 lives were lost, but 1,662 passengers and crew were rescued, many by the *Île de France*, which had hurried to the scene. The *Stockholm* managed to limp back to port – with a jagged stump where once her bow had been.

Within a year of the record-breaking Blue Riband runs of the *United States* there took place another series of maiden voyages. The 'De Havilland Comet' was the world's first commercial jetliner, a British development from wartime jet engine technology. In 1953 the Comet accomplished the seemingly miraculous feat of a flight from London to Tokyo in 36 hours. The Comets were bedevilled by technical troubles, but in 1958 Trans World Airlines opened a regular transatlantic service by jet airliner, the Boeing 707 – possibly the most successful commercial aircraft of all. The Atlantic could be spanned in six hours. By the mid-Sixties, 95 per cent of passenger traffic across the Atlantic would be by air.

Splendid liners continued to be built. The Italian Line replaced the *Andrea Doria* with the *Leonardo da Vinci*, 33,340 tons, launched at the Ansaldo yard on 7 December 1958 and introduced to the Atlantic route in 1960. She was withdrawn to become a cruise liner in 1976. She had a dramatic end when she caught fire in harbour at La Spezia in July 1980. Throughout the Sixties and Seventies many of the great liners would follow her into a sunset career as cruise ships, followed by the scrapyard.

The *United States*, new winner of the Blue Riband, being secured at her berth in Le Havre, France, July 1952. A superb photograph for *Picture Post* by John Chillingworth.

Die *United States*, neue Inhaberin des Blauen Bandes, wird im Juli 1952 am Kai in Le Havre festgezurrt. Eine großartige Aufnahme von John Chillingworth für die *Picture Post*.

Le *United States*, nouveau lauréat du Ruban bleu, est amarré au quai du Havre, en juillet 1952. Une superbe photographie pour le *Picture Post* de John Chillingworth.

Am 7. Juli 1952 erreichte die SS *United States*, der Stolz der United States Lines, auf dem Wege nach Southampton den westlichsten Leuchtturm Englands, Bishop Rock. Nur 3 Tage, 10 Stunden und 40 Minuten zuvor hatte sie das Ambrose-Feuerschiff vor New York passiert, den anderen Markierungspunkt einer Atlantiküberquerung. Der 53329-Tonner hatte mit einer Durchschnittsgeschwindigkeit von 35,59 Knoten somit schon auf seiner Jungfernfahrt einen neuen Rekord aufgestellt und das Blaue Band und die Hales Trophy errungen. Die Trophäe für die Weststrecke heimste das Schiff auf der Rückfahrt am 15. Juli ein, mit einer Geschwindigkeit von 34,51 Knoten. Es sollte das letzte Mal sein, daß ein Ozeanriese diese Auszeichnung errang.

Damit hatte die *United States* ihr Ziel erreicht, nämlich das Blaue Band für die Vereinigten Staaten zurückzuerobern und die Vorherrschaft der Cunard-*Queens* auf dem Atlantik zu brechen. Konstruktion und Bau waren unter großer Geheimhaltung erfolgt, teils aus Reklame-, teils aus Sicherheitsgründen, vor allem aber aus schierem amerikanischem Stolz. Das Schiff konnte als Truppentransporter 14.000 Mann befördern, die Kapazität für zivile Passagiere betrug 1998 Personen, davon 913 in der Ersten, 558 in der Kabinen- und 537 in der Touristenklasse. Hauptkonstrukteur war William Gibbs, der Doyen der amerikanischen Schiffsbaumeister, der auch einen anderen Star der United States Lines entworfen hatte, die *America*. Er beanspruchte jedoch die Ehre nicht für sich, sondern wehrte ab: »50 Prozent der Schiffskonstrukteure des Landes haben an diesem Projekt mitgewirkt.« Der Bau kostete die gewaltige Summe von 70 Millionen Dollar. Das Schiff war in mehrerlei Hinsicht revolutionär und um eine ganze Generation fortschrittlicher als seine großen Rivalinnen *Queen Mary* und *Queen Elizabeth*.

Die *United States* hatte eine Breite von ungefähr 31 Metern, zirka 5 Meter weniger als die *Queen Mary*, und damit war sie schmal genug, um durch den Panamakanal zu passen. Bei der Konstruktion wurde auf größtmögliche Sicherheit geachtet, und sie hatte mehr wasserdichte Abteilungen als jedes andere Schiff ihrer Zeit. Da sie mit Blick auf den Militärdienst gebaut wurde – es war den Amerikanern sehr gegen die Ehre gegangen, daß sie im Krieg auf britische Truppentransporter angewiesen waren –, galten die meisten Sicherheitsmaßnahmen eher dem Schutz vor feindlichen Angriffen als dem Schutz vor den Unbilden der See, vor Wind, Nebel und Eis. Das Schiff verfügte über einen Notantrieb mit eigenem ölbefeuertem Kessel, der zwei der vier Schrauben weiter antreiben konnte, wenn die Hauptturbinen ausfielen. Ein Großteil der Aufbauten bestand aus einer Aluminiumlegierung, was nicht nur Gewicht sparte, sondern auch die Explosionsgefahr minderte. Die moderne Innenausstattung sagte nicht jedem zu, denn die Holzvertäfelungen und Plüschsessel traditionellerer Ozeandampfer waren verschwunden. Es fanden sich jedoch auch Bewunderer, darunter der Herzog und die Herzogin von Windsor, die von nun an mit dem neuen amerikanischen Flaggschiff fuhren.

Partner der *United States* im Liniendienst von New York nach Le Havre und Southampton war der 1940 fertiggestellte 33961-Tonner *America*, mit seinem hohen Komfort ein schönes Beispiel dafür, mit welcher Energie und Anpassungsfähigkeit die großen Liner nach dem Krieg ihren Dienst wiederaufnahmen. Gemeinsam boten die beiden Schiffe in den fünfziger Jahren den amerikanischen Passagieren, die gern unter ihrer eigenen Flagge fuhren, einen erstklassigen »Fährdienst« über den Atlantik. Das eindrucksvolle Debüt der *United States* eröffnete die letzte große Ära der Linienschiffahrt auf den Weltmeeren, die sich über die fünfziger bis in die frühen sechziger Jahre erstreckte.

Die fünfziger Jahre wurden weltweit zu einer Glanzzeit der Passagierflotten, denn überall wurden die Schiffe nach langem, hartem Kriegsdienst überholt und neu ausgestattet. Das Zeitalter des Massentourismus brach an, und die Reedereien bauten Dutzende von Schiffen dafür um oder gaben neue in Auftrag. Die Holland-Amerika-Linie machte aus zwei Neubauten, die ursprünglich als Frachtschiffe gedacht waren, Kreuzfahrtschiffe und taufte sie *Ryndam* und *Maasdam*. Dieser neue Typus öffnete den 845 Reisenden der Touristenklasse fast das gesamte Schiff, und nur ein kleiner Bereich blieb ausschließlich den nur 39 Passagieren der Ersten Klasse vorbehalten. Das Konzept erwies sich als so erfolgreich, daß andere es bald kopierten, die American Banner Lines mit der *Atlantic* und die Deutsche Atlantiklinie mit der *Hanseatic*, hinter der sich die von Grund auf renovierte *Empress of Scotland* verbarg.

Auch die Linien nach Südafrika, Australien, Neuseeland und in den Pazifik blühten mit neuen Konzepten auf. Union Castle, Canadian Pacific, Shaw Savill, Orient Line und Cunard expandierten mit neuen Schiffen für ein neues Kreuzfahrtpublikum. Zugleich war es auch eine Zeit der Auswanderung aus und nach Europa, nach Südamerika und Australasien. Neue, hoch angesehene Schiffe der Union Castle Line waren die *Edinburgh Castle* und die *Pretoria Castle*, und weitere folgten: *Bloemfontein, Rhodesia, Kenya, Braemar* und *Pendennis Castle*.

P & O stellte zwischen 1948 und 1954 sieben neue Schiffe in Dienst. Unverwechselbar war die Silhouette der *Southern Cross* von Shaw Savill, die einen neuen Bautyp einführte, mit Maschinen und Schornsteinen im Heck, ohne Laderaum und folglich mit viel Platz für die 1100 Passagiere der Touristenklasse, die sich auf den oberen Decks frei bewegen konnten. Ihr Partner war die *Dominion Monarch*, die zwar schon 1939 vom Stapel lief, jedoch erst in den Fünfzigern zu Ehren kam und als ausgesprochenes Luxusschiff galt.

Bevor die *United States* kam, war die *Constitution* das schnellste amerikanische Schiff. Der 30293-Tonner nahm für die American Export Lines 1951 den Dienst zwischen den USA und dem Mittelmeerraum auf und hatte wie das Schwesterschiff *Independence* mit der gleichen Tonnage ein auffällig schlankes Profil mit spitz zulaufenden Schornsteinen und gegenläufigen Steven.

Auch wenn die Zeichen der Zeit auf Tourismus standen, stellte die Ausstattung der Schiffe immer noch den Luxus heraus. 1952 hatten die beiden neuen Liner *Antilles* und *Flandre* der französischen CGT jeweils über 400 Betten in der Ersten, jedoch nur knapp 300 in der Kabinen- und Touristenklasse, und im nächsten Jahr folgte die *Kungsholm* der Schweden-Amerika-Linie, deren Service einen solchen Ruf genoß, daß sie außerhalb der Saison ihre Fahrten ausschließlich Erster Klasse anbot. Die Furness-Bermuda-Linie ließ ihr neues Schiff, die *Ocean Monarch*, zusammen mit der *Queen of Bermuda* die Hälfte des Jahres ausdrücklich als Kreuzfahrtschiff in der Karibik fahren.

Die Fünfziger waren auch das letzte Jahrzehnt der »Prunkschiffe«. Die CGT nahm die *Liberté* in Dienst, wie die *Europa*, die ehemals für den Norddeutschen Lloyd das Blaue Band errungen hatte, nach ausgiebigen Umbauten nun hieß, und ihr zur Seite stand eine weitere Vorkriegslegende, die *Île de France*. Ebenfalls prachtvoll restauriert war die *Nieuw-Amsterdam*, das Flaggschiff der Holland-Amerika-Linie. Die Deutschen kehrten mit einer neuen *Bremen* auf den Atlantik zurück, den sie vor dem Krieg so erfolgreich befahren hatten; der Rumpf des Schiffes stammte von dem französischen Truppentransporter *Pasteur*.

Der Stolz der wiederauferstandenen italienischen Flotte, der 29083-Tonner *Andrea Doria*, entstand 1953 auf der Ansaldo-Werft in Genua. Am 25. Juli 1956 glitt sie durch die Nebelbänke vor der Insel Nantucket mit Kurs auf New York, als ein Wachoffizier den schwedischen Liner *Stockholm* sichtete. Keiner weiß, warum die beiden Schiffe, obwohl sie in Sichtweite waren, trotzdem weiter Kurs aufeinander hielten. Um 23 Uhr 10 bohrte sich der Eisbrecherbug der *Stockholm* hinter der Brücke in die Steuerbordseite der *Andrea Doria*. Binnen kurzem hatte sie so starke Schlagseite, daß man nur noch mit Mühe die Rettungsboote zu Wasser lassen konnte. Kurz nach 6 Uhr am Morgen des 26. Juli kenterte sie und sank; insgesamt kamen 52 Menschen um, doch 1662 Passagiere und Besatzungsmitglieder wurden gerettet, viele davon von der *Île de France*, die mit voller Kraft zu Hilfe geeilt war. Die *Stockholm* konnte sich in den Hafen schleppen – mit einem schartigen Stummel, wo einst ihr Bug gewesen war.

Nur knapp ein Jahr nach der Rekordfahrt der *United States* fand eine Reihe ganz anderer Jungfernreisen statt. Die »De Havilland Comet« war das erste Düsen-Verkehrsflugzeug der Welt, in Großbritannien mit den im Krieg entwickelten Strahltriebwerken gebaut. 1953 flog eine Comet in 36 Stunden von London nach Tokio, eine damals unerhörte Leistung. Die Comets hatten noch mit technischen Schwierigkeiten zu kämpfen, doch 1958 eröffnete Trans World Airlines den ersten Atlantik-Liniendienst per Düsenflugzeug mit einer Boeing 707 – vielleicht dem erfolgreichsten Passagierflugzeug aller Zeiten. Nun ließ sich der Atlantik in sechs Stunden überqueren. Mitte der sechziger Jahre reisten bereits 95 Prozent der Atlantikpassagiere mit dem Flugzeug.

Doch noch immer baute man prachtvolle Ozeandampfer. Die Italia-Linie ließ bei Ansaldo als Ersatz für die *Andrea Doria* die *Leonardo da Vinci* bauen, die mit einer Kapazität von 33340 Tonnen am 7. Dezember 1958 vom Stapel lief und 1960 ihre Transatlantikfahrten aufnahm. 1976 wurde sie zum Kreuzfahrtschiff umgebaut und fand im Juli 1980 ein dramatisches Ende, als sie im Hafen von La Spezia ausbrannte. Viele große Passagierschiffe verbrachten in den sechziger und siebziger Jahren ihre letzten Tage als Kreuzfahrtschiffe, doch am Ende wartete auf fast alle die Abbruchwerft.

Work on the stabilizers for the new Canadian Pacific liner *Empress of Britain* a month before she is launched by Queen Elizabeth at the Fairfield yard, Govan, Scotland, May 1955.

Arbeiten an den Stabilisatoren des neuen Canadian-Pacific-Liners *Empress of Britain*, aufgenommen in der Fairfield-Werft im schottischen Govan einen Monat vor der Schiffstaufe, die Königin Elisabeth im Mai 1955 vollzog.

La mise en place des stabilisateurs du nouveau paquebot de la Canadian Pacific, l'*Empress of Britain*, un mois avant son lancement par la reine Elizabeth aux chantiers Fairfield de Govan (Écosse), en mai 1955.

Le 7 juillet 1952, l'élégante carène du SS *United States*, fierté de la flotte des United States Lines, franchit Bishop Rock, le phare le plus à l'ouest de l'Angleterre, en remontant vers Southampton. Il a passé le bateau-phare d'Ambrose, au large de New York, seulement 3 jours 10 heures et 40 minutes auparavant. Ce paquebot de 53 329 tonneaux pulvérise ainsi le record de la traversée de l'Atlantique lors de son voyage inaugural, à la vitesse moyenne de 35,59 nœuds, et remporte le Ruban bleu et le trophée Hales. Il s'arroge également le record sur la route Est-Ouest à son retour, le 15 juillet, effectué à la vitesse moyenne de 34,51 nœuds. C'est le dernier grand paquebot à réussir ce double exploit.

En réalité, il a accompli l'exploit pour lequel il a été spécifiquement conçu : reprendre le Ruban bleu en défiant les *Queens* de la Cunard qui dominent l'Atlantique. Dessiné et construit dans le plus grand secret, pour des raisons tant commerciales que de sécurité – mais aussi par pure fierté américaine –, le *United States* peut transporter 14 000 soldats alors que sa capacité en passagers n'est que de 1998 personnes (913 en première classe, 558 en deuxième classe et 537 en classe touriste). Son principal architecte est William Gibbs, doyen des architectes navals américains, auteur également d'un autre paquebot vedette américain, l'*America*. Il refuse cependant de s'en attribuer le mérite de la conception, disant – en grinçant – que « près de 50 pour cent des cerveaux des ingénieurs navals du pays se sont penchés sur le navire ». L'énorme somme de 70 millions de dollars est investie dans le projet. Le nouveau navire bénéficie de plusieurs nouveautés révolutionnaires qui le placent une génération d'avance par rapport à ses grands rivaux que sont le *Queen Mary* et le *Queen Elizabeth*.

Le *United States* a une largeur au barrot d'environ 31 mètres, soit 5 mètres de moins que le *Queen Mary*, caractéristique qui lui permet de franchir le canal de Panama. Il a été construit en suivant les spécifications les plus sévères en matière de sécurité, ce qui implique la création d'un plus grand nombre de compartiments étanches que tout autre navire de l'époque. Dans l'optique d'éventuels conflits – les Américains n'ayant pas apprécié de devoir utiliser les transports de troupes anglais pendant la Seconde Guerre mondiale – la plupart des éléments de sécurité visent à le protéger plus des attaques navales que d'une mer turbulente, du vent, du brouillard ou de la glace. Il dispose d'un ensemble moteur de rechange complet, avec une chaudière à mazout indépendante permettant d'actionner deux des hélices dans le cas où la turbine principale serait endommagée. La plus grande partie de la structure est en alliage d'aluminium, autant pour réduire le poids que pour minimiser les risques d'explosion. Sa décoration intérieure, malgré sa modernité, ne plait pas à tous les passagers, qui lui reprochent l'absence des panneaux vernissés et du confort douillet de paquebots plus traditionnels. Il a pourtant des admirateurs, parmi lesquels le duc et la duchesse de Windsor, qui font ainsi allégeance au nouveau navire amiral américain.

Le *United States* effectue le trajet régulier entre New York, Le Havre et Southampton, conjointement avec l'*America*, un navire de 33 961 tonneaux construit en 1940, dont le niveau de confort est un remarquable témoignage de la renaissance et de l'adaptabilité des paquebots de passagers après guerre. Dans les années 1950, ces deux paquebots offrirent aux Américains un superbe « ferry transatlantique » aux couleurs nationales. Les éblouissants débuts du *United States* sont le prélude de la dernière grande époque des voyages transatlantiques par voie maritime, celle des années 1950 et 1960.

On assiste en effet, dans les années 1950, à la formidable renaissance des marines marchandes du monde. Les compagnies maritimes répondent à l'avènement de la classe touriste en construisant ou en reconditionnant des douzaines de paquebots. La Holland-America Line stoppe ainsi la construction de deux cargos pour les transformer en paquebots touristiques, baptisés *Ryndam* et *Maasdam*. La conception adoptée permet ainsi aux 845 passagers de la classe touriste de disposer de pratiquement toute la longueur du navire, à l'exception d'une petite zone réservée à l'accueil de 39 passagers de première classe. Cette disposition a tant de succès que les autres compagnies n'hésitent pas à la copier aussitôt : notamment les American Banner Lines pour l'*Atlantic* et la German Atlantik Line avec l'*Hanseatic*, totalement reconstruit à partir de l'ancien *Empress of Scotland*.

Les nombreuses lignes ouvertes vers l'Afrique du Sud, l'Australie, la Nouvelle-Zélande et le Pacifique obligent aussi à mettre en service des navires de conception nouvelle. Des compagnies comme la Union Castle, la Canadian Pacific, la Shaw Savill, l'Orient Line et la Cunard se développent, introduisant des navires modernes destinés à une clientèle friande de croisières.

Ces années sont également marquées par une nouvelle vague de migrations de et vers l'Europe, l'Amérique du Sud et l'Australasie. La compagnie P & O affrète sept navires entre 1948 et 1954, tandis que la Union Castle lance plusieurs célèbres paquebots comme le *Edinburgh Castle* et le *Pretoria Castle*, bientôt suivis par les *Bloemfontein*, *Rhodesia*, *Kenya*, *Braemar* et *Pendennis Castle*. Le *Southern Cross*, de la compagnie Shaw Savill, présente une silhouette reconnaissable et de conception résolument moderne pour l'époque : les moteurs et les cheminées étant à l'arrière et les cales pour le fret entièrement supprimées, une vaste zone s'étendant sur toute la longueur du navire est libérée aux ponts supérieurs au bénéfice des 1100 passagers de classe touriste. Ce paquebot allait être doublé par le *Dominion Monarch*, construit en 1939 mais qui se fit une réputation de luxe dans les années 1950.

Avant le *United States*, le paquebot américain le plus rapide avait été le *Constitution* (30293 tonneaux), armé en 1951 par les American Export Lines pour assurer la liaison États-Unis–Méditerranée. Ce navire, et son « sister ship » *Independence*, avait un profil fin très particulier, des cheminées fuselées et des contre-étraves.

Si la clientèle se démocratise quelque peu, le paquebot demeure bien souvent un luxe. En 1952, les nouveaux paquebots *Antilles* et *Flandre*, armés par la CGT, offrent chacun plus de 400 couchettes de première classe, et moins de 300 en deuxième et classe touriste. Ils sont suivis en 1953 par le *Kungsholm*, de la Swedish American Line, qui a une telle réputation pour la qualité de son service à bord qu'il peut proposer des croisières hors saison dans une seule classe. La Furness-Bermuda Line met également en service un nouveau navire, l'*Ocean Monarch*, qui vient en complément du *Queen of Bermuda* pour des croisières dans les Caraïbes la moitié de l'année.

Les années 1950 sont la dernière grande époque du « style paquebot ». La Compagnie Générale Transatlantique met ainsi en service le *Liberté* après avoir somptueusement transformé l'ancien *Europa*, le lauréat allemand du Ruban bleu avant-guerre, en l'associant sur la ligne transatlantique à cette autre légende qu'est l'*Île de France*. De même, la Holland-America Line rénove magnifiquement le *Nieuw-Amsterdam* pour en faire le navire amiral de sa flotte. Les Allemands reviennent également sur l'Atlantique, où ils connurent tant de succès maritimes, en armant un nouveau *Bremen*, construit sur la base du *Pasteur*, l'ancien transport de troupes français.

Le fleuron de la flotte italienne ressuscitée, l'*Andrea Doria* (29083 tonneaux) est construit aux chantiers Ansaldo de Gênes en 1953. Le soir du 25 juillet 1956, il approche de New York et se trouve pris dans les bancs de brouillard autour de l'île de Nantucket lorsque l'officier de quart aperçoit le *Stockholm*, appartenant à la compagnie suédoise. Pour une raison inexpliquée, les deux navires, qui naviguent cependant à vue, font route de collision. À 23 h 10, la proue brise-glace du *Stockholm* vient enfoncer le côté tribord arrière du pont de l'*Andrea Doria*, qui se met aussitôt à gîter si fortement qu'il est difficile de mettre les canots de sauvetage à la mer. Peu après 6 heures du matin, le 26 juillet, il chavire et coule. Grâce notamment à la présence sur les lieux de l'*Île de France*, qui s'est dérouté, la majorité des 1662 passagers et membres d'équipage ont été recueillis ; mais 52 personnes ont disparu. Le *Stockholm* parvient à rejoindre un port par ses propres moyens, montrant un moignon déchiqueté à la place de la proue.

C'est l'année suivant l'attribution du Ruban bleu au *United States* que commencent les premiers voyages au long cours par avion à réaction. En 1953, un « De Havilland Comet » accomplit l'exploit de relier Londres à Tokyo en 36 heures. Cet appareil est le premier avion commercial du monde, construit par les Britanniques à partir de la technologie des moteurs à réaction inventés pendant la guerre. En 1958, la compagnie aérienne Trans World Airlines ouvre un service transatlantique régulier par avion, un Boeing 707 – sans doute l'appareil qui aura le plus de succès. L'Atlantique peut désormais être franchi en six heures. Au milieu des années 1960, 95 pour cent du trafic passager transatlantique se fait désormais par voie aérienne.

De splendides paquebots continuèrent d'être construits. La ligne Italia remplaça l'*Andrea Doria* par le *Leonardo da Vinci* (33340 tonneaux), lancé sur le chantier Ansaldo le 7 décembre 1958 et mis en service sur la ligne Atlantique en 1960. Il fut retiré du service pour devenir un paquebot de croisière en 1976. Il connut une fin dramatique lorsqu'il prit feu dans le port de La Spezia en juillet 1980. Pendant toutes les années 1960 et 1970, nombre des grands paquebots le suivrait dans une nouvelle carrière comme navires de croisière, avant de terminer dans les chantiers de ferrailleurs.

The *Queen Elizabeth* in dry dock at Southampton, May 1955. She was being fitted with Denny-Brown stabilizers to check her famous roll.

Die *Queen Elizabeth* im Trockendock in Southampton, Mai 1955. Sie wird mit Stabilisatoren von Denny-Brown ausgestattet, um das berüchtigte Schlingern einzudämmen.

Le *Queen Elizabeth* en cale sèche à Southampton, en mai 1955, est désormais équipé de stabilisateurs Denny-Brown permettant de réduire son roulis.

Docks and Docklands

(Above) The 20,204-ton *Southern Cross* of the Shaw Savill Line at Southampton being readied for her maiden round-the-world voyage, March 1955. She is now *Ocean Breeze*. (Right) The same line's *Dominion Monarch*, 27,155 tons, towers above the houses in Saville Street in London's Docklands.

Docks und Docklands

(Oben) Die *Southern Cross* von Shaw Savill, 20 204 Tonnen, im März 1955 in Southampton, wo sie für ihre Jungfernfahrt um die Welt vorbereitet wird. Sie fährt heute noch unter dem Namen *Ocean Breeze*. (Rechts) Die *Dominion Monarch* derselben Reederei, 27 155 Tonnen, überragt die Häuser der Saville Street im Londoner Hafenviertel.

Docks et Docklands

Le *Southern Cross* – aujourd'hui l'*Ocean Breeze* (20 204 tonneaux) –, de la Shaw Savill Line, lors de ses préparatifs à Southampton avant d'effectuer son tour du monde inaugural, en mars 1955 (ci-dessus). Le *Dominion Monarch* (27 155 tonneaux), de la même compagnie, domine les maisons de Saville Street dans le quartier londonien des Docklands (à droite).

Fifties Deco
The Fifties style aboard the Furness-Bermuda's *Ocean Monarch*: (top left) the air-conditioned cinema and theatre, (top right) the dining room, (below left) the cocktail bar, (below right) the lounge, complete with fireplace.
(Right) The liner puts in for a major overhaul in 1959 after eight years on the New York to Bermuda run.

Stil der Fünfziger
Die *Ocean Monarch* der Furness-Bermuda-Linie ist ganz im Stil der fünfziger Jahre ausgestattet: (Oben links) das Kino und Theater mit Klimaanlage, (oben rechts) der Speisesaal, (unten links) die Cocktailbar, (unten rechts) der Salon mit echtem Kamin. (Rechts) 1959 kam der Liner nach acht Jahren auf der Strecke New York–Bermuda zu einer größeren Überholung ins Dock.

Le style des années 1950
Le style des années 1950 marque l'intérieur de l'*Ocean Monarch*, de la compagnie Furness-Bermuda. On reconnaît : la salle de cinéma et de théâtre, pourvue de l'air conditionné (en haut, à gauche) ; la salle à manger (en haut, à droite) ; le bar (en bas, à gauche) ; le salon, avec sa cheminée (en bas, à droite). Le paquebot entre dans le bassin de radoub pour une remise en état complète en 1959, après avoir servi huit années sur la route New York–Bermudes (à droite).

Winner's reception
(Left) Passengers form a conga line during the festivities as the *United States* grasps the trophy on her maiden voyage. (Right) What was to become the official portrait of the last big liner to win the Blue Riband and Hales Trophy. (Overleaf) She is given the full fire-float welcome at Le Havre after winning the Blue Riband from the *Queen Mary*.

Eine Party für den Sieger
(Links) Passagiere tanzen eine Polonaise bei dem großen Fest, mit dem auf der *United States* das schon auf der Jungfernfahrt errungene Band gefeiert wurde. (Rechts) Dieses Bild sollte zum offiziellen Porträt des letzten Ozeanriesen werden, der das Blaue Band und die Hales Trophy erringen konnte. (Folgende Doppelseite) Feuerlöschboote sprühen ihre Fontänen, als die *United States* nach der Rekordfahrt in Le Havre eintrifft.

Réception du vainqueur
Les passagers dansent une conga à la queue leu leu pendant les festivités organisées à bord du *United States*, nouveau détenteur du Ruban bleu lors de son voyage inaugural (à gauche). Cette photographie (à droite) allait devenir le portrait officiel du dernier grand paquebot à remporter à la fois le Ruban bleu et le trophée Hales. Il reçoit un accueil chaleureux des bateaux-pompes du Havre après avoir repris le Ruban bleu au *Queen Mary* (pages suivantes).

Passage to Australia

(Above left) The clean line of the funnel and after-decks of the
P & O *Arcadia*, 29,734 tons, at Tilbury before her maiden voyage
to Australia on 22 February 1954. (Above right) The starboard
promenade deck of the *Iberia*, 29,614 tons, P & O sister to the
Arcadia. The shape of their yellow stacks was a characteristic
of the P & O liners. (Right) Streamers make a blizzard as
Orient Line's *Orsova* departs for Australia in 1955.

Die Reise nach Australien

(Oben links) Klare Linien von Schornstein und Achterdeck –
die *Arcadia* der P & O, 29 734 Tonnen, in Tilbury kurz vor
ihrer Jungfernfahrt, zu der sie am 22. Februar 1954 nach
Australien auslief. (Oben rechts) Das Promenadendeck auf
der Steuerbordseite der *Iberia*, 29 614 Tonnen, des Schwesterschiffs der *Arcadia*. Die Form der gelben Schornsteine war
charakteristisch für die Schiffe der P & O. (Rechts) Ein ganzer
Blizzard aus Luftschlangen weht von Deck des Orient-Liners
Orsova, der hier 1955 zur Australienüberfahrt ablegt.

Passage en Australie

Les lignes pures de la cheminée et des ponts arrière de
l'*Arcadia* (29734 tonneaux), appartenant à la P & O, amarré
à Tilbury avant d'effectuer son voyage inaugural vers
l'Australie, le 22 février 1954 (ci-dessus, à gauche). Le
pont promenade tribord de l'*Iberia* (29614 tonneaux),
frère d'armement de l'*Arcadia* (ci-dessus, à droite). La
forme des cheminées jaunes caractérise les paquebots de
la P & O. Les serpentins lancés par les passagers forment
une véritable muraille de papier lors du départ pour
l'Australie de l'*Orsova*, de l'Orient Line, en 1955 (à droite).

Two ships, many names

(Left) The 20,469-ton *Flandre* of the French Line as she enters service from Le Havre to New York in 1952. In 1968 she became the Italian Costa Line's *Carla C.* She ended her days as Epirotiki Line's *Pallas Athena.* (Right) The Swedish-American *Kungsholm*, 21,141 tons, built in 1953. Renamed *Europa* (Norddeutscher Lloyd), then *Columbus C* (Costa Line), she sank after hitting a breakwater at Cadiz on 29 July 1984.

Zwei Schiffe, viele Namen

(Links) Die *Flandre* der CGT, 20.469 Tonnen, als sie 1952 auf der Route Le Havre–New York in Dienst gestellt wird. 1968 ging sie an die italienische Costa-Linie und hieß von da an *Carla C.* Ihre letzten Tage verbrachte sie als *Pallas Athena* der Epirotiki-Linie. (Rechts) Die *Kungsholm* der Schweden-Amerika-Linie, 21.141 Tonnen, wurde 1953 gebaut. Später fuhr sie als *Europa* für den Norddeutschen Lloyd, dann als *Columbus C.* für Costa; am 29. Juli 1984 prallte sie gegen einen Wellenbrecher im Hafen von Cadiz und sank.

Deux navires, plusieurs noms

(À gauche) Le *Flandre*, un paquebot de 20.469 tonneaux appartenant à la CGT, au moment de sa mise en service sur la ligne Le Havre–New York, en 1952. Racheté en 1968 par la compagnie italienne Costa Line, il est rebaptisé *Carla C.* et finira ses jours aux couleurs de la Epirotiki Line sous le nom de *Pallas Athena.* (À droite) Le paquebot américano-suédois *Kungsholm* (21.141 tonneaux), construit en 1953, sera successivement rebaptisé *Europa* (Norddeutscher Lloyd), puis *Columbus C.* (Costa Line). Il fera naufrage le 29 juillet 1984 après avoir heurté un brise-lames de Cadiz.

Italian elegance

(Left) The bow and main sea-anchor chain of the elegant but ill-fated *Andrea Doria*, 29,085 tons, the flagship and pride of the Italian Line, and the largest Italian liner built since the Thirties. She sank after colliding with the Swedish liner *Stockholm* off Nantucket on 25 July 1956. (Right) The launch of her replacement, the 33,340-ton *Leonardo da Vinci*, on 7 December 1958.

Italienische Eleganz

(Links) Bug und Ankerkette der eleganten *Andrea Doria*, deren kurzes Schiffsleben tragisch enden sollte. Mit 29085 Tonnen war sie Stolz und Flaggschiff der Italia-Linie, der größte Passagierdampfer, der in Italien seit den dreißiger Jahren entstanden war. Sie sank am 25. Juli 1956 nach einer Kollision mit dem schwedischen Liner *Stockholm* vor Nantucket. (Rechts) Stapellauf des Nachfolgers, des 33340-Tonners *Leonardo da Vinci*, am 7. Dezember 1958.

Élégance italienne

(À gauche) La proue et la chaîne de l'ancre principale de l'élégant mais infortuné paquebot *Andrea Doria* (29085 tonneaux), navire amiral et fierté de la compagnie italienne. Le plus grand paquebot italien construit depuis les années 1930 fit naufrage le 25 juillet 1956 après une collision avec le paquebot suédois *Stockholm* au large de Nantucket. (À droite) Il fut remplacé par le *Leonardo da Vinci* (33340 tonnes), lancé le 7 décembre 1958.

Union Castle liners

(Left) The *Bloemfontein Castle*, 18,400 tons, moored in King George V Dock, London, preparing to sail for South Africa, October 1951. To the right are two fleet-mates, the *Rhodesia Castle*, 17,041 tons, and *Dunnottar Castle*, 15,007 tons. (Above) Scrubbing the upperworks and hull of the *Capetown Castle*, 27,002 tons, Southampton docks, December 1958.

Union-Castle-Schiffe

(Links) Die *Bloemfontein Castle*, 18400 Tonnen, macht sich im Oktober 1951 im Londoner King George V Dock für die Fahrt nach Südafrika bereit. Rechts im Hintergrund zwei Schiffe derselben Flotte, die *Rhodesia Castle*, 17041 Tonnen, und die *Dunnottar Castle*, 15007 Tonnen. (Oben) Deck und Rumpf der *Capetown Castle*, 27002 Tonnen, werden in den Docks von Southampton geschrubbt, Dezember 1958.

Les paquebots de la Union Castle

(À gauche) Le *Bloemfontein Castle* (18400 tonneaux), amarré au King George V Dock de Londres, est prêt à appareiller pour l'Afrique du Sud, en octobre 1951. À droite deux autres navires de la compagnie : le *Rhodesia Castle* (17041 tonneaux) et le *Dunnottar Castle* (15007 tonneaux). (Ci-dessus) Les œuvres vives et la coque du *Capetown Castle* (27002 tonneaux) sont nettoyées dans les docks de Southampton, en décembre 1958.

'Luxury liner row'

(Left) The SS *Constitution*, 30,293 tons, alongside in Manhattan, 1955. (Above) A Who's Who of the great North Atlantic liners at their Manhattan berths, October 1952: from left, Cunard's *Media*, *Mauretania*, *Queen Elizabeth*, *Georgic* (still in White Star colours), French Line's *Liberté*, United States Line's *United States*, and Italian Line's *Conte Biancamano*.

»Straße der Ozeanriesen«

(Links) Die SS *Constitution*, 30293 Tonnen, in Manhattan vertäut, 1955. (Oben) Ein Who's Who der großen Atlantikliner an den Piers von Manhattan, im Oktober 1952. Von links: Cunards *Media*, *Mauretania*, *Queen Elizabeth*, *Georgic* (noch in den Farben der White Star Line), die *Liberté* der französischen CGT, die *United States* der United States Line und die italienische *Conte Biancamano*.

Le quai des paquebots de luxe

(À gauche) Le SS *Constitution* (30293 tonneaux), amarré à Manhattan en 1955. (Ci-dessus) Cette photographie présente le Who's Who des grands paquebots transatlantiques, en octobre 1952. De gauche à droite, les paquebots *Media*, *Mauretania*, *Queen Elizabeth* et *Georgic* (encore sous les couleurs de la White Star), appartenant à la Cunard ; le *Liberté* de la CGT ; l'américain *United States*, et l'italien *Conte Biancamano*.

A new *Bremen*

The French *Pasteur* was rebuilt in 1957–1959 as the Nord-deutscher Lloyd *Bremen*, 32,336 tons. (Left) The first-class dining room. (Above right) The tourist-class lounge (right), convertible into a ballroom, and the first-class lounge. (Opposite) Berthed at Bremerhaven just before her maiden voyage to America, 6 July 1959.

Eine neue *Bremen*

Die französische *Pasteur* wurde von 1957 bis 1959 für den Nord-deutschen Lloyd zur neuen *Bremen* umgebaut, 32 336 Tonnen. (Links) Der Speisesaal der Ersten Klasse. (Oben rechts) Der Salon der Touristenklasse (rechts), der auch als Tanzsaal diente, und der Salon der Ersten Klasse. (Gegenüber) Am Kai in Bremerhaven kurz vor dem Aufbruch zur Jungfernfahrt nach Amerika, am 6. Juli 1959.

Un nouveau *Bremen*

Le paquebot français *Pasteur* fut reconstruit en 1957–1959 et prit alors le nom de *Bremen* (32 336 tonneaux), armé par la Norddeutscher Lloyd. La salle à manger et le salon des première classe (à gauche et en haut, à droite), et le salon de la classe touriste, transformable en salle de bal (à droite). (Ci-contre) Le *Bremen* à son quai de Bremerhaven juste avant d'effectuer son voyage inaugural en Amérique, le 6 juillet 1959.

7

Into the Sunset:
The Sixties and After

At the end of the 1950s debate arose in Britain about the desirability of a successor to the *Queen Mary* and *Queen Elizabeth*, and in 1960 a government loan of £18 million was allocated to Cunard for a new liner of about 75,000 tons. She was codenamed 'Q3'. After some heart-searching by the company, it was decided that a large ship designed only for the Europe–America service was not economically viable. A smaller liner was proposed, narrow enough and with a shallow enough draft to navigate both the Panama and Suez Canals, as her role would be as much to cruise the world as to make regular scheduled voyages across the Atlantic. The new project was, unsurprisingly, codenamed 'Q4'.

On 20 September 1967 she was launched from the yard of Upper Clyde Shipbuilders by Queen Elizabeth II, who named her *Queen Elizabeth 2*. Due to continuing labour disputes and technical problems her maiden voyage had to be put off until 18 April 1969. Mechanical troubles were to dog her life at critical stages. Even so, the new slimline 'greyhound', 963 feet long and 65,000 tons, proved a great commercial success.

The *Queen Elizabeth 2* at first sight seems the epitaph to the great era of the liners. She was the last great ship to appear in the 20th century with the familiar Cunard livery of red funnel with black and white hull and superstructure. Despite obvious troubles, such as the decline in regular passenger traffic and industrial disputes with dock hands on both sides of the Atlantic, she has proved remarkably durable, surviving not a few excitements.

In January 1971 she went to the rescue of the French liner *Antilles*, ablaze off the island of Mustique, and with the help of two other French ships landed the passengers on Barbados. A bomb scare in 1972 proved false. Her biggest adventure was to follow her sisters into war service in 1982, when she was commissioned as a troopship to take some 3,000 troops to the Falklands War.

Meanwhile, in 1960, the merger of two well-established companies resulted in the world's largest passenger fleet. P & O-Orient Lines now had 16 liners, of which *Oriana* and *Canberra* were the new stars. The stylish *Oriana*, at 41,932 tons the largest British ship to be built since the *Queen Elizabeth*, entered service in December 1960; *Canberra* set out on her maiden voyage from Southampton to Australia on 2 June 1961, heralded as 'the ship that will shape the future'. P & O-Orient planned to develop the trans-Pacific and other new routes, challenging the ascendancy of the world's airlines with a far more agreeable mode of travel.

At the onset of the Falklands War it was the *Canberra*, 45,733 tons, that did most of the work in delivering the troops to the battle zone. Her conversion to troop carrier for the Falklands in April 1982 was dramatic and bruising. Flight decks were bolted on fore and aft of the bridge. Instead of 2,700 elderly cruise passengers, she carried three and a half battalions of paratroopers and marines. After six months at sea, this extraordinarily tough and reliable vessel began to show signs of wear and tear, but she survived attack by low-flying aircraft to come through the war remarkably unscathed.

The *Canberra* was in service for 36 years. Her place as flagship of the P & O fleet was filled in 1995 by a new *Oriana*, built in Germany. The company also undertook a $3 billion expansion programme of their Princess Cruises division, for which it took delivery in 1998 of the *Grand Princess*. This enormous vessel (109,000 tons) is a piece of fantasy marine architecture, including a glass-roofed nightclub suspended over the stern, a chapel for renewing wedding vows, and 760 individual cabins with their own balconies for her 2,600 passengers.

Among other lines that successfully reinvented themselves was the Holland-America Line. Their *Nieuw-Amsterdam*, 36,287 tons, launched at Rotterdam in 1938, served from 1940 to 1945 as an Allied troopship, and successfully flew the line's flag on the Rotterdam–New York route until 1971, spending her last two years cruising the Caribbean. In 1959 she was superseded as flagship by the *Rotterdam*, 38,645 tons, on which both first- and tourist-class passengers had the full run of the ship.

By the mid-Sixties, however, the scheduled services of most of the great ships and companies had struck rough commercial waters. Both the *United States* and the *QE2* were to be hit by industrial action. Between 1961 and 1969 the *United States* suffered the cancellation of no fewer than eleven voyages due to strike action. On her 726th crossing of the Atlantic she was ordered to proceed next for an early refit at Newport News, in order to head off the effects of a threatened strike. She was never to leave there again under her own power.

An even worse fate had overtaken the old *Queen Elizabeth*, withdrawn in 1968. She was sold to a Taiwanese shipping tycoon, who planned to turn her into a learning centre cruising the world as the *Seawise University*. When rebuilding in Hong Kong was almost complete, in January 1972, she caught fire, rolled on to her side and continued to burn for a week. Later it was confirmed that this was the work of an arsonist, though nobody was ever charged with the crime.

The French Line's glamorous new flagship, *France*, made her appearance in 1962. Built at a total cost of £30 million, she was the longest liner ever at 1,035 feet; her design and layout were the last word in up-to-date elegance. Her owners were confident that there was sufficient demand for such exceptional quality. By the early 1970s, however, with more than 90 per cent of all passenger traffic across the Atlantic by air, the French Line was in difficulties. In 1974 it was announced that the company 'most regrettably will have to discontinue its regular transatlantic service after 110 years'. The *France* was due to make her last voyage, from New York to Cannes, on 18 October. However, on 11 September, as she was approaching Le Havre, a party of crew members entered the bridge and took control of the ship, blocking the main channel to force the government to withdraw its threat. After eleven days, with supplies running low, the crew decided to continue their protest ashore. Thus *France*'s career ended; she later became the cruise ship *Norway*.

Even so, the Sixties saw some great and bold designs of new liners. Most outstanding were Italian Line's twin ships of 1965, the 45,911-ton *Michelangelo* and *Raffaello*, 45,933 tons. With their latticework funnels, unusual profiles and six swimming-pools apiece, these two promoted a new ideal of Italian liner architecture. Their projected profitability never materialized, and after barely ten years they were bought by the Iranian government and became floating barracks. *Michelangelo* was scrapped in 1992; *Raffaello* was sunk by an Iraqi aircraft missile attack in 1983.

The strangest saga was that of the *Achille Lauro*, 21,119 tons. She had begun life as Rotterdam Royal Line's *Willem Ruys* in 1939, and was rebuilt in 1965. Some 20 years later she was cruising the eastern Mediterranean with a party of Americans bound for Israel when she was hijacked by PLO terrorists. An elderly wheelchair-bound New Yorker, Leon Klinghoffer, argued with the terrorists; he was thrown overboard and drowned. The Italians parlayed the group into leaving the ship, but then let the leader go free. The whole episode was a severe jolt to the Mediterranean cruise business. On 30 November 1994, the *Achille Lauro* was swept by a catastrophic fire off Somalia, and sank two days later.

At the close of the 20th century passenger travel by sea is booming, not as the fastest or most efficient way to reach a

destination, but as a destination and experience in itself. Cruises offer adventure; they go to all seas and continents, to the Arctic, and, more controversially because of their environmental effect, to the Antarctic. Cruises can be customized for learning, soaking up the sun, making journeys into history, even gambling, dancing and the pleasures of Dionysus.

But the era of the liner, epitomized by the *Queen Mary* and the *Normandie*, the *Raffaello* and the *Nieuw-Amsterdam*, the great German monsters of Albert Ballin and the Atlantic Express, may not be dead. Cunard, one of the original players in the transatlantic race, has placed an order for a new liner, to be larger than the old *Queen Elizabeth* and longer than the *France*. The transatlantic sea crossing is about to make a comeback.

The P & O-Orient Line *Oriana*, 42,000 tons, passes through the Panama Canal, July 1961. She was the largest ship up to then to go through the canal.

Die *Oriana* der P & O-Orient Line, 42 000 Tonnen, bei der Durchfahrt durch den Panamakanal im Juli 1961. Sie war das größte Schiff, das bis dahin den Kanal passiert hatte.

En juillet 1961, l'*Oriana* (42 000 tonneaux), de la P & O-Orient Line, empruntait le canal de Panama. C'était alors le plus gros navire à franchir le canal.

– 7 –
In den Sonnenuntergang:
Die sechziger Jahre und
die Zeit danach

A view of the *Queen Elizabeth 2*'s
stabilizers in dry dock,
Southampton, March 1969.
She was being checked after
troubles with her turbines
in earlier acceptance trials.

Eine Ansicht der Stabilisatoren der
Queen Elizabeth 2 im Trockendock
in Southampton, März 1969.
Nachdem bei Probefahrten die
Turbinen nicht zur Zufriedenheit
gelaufen waren, mußte sie noch
einmal ins Dock.

Une vue des stabilisateurs du
Queen Elizabeth 2 en cale sèche à
Southampton, en mars 1969, lors
d'une visite d'inspection nécessitée
par ses problèmes de turbine lors
des essais de réception.

Ende der fünfziger Jahre mehrten sich in Großbritannien die Stimmen, die einen Nachfolger für *Queen Mary* und *Queen Elizabeth* forderten, und 1960 gewährte die Regierung Cunard einen Kredit von 18 Millionen Pfund für den Bau eines neuen Passagierschiffes von etwa 75000 Tonnen. Das Projekt erhielt den Codenamen »Q3«. Nach langem Hin und Her kam die Leitung des Unternehmens zu dem Schluß, daß ein Schiff dieser Größe, nur für den Atlantikdienst gebaut, nicht profitabel sein würde. Sie schlug ein kleineres Schiff vor, das schmal genug und mit genügend niedrigem Tiefgang gebaut sein sollte, um den Panama- und den Suezkanal passieren zu können, denn neben dem Linienverkehr über den Atlantik sollte es auch für Kreuzfahrten eingesetzt werden. Das neue Projekt hörte, wie nicht anders zu erwarten, auf den Namen »Q4«.

Am 20. September 1967 lief das Schiff bei den Upper Clyde Shipbuilders vom Stapel, und Königin Elisabeth II. taufte es auf den Namen *Queen Elizabeth 2*. Wegen zahlreicher Streiks und technischer Schwierigkeiten verzögerte sich die Jungfernfahrt bis zum 18. April 1969. Das Schiff sollte auch später immer wieder mit technischen Mängeln zu kämpfen haben, doch trotzdem erwies sich dieser neue, schlanke »Windhund der Meere« mit 293 Metern Länge und 65000 Bruttoregistertonnen als großer Erfolg.

Die *Queen Elizabeth 2* war eine Art Abgesang auf die Zeit der großen Ozeanriesen. Sie war die letzte, die im 20. Jahrhundert den altvertrauten Cunard-Anstrich mit rotem Schornstein und mit Rumpf und Aufbauten in Schwarz und Weiß erhielt. Obwohl von rückläufigen Passagierzahlen und Streiks beiderseits des Atlantiks geplagt, hat sie sich als bemerkenswert zäh erwiesen und eine ganze Reihe von Krisen überstanden.

Im Januar 1971 eilte sie zur Rettung, als der französische Dampfer *Antilles* vor der Insel Mustique in Flammen stand, und evakuierte zusammen mit zwei weiteren französischen Schiffen die Passagiere nach Barbados. 1972 hieß es »Bombe an Bord«, doch der Alarm erwies sich als falsch. Ihr größtes Abenteuer kam 1982, als sie, wie ihre Schwestern zuvor, zum Kriegsdienst gerufen wurde und etwa 3000 Mann in den Falklandkrieg brachte.

Schon 1960 hatten zwei altehrwürdige Gesellschaften fusioniert und damit die weltweit größte Passagierflotte geschaffen. Die neuen Stars der P & O-Orient Lines, die über

insgesamt 16 Dampfer verfügte, hießen *Oriana* und *Canberra*. Die elegante *Oriana*, mit 41932 Tonnen das größte Schiff, das seit der *Queen Elizabeth* in Großbritannien entstanden war, wurde im Dezember 1960 in Dienst gestellt; die *Canberra*, »das Schiff, das die Zukunft prägen wird«, lief am 2. Juni 1961 von Southampton zur Jungfernfahrt nach Australien aus. P & O-Orient Lines wollte den Pazifikverkehr und andere neue Routen ausbauen und den auch dort immer stärker werdenden Fluggesellschaften mit einer bequemeren Art des Reisens Paroli bieten.

Als der Falklandkrieg ausbrach, trug die *Canberra* mit ihren 45733 Tonnen die Hauptlast und brachte Truppen in großer Zahl ins Einsatzgebiet. Der Umbau zum Truppentransporter im April 1982 ging recht unsanft vonstatten, und vor und hinter der Brücke wurden Flugdecks aufgenietet. Anstelle von 2700 betagten Kreuzfahrtpassagieren beförderte sie dreieinhalb Bataillone Fallschirmspringer und Marineinfanteristen. Nach sechs Monaten auf See war diesem außerordentlich kräftigen und zuverlässigen Schiff die Erschöpfung anzusehen, doch sie überstand sogar Tieffliegerangriffe und kehrte fast unbeschädigt von ihrem Einsatz zurück.

Die *Canberra* war 36 Jahre lang im Dienst. 1995 trat eine in Deutschland gebaute neue *Oriana* ihre Nachfolge als P & O-Flaggschiff an. Drei Milliarden Dollar steckte die Firma in ihren Ableger Princess Cruises und ließ dafür die 1998 fertiggestellte *Grand Princess* bauen. Dieses gewaltige Kreuzfahrtschiff (109000 Tonnen) ist eine Art schwimmendes Märchenschloß, unter anderem mit einem glasüberdachten, jenseits des Hecks über dem Meer schwebenden Nachtclub, einer Kapelle, in der man den ehelichen Bund erneuern kann, und 760 Kabinen für die 2600 Passagiere, jede mit einem eigenen Balkon.

Auch der Holland-Amerika-Linie gelang der Sprung in die neue Ära. Der 36287-Tonner *Nieuw-Amsterdam*, 1938 in Rotterdam vom Stapel gelaufen, diente im Zweiten Weltkrieg als alliierter Truppentransporter, befuhr dann bis 1971 erfolgreich die Route Rotterdam–New York und verbrachte seine letzten beiden Jahre als Kreuzfahrtschiff in der Karibik. Flaggschiff war seit 1959 jedoch mit 38645 Tonnen die *Rotterdam*, die das ganze Schiff für die Passagiere beider Klassen öffnete.

Schon Mitte der sechziger Jahre gab es kaum noch einen Ozeandampfer, der im Liniendienst Gewinn erwirtschaftete. Die *United States* und die *QE 2* wurden zudem von

328

Streiks geplagt. Zwischen 1961 und 1969 mußte die *United States* elfmal eine Fahrt wegen Streiks absagen. Auf ihrer 726. Atlantiküberfahrt erhielt sie Order, zu vorgezogenen Wartungsarbeiten in Newport News anzulegen, um einem weiteren drohenden Streik zu entgehen, und mit eigener Kraft sollte sie das dortige Dock nie wieder verlassen.

Noch schlimmer erging es der alten *Queen Elizabeth*, 1968 außer Dienst gestellt. Ein Schiffahrtsmagnat aus Taiwan erwarb sie und wollte ein schwimmendes Lehrinstitut daraus machen, das als *Seawise University* die Weltmeere befahren sollte. Im Januar 1972, als die Umbauarbeiten in Hongkong fast abgeschlossen waren, geriet sie in Brand, legte sich auf die Seite und brannte eine ganze Woche lang. Ermittlungen ergaben, daß es sich um Brandstiftung gehandelt hatte, doch der Täter wurde nie gefaßt.

Das prachtvolle neue Flaggschiff der Compagnie Générale Transatlantique, die *France*, nahm 1962 die Fahrt auf. Mit 315 Metern Länge war sie der größte Liniendampfer aller Zeiten, und der Bau verschlang den Gegenwert von 30 Millionen Pfund; Aufbauten und Ausstattung waren von erlesener Eleganz. Die Betreiber waren zuversichtlich, daß für solche Luxusüberfahrten auch weiterhin ein Markt bestand, doch schon Anfang der siebziger Jahre wählten über 90 Prozent der Atlantikpassagiere das Flugzeug, und die Reederei geriet in Schwierigkeiten. 1974 wurde bekanntgegeben, daß man »mit größtem Bedauern nach 110 Jahren den Liniendienst auf dem Atlantik einstellen« müsse. Die letzte Fahrt, von New York nach Cannes, war für den 18. Oktober angesetzt. Doch als die *France* am 11. September in Le Havre einlief, enterte ein Trupp Besatzungsmitglieder die Brücke, übernahm das Kommando und blockierte mit dem Schiff die Hafeneinfahrt, um die Regierung zum Weiterbetrieb zu zwingen. Als nach elf Tagen die Nahrungsvorräte zu Ende gingen, beschloß die Mannschaft, ihren Protest an Land fortzusetzen. So endete die Karriere der *France*; später wurde sie zum Kreuzfahrtschiff *Norway* umgebaut.

Doch selbst in den sechziger Jahren entstanden noch imposante neue Liner. Die eindrucksvollsten waren die beiden 1965 in Dienst gestellten neuen Schiffe der Italia-Linie, die *Michelangelo* mit 45911 Tonnen und die *Raffaello* mit 45933 Tonnen. Mit ihren Gitterwerkschornsteinen, dem markanten Profil und den sechs Swimmingpools pro Schiff sollten sie das neue Ideal italienischer Schiffsbaukunst verkörpern. Rentabel waren sie jedoch nie, und nach nicht einmal zehn Jahren wurden sie an den Iran verkauft, wo sie als schwimmende Kasernen dienten. Die *Michelangelo* kam 1992 zum Verschrotten, die *Raffaello* sank 1983 nach einem irakischen Raketenangriff.

Das seltsamste Schicksal ereilte die *Achille Lauro*. Der 21119-Tonner war 1939 bei der Rotterdam Royal Line als *Willem Ruys* in Dienst gestellt und 1965 neu aufgebaut worden. Als das Schiff etwa 20 Jahre darauf mit einer amerikanischen Reisegesellschaft mit Kurs auf Israel im östlichen Mittelmeer unterwegs war, wurde es von PLO-Terroristen gekapert. Ein älterer, an den Rollstuhl gefesselter New Yorker namens Leon Klinghoffer legte sich mit den Terroristen an; sie warfen ihn über Bord, und er ertrank. Der italienischen Regierung gelang es, die Gruppe zum Verlassen des Schiffes zu bewegen, doch den Anführer ließ man laufen. Nach diesem Zwischenfall ging der Kreuzfahrttourismus im Mittelmeer stark zurück. Am 30. November 1994 brannte die *Achille Lauro* vor der somalischen Küste aus und sank zwei Tage darauf.

Heute blüht der Passagierverkehr auf den Weltmeeren; nicht mehr als die schnellste und einfachste Art, ein Ziel zu erreichen, sondern als Reise an sich. Eine Kreuzfahrt ist ein Abenteuer; man kann sämtliche Meere des Erdballs bereisen, sämtliche Kontinente anlaufen; Schiffe sind in der Arktis unterwegs und auch – obwohl wegen der Umweltbelastung umstritten – in der Antarktis. Ob Studienfahrt, ob nostalgisches Erlebnis, zum Sonnenbad, Glücksspiel, Tanz oder zu dionysischen Freuden, für alles findet man das richtige Schiff.

Doch auch die Zeit der Ozeanriesen, der großen Passagierdampfer vom Schlage einer *Queen Mary* oder *Normandie*, die Zeit der *Raffaello*, der *Nieuw-Amsterdam* und der Giganten Albert Ballins, der Expreßrouten über den Atlantik, ist vielleicht noch nicht vorbei. Cunard, einer der ältesten Teilnehmer am großen atlantischen Wettrennen, hat einen neuen Liner in Auftrag gegeben, der größer als die alte *Queen Elizabeth* und länger als die *France* werden soll. Die Atlantiküberfahrt per Schiff wird schon bald ihre Wiedergeburt erleben.

Labour intensive! Dockyard workers painting the funnel of a liner in dock at Hamburg, Germany, November 1969.

Das schafft Arbeitsplätze! In einem Dock in Hamburg wird im November 1969 ein Schiffsschornstein gestrichen.

Un travail de fourmis ! Les ouvriers d'un chantier naval de Hambourg (Allemagne) repeignent la cheminée d'un paquebot, en novembre 1969.

Un débat s'ouvre en Grande-Bretagne à la fin des années 1950 quant à la nécessité de donner un successeur au *Queen Mary* et au *Queen Elizabeth*. En 1960, un prêt gouvernemental de 18 millions de livres est accordé à la Cunard pour la construction d'un nouveau paquebot de 75 000 tonneaux environ, dont le nom de code est « Q3 ». Après s'être longuement interrogé, la compagnie juge qu'un grand navire conçu uniquement pour un service Europe–Amérique n'est pas économiquement viable. On leur propose un paquebot plus petit, assez étroit et d'un tirant d'eau suffisamment faible pour franchir le canal de Panama et celui de Suez, prévoyant qu'il devrait non seulement parcourir toutes les mers du monde mais aussi effectuer des traversées régulières de l'Atlantique. Ce nouveau projet est alors évidemment baptisé « Q4 ».

Le nouveau navire est lancé le 20 septembre 1967 aux chantiers Upper Clyde Shipbuilders par la reine Elizabeth II, qui le baptise *Queen Elizabeth 2*. Mais, une série de grèves et des problèmes techniques continuels contribuent à retarder son voyage inaugural au 18 avril 1969. Si ces problèmes mécaniques allaient poursuivre le navire toute sa vie durant, ce nouveau « lévrier des mers », de 293 mètres de longueur pour 65 000 tonnes de déplacement, se révèle être un succès commercial.

Le *Queen Elizabeth 2* semble tout d'abord graver l'épitaphe de l'ère glorieuse des paquebots. C'est en effet le dernier grand navire du XXe siècle à porter les couleurs traditionnelles de la Cunard – cheminées rouges avec coque et superstructure noire et blanche. Malgré d'évidentes difficultés, tel que la baisse du trafic régulier de passagers et les conflits avec les dockers des deux côtés de l'Atlantique, il se montrera remarquablement solide et durable.

En janvier 1971, le *Queen Elizabeth 2* participe au sauvetage du paquebot français *Antilles*, en feu au large de l'île Moustique, et, aidé par deux autres navires français, en débarque sains et saufs les passagers à la Barbade. En 1972, il connaît une fausse alerte à la bombe. Sa plus grande aventure, suivant l'exemple de ses aînés britanniques, est de participer comme transport de troupes, lors de la guerre des Malouines en 1982, au débarquement de 3000 soldats.

En 1960, deux des anciennes compagnies britanniques fusionnent sous le nom des P & O-Orient Lines. La nouvelle compagnie dispose alors de la flotte de navires passager la plus importante du monde, composée de 16 paquebots, dont l'*Oriana* et le *Canberra* sont les nouvelles stars. L'élégant *Oriana*, qui, avec ses 41 932 tonneaux, est le plus grand navire britannique construit depuis le *Queen Elizabeth*, entre en service en décembre 1960 ; le *Canberra*, annoncé comme « le navire qui marquera le futur », effectue son voyage inaugural de Southampton vers l'Australie le 2 juin 1961. La P & O-Orient prévoit d'ouvrir les routes transpacifiques et quelques autres lignes importantes en offrant un mode de voyage bien plus agréable capable de concurrencer la domination croissante des compagnies aériennes.

La transformation du *Canberra* (45 733 tonneaux) en transport de troupes, en avril 1982, est spectaculaire, notamment avec le boulonnage de ponts d'envol à sa proue et à sa poupe. Au début de la guerre des Malouines, c'est lui qui accomplit le plus gros travail en débarquant les troupes britanniques dans la zone des combats. Au lieu d'embarquer 2700 passagers pour une croisière paisible, il transporte trois bataillons et demi de parachutistes et de fusiliers marins. Après six mois de mer, ce navire fiable et extraordinairement résistant commence à montrer des signes de fatigue mais sort de la guerre relativement indemne, après avoir réussi à échapper à une attaque en rase-mottes d'avions.

Le *Canberra* reste en service pendant 36 ans. En 1995, sa place de navire amiral de la flotte P & O est prise par un nouvel *Oriana*, construit en Allemagne. La compagnie lance également un programme de 3 milliards de dollars pour le développement de leur département croisière, les Princess Cruises, qui prennent livraison en 1998 du *Grand Princess*. Cet énorme vaisseau de 109 000 tonneaux est un chef-d'œuvre fantasque de l'architecture maritime, puisqu'on y trouve un night-club d'acier et de verre en porte-à-faux à la poupe, une chapelle pour que les 2600 passagers puissent y renouveler leurs vœux de mariage et 760 cabines individuelles avec un balcon indépendant.

D'autres compagnies se réorganisent, comme la Holland-Amerika Line. Le *Nieuw-Amsterdam*, un paquebot de 36 287 tonneaux lancé à Rotterdam en 1938 et qui servit aux Alliés de transport de troupes entre 1940 à 1945, est jusqu'en 1971 le nouveau porte-drapeau de la compagnie sur la route Rotterdam-New York, passant ses deux dernières années en croisière dans les Caraïbes. En 1959, il a cédé la place de navire amiral au *Rotterdam* (38 645 tonneaux), un paquebot où les passagers de première et de classe touriste disposent de toute la longueur du bateau.

Au milieu des années 1960, les lignes régulières de la plupart des grandes compagnies connaissent une période difficile. Le *United States* et le *Queen Elizabeth 2* sont frappés par des mouvements sociaux. Entre 1961 et 1969, le *United States* voit ainsi annuler onze de ses voyages à cause des grèves. Lors de sa 726e traversée de l'Atlantique, son armateur lui ordonna de se rendre à Newport News pour y subir une remise en état prématurée, ce afin de parer à la menace d'une grève. Il n'allait jamais en repartir par ses propres moyens.

Un sort moins enviable encore est réservé au vieux *Queen Elizabeth*, désarmé en 1968. Il est vendu à un gros entrepreneur de Taiwan, qui prévoit d'en faire une université itinérante en croisière autour du monde, baptisée la *Seawise University*. En janvier 1972, le réarmement du paquebot, réalisé à Hong Kong, est presque terminée lorsqu'il prend brusquement feu. Couché sur le flanc, il va brûler encore pendant une semaine. L'enquête indiquera par la suite que c'était l'œuvre d'un pyromane.

Le *France*, le dernier et le plus magnifique navire de la Compagnie Générale Transatlantique, naît en 1962. Ce paquebot, dont la conception et les aménagements élégants sont du dernier cri – il a coûté 30 millions de livres –, est aussi le plus long paquebot jamais construit au monde (315 mètres). Ses propriétaires pensent alors qu'il existe une clientèle suffisante capable d'apprécier une aussi exceptionnelle qualité. Mais, au début des années 1970, plus de 90 pour cent du trafic passager transatlantique s'effectue par avion et la CGT commence à connaître quelques difficultés. En 1974, la compagnie annonce qu'elle « doit malheureusement interrompre son service régulier sur la ligne transatlantique, 110 ans après son ouverture » et que le *France* va effectuer son dernier voyage, de New York à Cannes, le 18 octobre. Le 11 septembre, à l'approche du Havre, une partie de l'équipage prend le contrôle de la passerelle et, mouillant en rade, bloque le chenal principal du port pour forcer le gouvernement à retirer sa menace d'arrêt des subventions. Onze jours plus tard, alors que les provisions s'épuisent, les marins grévistes décident de poursuivre leur action à terre. Rien n'y fera et le *France* achèvera sa carrière avant d'être transformé en paquebot de croisière et rebaptisé *Norway*.

Malgré tout, les années 1960 voient apparaître quelques superbes grands paquebots. Les plus extraordinaires sont, en 1965, les deux navires jumeaux de la ligne Italia, le *Michelangelo* (45 911 tonneaux) et le *Raffaello* (45 933 ton-

neaux). Avec leurs cheminées treillissées, leurs étranges silhouettes et leurs six piscines chacun, ils matérialisent le nouvel idéal de l'architecture navale italienne. Les prévisions sur leur rentabilité ne seront toutefois jamais réalisées et, un an à peine après leur lancement, ils sont rachetés par le gouvernement iranien et transformés en casernes flottantes. Le *Michelangelo* est mis à la ferraille en 1992 tandis que le *Raffaello* est coulé en 1983 par un missile irakien.

L'histoire la plus dramatique est sans doute celle de l'*Achille Lauro* (21 119 tonneaux), lancé en 1939 aux couleurs de la Rotterdam Royal Line sous le nom de *Willem Ruys* et reconstruit en 1965. Près de 20 ans plus tard, il est pris en otage par des membres de l'OLP alors qu'il croise dans l'est de la Méditerranée pour amener des Américains en Israël. Leon Klinghoffer, un New-yorkais âgé en chaise roulante, tente de parlementer avec les terroristes mais est aussitôt jeté par dessus bord et se noie. Le gouvernement italien parvient à négocier et à faire libérer le navire mais laisse s'enfuir leur chef. Cet épisode porte un coup sévère aux croisières en Méditerranée. Le 30 novembre 1994, l'*Achille Lauro* est dévasté par un incendie au large de la Somalie et sombre deux jours plus tard.

En cette fin du XXe siècle, les voyages et les croisières en mer connaissent un regain d'intérêt, non pas pour être le moyen le plus rapide et le plus efficace d'atteindre une destination mais bien en tant que destination et expérience en soi. Les croisières proposent l'aventure ; elles permettent d'aller sur toutes les mers et de gagner tous les continents, de l'Arctique à l'Antarctique (malgré les controverses au sujet de leurs effets sur l'environnement). Les croisières peuvent également être personnalisées, « thématiques », dans un but éducatif (histoire) ou de loisirs (jeu, danse ou plaisirs dionysiaques).

L'époque des paquebots, dont les fleurons sont le *Queen Mary* et le *Normandie*, le *Raffaello* et le *Nieuw-Amsterdam*, ainsi que les géants dus à Albert Ballin et ceux de l'Atlantic Express, n'est pas encore achevée. La Cunard, l'une des premières compagnies à exploiter les lignes transatlantiques, vient de commander un nouveau paquebot, encore plus grand que le vieux *Queen Elizabeth* et plus long que le *France*. La traversée de l'Atlantique revient à la mode.

The stern of the French Line's SS *France*, the longest liner in the world, as she undergoes a clean in Le Havre before a Christmas cruise.

Das Heck der SS *France*, des der CGT gehörenden längsten Passagierschiffes der Welt; hier wird sie in Le Havre für eine Weihnachtskreuzfahrt auf Hochglanz gebracht.

La poupe du SS *France*, le paquebot passager le plus long du monde de la CGT, lors d'un radoub au Havre avant la croisière de Noël.

Oriana and Canberra

(Right) The 41,923-ton *Oriana* at Southampton before
her maiden voyage to Australia, November 1960.
(Above) Arrival at the new Ocean Terminal, Sydney,
January 1961. (Previous pages, left to right) The launch
of the *Canberra*, 45,733 tons, Belfast, 16 March 1960; the swept
funnels aft that became her trademark; the bulbous bow.

Oriana und *Canberra*

(Rechts) Die *Oriana*, 41 923 Tonnen, in Southampton vor
ihrer Jungfernfahrt nach Australien im November 1960. (Oben)
Ankunft am neuen Ocean Terminal in Sydney, Januar 1961.
(Vorherige Seiten, von links nach rechts) Stapellauf der
Canberra in Belfast am 16. März 1960; die geschwungenen,
weit hinten sitzenden Schornsteine, die das Markenzeichen
des 45733-Tonners werden sollten; der Bug mit Bugwulst.

Oriana* et *Canberra

Le paquebot *Oriana* (41 923 tonneaux) prêt à appareiller
de Southampton pour son voyage inaugural vers l'Australie, en
novembre 1960 (à droite), où il arrive au nouvel Ocean Terminal
de Sydney, en janvier 1961 (ci-dessus). (Pages précédentes, de
gauche à droite) Le Canberra (45773 tonneaux) sur son ber de
lancement à Belfast, le 16 mars 1960 ; le profil de ses cheminées
avant est une de ses caractéristiques ; le bulbe de proue.

Unmistakably French
The extravagant lettering of the French Line's *France*, 66,348 tons, photographed on her first visit to Southampton for docking trials in January 1962. (Right) The launch of the 1035-foot liner, the longest in the world, at Saint-Nazaire, 11 May 1960, by Madame de Gaulle, wife of the French President.

Unverkennbar französisch
In großen Lettern zeigt der neue 66348-Tonner der CGT seinen Namen, aufgenommen beim ersten Besuch der *France* in Southampton zwecks Andockübung ,im Januar 1962. (Rechts) Stapellauf am 11. Mai 1960 in Saint-Nazaire. Madame de Gaulle, Gattin des Staatspräsidenten, taufte das Schiff – mit 315 Metern damals das längste der Welt.

Indiscutablement français
Le lettrage extravagant du *France* (66348 tonneaux), de la CGT, photographié lors de sa première visite à Southampton pour des essais en bassin, en janvier 1962. (À droite) Ce paquebot de 315 mètres de longueur, le plus long du monde, fut lancé à Saint-Nazaire, le 11 mai 1960, par Madame de Gaulle, l'épouse du président français.

Pride of France

The *France* leaving Southampton after completing her docking trials, January 1962. She was withdrawn from service following an act of mutiny when the French Line had to close its regular passenger service across the Atlantic in 1974. In 1979 she was sold to Norwegian Caribbean Lines and converted into their flagship *Norway*. She still makes occasional transatlantic voyages.

Der Stolz der Nation

Nach absolvierter Andockübung verläßt die *France* Southampton im Januar 1962 wieder. Als die CGT 1974 bekanntgab, daß sie den Liniendienst über den Atlantik einstellen müsse, meuterten die Matrosen, und die *France* wurde aufgelegt. 1979 ging sie an die Norwegian Carribbean Lines und wurde zu deren Flaggschiff, der *Norway*, umgebaut. Sie unternimmt auch heute noch von Zeit zu Zeit Atlantikfahrten.

La fierté de la France

Le *France* quitte Southampton en janvier 1962 après ses essais en bassin. Il fut retiré du service par la CGT après que l'équipage se soit mutiné pour protester contre la fermeture de la ligne transatlantique en 1974. Le *France* fut vendu en 1979 comme navire amiral aux Norwegian Caribbean Lines. Rebaptisé *Norway*, il effectue aujourd'hui encore quelques voyages transatlantiques.

Elegance and lattice

The Italian Line's *Raffaello* and *Michelangelo*, two of the most distinctive liners introduced in the Sixties. (Above) The 45,933-ton *Raffaello* slipping from the piers at Genoa at the start of her maiden voyage to New York, 26 July 1965. (Right) The lattice frame on the funnel of her sister, the *Michelangelo*, 45,911 tons, the most visible individual feature of these ships. Both ships were to have only brief careers under the Italian flag.

Zierlich und elegant

Die *Raffaello* und die *Michelangelo* der Italia-Linie, zwei der bemerkenswertesten Passagierschiffe der sechziger Jahre. (Oben) Die *Raffaello*, 45933 Tonnen, legt am 26. Juli 1965 zu ihrer Jungfernfahrt nach New York vom Pier in Genua ab. (Rechts) Der mit Gitterwerk eingefaßte Schornstein ihres Schwesterschiffs *Michelangelo*, 45911 Tonnen; dieser Schornstein war bei beiden Schiffen der charakteristischste Zug. Beide sollten nur kurze Zeit unter italienischer Flagge fahren.

Élégance et treillissage

Le *Raffaello* (45933 tonneaux) et le *Michelangelo* (45911 tonneaux), de la ligne Italia, sont deux des paquebots les plus élégants mis en service dans les années 1960. (Ci-dessus) Le *Raffaello* quitte les quais de Gênes pour effectuer son voyage inaugural vers New York, le 26 juillet 1965. (À droite) La charpente treillissée de leurs cheminées (ici celle du *Michelangelo*) est la caractéristique la plus visible de ces navires. Ces deux paquebots ne connurent qu'une brève carrière sous le pavillon italien.

Last days of the
Queen Elizabeth

(Above) The liner in her new guise
as the floating university and
learning centre, *Seawise University*,
of the C.Y. Tung Shipping Group of
Hong Kong, her purchaser at
auction in 1970. (Right) The fires
which gutted her on 9 January 1972,
ascribed to arson. Later the hull
rolled over, spilling oil into the
waters off Hong Kong; it was
decided to scrap her where she lay.

Die letzten Tage der
Queen Elizabeth

(Oben) Die C. Y. Tung Shipping
Group in Hongkong hatte den
Liner im Jahre 1970 ersteigert
und zu einer schwimmenden
Unterrichtsstätte, der *Seawise
University*, umgerüstet. (Rechts)
Am 9. Januar 1972 brannte sie aus,
vermutlich durch Brandstiftung.
Später kenterte sie, und Öl lief in
die Gewässer vor Hongkong; man
beschloß, sie an Ort und Stelle
abzuwracken.

Les derniers jours du
Queen Elizabeth

Le paquebot arbore les nouvelles
couleurs de la *Seawise University*,
université et centre d'enseignement
flottants, appartenant au C. Y. Tung
Shipping Group de Hong Kong,
qui l'a acquis lors de sa vente aux
enchères en 1970 (ci-dessus). Le
paquebot fut dévasté le 9 janvier
1972 par un incendie d'origine
probablement criminelle (à droite).
Il se coucha ensuite sur le flanc
en déversant du mazout dans les
eaux au large de Hong Kong. Les
autorités décidèrent de le détruire
à l'endroit où il était échoué.

Sailing to retirement

(Above) The *Queen Mary* is given a heroine's welcome as she sails to retirement at Long Beach, California, December 1967. She had been bought by an American consortium for £16,500,000, to be turned into a conference centre, hotel and museum (right). This has been the most successful retirement for any of the great liners.

In den Ruhestand

(Oben) Die *Queen Mary* wird mit allen Ehren begrüßt, als sie im Dezember 1967 an ihrem Ruheplatz im kalifornischen Long Beach ankommt. Ein amerikanisches Konsortium hatte sie für £16 500 000 erworben und machte ein Konferenzzentrum mit Hotel und Museum daraus (rechts). Einen schöneren Ruhestand hat keiner der klassischen Ozeanriesen bekommen.

Navigation de retraite

(Ci-dessus) Le *Queen Mary* reçoit un accueil de héros en arrivant à sa dernière retraite à Long Beach (Californie), en décembre 1967. Il a été acheté 16 500 000 £ par un consortium américain pour être transformé en centre de conférences, hôtel et musée (à droite). C'est le paquebot à avoir le mieux réussi sa retraite.

345

A new *Queen*

The launch of the *Queen Elizabeth 2*, 20 September 1967. Dockyard workers flat on the fore-peak (left) to catch the magic moment when Queen Elizabeth II will launch this great Cunard Atlantic liner, naming her in memory of the previous *Queen Elizabeth*. Television vans are lined up to record the event. (Right) Next morning the liner is manoeuvred into the fitting-out berth of Upper Clyde Shipbuilders.

Eine neue *Queen*

Taufe der *Queen Elizabeth 2*, am 20. September 1967. Werftarbeiter haben sich einen Platz an der Reling gesichert (links), um den großen Augenblick nicht zu verpassen, wenn Königin Elisabeth II. den neuen Cunard-Liner vom Stapel läßt; seinen Namen trägt er im Gedächtnis an den Vorläufer, die alte *Queen Elizabeth*. Das Fernsehen ist dabei und hält das Ereignis fest. (Rechts) Am nächsten Morgen wird das Schiff ins Ausrüstungsdock der Upper Clyde Shipbuilders geschleppt.

Une nouvelle *Queen*

Le lancement du *Queen Elizabeth 2*, le 20 septembre 1967. Les ouvriers des docks se sont allongés à la proue (à gauche) pour voir le moment magique où la reine Elizabeth II lancera ce grand paquebot transatlantique de la Cunard, dont le nom évoque la mémoire du premier *Queen Elizabeth*. L'évènement est retransmis à la télévision. (À droite) Le lendemain, le paquebot manœuvre pour entrer dans le bassin d'armement des chantiers Upper Clyde Shipbuilders.

Sailing into a bright future
The *Queen Elizabeth 2* on her speed trials off the Isle of Arran, November 1968. Despite huge ups and downs in her career, strikes, bomb scares and war, the liner has proved her worth and is considered good value for the initial £30 million she cost: so much so, that a running mate is under active consideration after 30 years of dedicated service from her. The age of the liner is not dead yet!

In eine strahlende Zukunft
Die *Queen Elizabeth 2* bei der ersten Probefahrt unter Volldampf im November 1968 vor der Insel Arran. Sie hat Höhen und Tiefen erlebt, Streiks, Bombendrohungen und Krieg, doch heute gilt es als ausgemacht, daß die 30 Millionen Pfund, die sie kostete, gut investiert waren, und nach 30 Jahren treuer Dienste wird nun sogar der Bau eines Schwesterschiffes erwogen. Die Zeit der Ozeanriesen ist noch nicht vorbei!

En route pour l'avenir
Le *Queen Elizabeth 2* lors de ses essais de vitesse au large de l'île d'Arran, en novembre 1968. Malgré les hauts et les bas de sa carrière, les grèves, les alertes à la bombe et la guerre, ce paquebot s'est révélé rentable. Il est considéré comme un bon investissement malgré son coût initial de 30 millions de livres, si bien qu'on envisage de lui donner un frère d'armement, 30 ans après la mise en service de ce navire. L'ère des paquebots n'est pas encore révolue !

Index

351

gettyimages

This book was created by Getty Images, 21-31 Woodfield Road, London W92BA

Over 70 million images and 30,000 hours of film footage are held by the various collections owned by Getty Images.
These cover a vast number of subjects from the earliest photojournalism to current press photography, sports, social history
and geography. Getty Images' conceptual imagery is renowned amongst creative end users.
www.gettyimages.com

Über 70 Millionen Bilder und 30 000 Stunden Film befinden sich in den verschiedenen Archiven von Getty Images.
Sie decken ein breites Spektrum an Themen ab – von den ersten Tagen des Fotojournalismus bis hin zu aktueller
Pressefotografie, Sport, Sozialgeschichte und Geographie. Bei kreativen Anwendern ist das Material von Getty Images
für seine ausdrucksstarke Bildsprache bekannt.
www.gettyimages.com

Plus de 70 millions d'images et 30 000 heures de films sont détenus par les différentes collections dont Getty Images
est le propriétaire. Cela couvre un nombre considérable de sujets – des débuts du photojournalisme aux photographies actuelles de
presse, de sport, d'histoire sociale et de géographie. Le concept photographique de Getty Images est reconnu des créatifs.
www.gettyimages.com

Picture acknowledgements:
Charles Dragonette Collection *270*, Clive Harvey Collection *169*, *315*, International News Photo *265*, Sky Photos *314*,
Ulster Folk & Transport Museum *65*, US Naval Historical Center *271*.

All other images in this book were supplied by Getty Images.

352